British Elections & Parties Review
VOLUME 9

BRITISH
ELECTIONS
& PARTIES
REVIEW
VOLUME 9

EDITORS

Justin Fisher • Philip Cowley
David Denver • Andrew Russell

FRANK CASS
LONDON • PORTLAND, OR

First published in 1999 in Great Britain by
FRANK CASS PUBLISHERS
Newbury House, 900 Eastern Avenue, London IG2 7HH

and in the United States of America by
FRANK CASS PUBLISHERS
5804 N.E. Hassalo Street
Portland, Oregon 97213-3644

Website www.frankcass.com

British Library Cataloguing in Publication Data

British elections & parties review
Vol. 9
1. Elections – Great Britain 2. Political parties – Great
Britain 3. Great Britain – Politics and government – 1998 –
I. Fisher, Justin
324.9'41'0895

ISBN 0714650153

ISBN 0 7146 5015 3 (cloth)
ISBN 0 7146 8072 9 (paper)
ISSN 1368 9886

Library of Congress Cataloging-in-Publication Data applied for

Printed in Great Britain by MPG Books Ltd, Bodmin, Cornwall

CONTENTS

PREFACE

This is the ninth annual volume published under the auspices of the Elections, Public Opinion and Parties (EPOP) specialist group of the Political Studies Association. The articles contained here were originally presented at EPOP's annual conference hosted by the University of Manchester in September 1998. As in all previous volumes, the papers have been substantially revised and the articles finally published have all been independently and extensively refereed. The Review also includes the annual reference section. This contains comprehensive data, which we believe will be extremely useful for readers.

We are grateful to a number of people and organizations for helping to make this publication and the activities of EPOP so successful. First, we would like to thank the authors of the articles contained here for revising their original papers and responding both positively and swiftly to requests for amendments. Second, we would like to thank all the paper-givers at our conferences for helping to ensure that the fields of elections, public opinion and parties are studied in such depth and quality in the United Kingdom. Third, we would like to thank the conference attenders who frequently and helpfully alert paper-givers to ways in which their work could be improved. Fourth we would like to thank the following for invaluable financial and other support: the Economic and Social Research Council (Award Number L477 09 4001 98), the McDougall Trust, the European Policy Research Unit, the Political Studies Association, the Department of Government at the University of Manchester, and the three journals edited from the Department – *Government & Opposition*, *Party Politics* and *Political Studies*. Finally, we are grateful to Frank Cass publishers and to Cathy Jennings in particular who continues to be a source of support, encouragement and invaluable advice to the editors.

EPOP remains the largest and most active specialist group within the PSA, and these volumes testify to the breadth and the high quality of work produced by group members. Further details about EPOP can be obtained from any of the editors, or by visiting our website at www.psa.ac.uk/spgrp/epop.htm.

Justin Fisher   Philip Cowley   David Denver   Andrew Russell

April 1999

NOTES ON CONTRIBUTORS

David Baker is Reader in British Politics at Nottingham Trent University and co-founder with Andrew Gamble of the Members of Parliament Project. He recently co-edited *Britain For and Against Europe: British Politics and the Question of European Integration* (Oxford University Press) and is currently writing two books, *Models of Fascism* (I.B. Tauris) and *British Political History 1640–2000* (Macmillan). He is also (with Sean Kelly) preparing a Reader to accompany the political history book.

John Bartle is a lecturer and British Academy Post-Doctoral Fellow at the University of Essex. He has published articles in *The British Journal of Political Science*, *British Elections and Parties Review* and, with Ivor Crewe and Brian Gosschalk, has edited *Political Communications: Why Labour Won the General Election of 1997* (Frank Cass, 1998).

Hugh Bochel is Professor and Head of the Department of Policy Studies, University of Lincolnshire and Humberside.

Katrina Bull is the ESRC research assistant working on the Members of Parliament Project survey of parliamentarians. She holds degrees in politics from Sussex and Aberdeen Universities.

Harold D. Clarke is Regents Professor and Chair of the Department of Political Science, University of North Texas. His research focuses on voting, elections and the political economy of party support in Anglo-American democracies. His articles have appeared in journals such as the *American Political Science Review*, the *American Journal of Political Science*, the *British Journal of Political Science*, and the *Journal of Politics*. Current projects include studies of voting behaviour in the 1995 Quebec sovereignty referendum and the dynamics of party support in Britain.

Matt Cole has been an associate lecturer in Social Sciences with the Open University since 1990, and is Head of History and Politics at Cadbury College, Birmingham. He is pursuing a PhD on the British Liberal Party at the University of Birmingham, and has published articles in *Politics Review*, *Modern History Review* and *Parliamentary Affairs*.

Philip Cowley is a lecturer at the University of Hull, and Deputy Director of the Centre for Legislative Studies. His publications include *Conscience* *and Parliament* (Frank Cass, 1998), as well as articles in a range of journals including the *British Journal of Political Science, Political Studies, Party Politics, Public Law,* and the *Journal of Legislative Studies.*

David Denver is Professor of Politics at Lancaster University and series editor of the *British Elections & Parties Review.*

Danny Dorling is a Reader in the School of Geographical Sciences at the University of Bristol. His research interests focus on the use of visualization in the exploration and analysis of statistical data in the social sciences, with particular reference to elections and health. He is the author of *A New Social Atlas of Britain* (Wiley) and co-editor of *Statistics in Society: The Arithmetic of Politics* (Arnold).

Patrick Dunleavy is Professor of Government at the London School of Economics and Political Science. He has worked on electoral reform issues in Britain and comparatively since 1992, and with Helen Margetts and Stuart Weir published *Replaying the General Election of 1992* (LSE Public Policy Group), *Making Votes Count* (Democratic Audit, 1997) and *The Politico's Guide to Electoral Reform in Britain* (Politicos, 1998). His current work is mainly on public choice issues including the rationality of participation, and public policy.

Justin Fisher is Senior Lecturer in Political Science at London Guildhall University. He has published widely in the fields of political parties and party finance. During 1998, he acted as a consultant to the Committee on Standards in Public Life in its investigations into the funding of political parties.

Andrew Gamble is Professor of Politics at the University of Sheffield and a director of the Political Economy Research Centre (PERC) in Sheffield. He is also a co-founder of the Members of Parliament Project with David Baker. He is well known for a number of books in the field of political economy including *Britain in Decline, The Free Economy and the Strong State* and *Hayek.* He is presently working on a number of projects associated with global political economy.

Matt Henn is Senior Lecturer in Social Science Research Methodology at the Nottingham Trent University. His research interests include electoral politics, party campaigning and political participation. His most recent publication is *Opinion Polls and Volatile Electorates: Problems and Issues in Polling European Societies* (Ashgate, 1998).

David W.F. Huang is Assistant Research Fellow, Institute of European and American Studies, Academia Sinica, Taipei, Taiwan.

Ron Johnston is a Professor in the School of Geographical Sciences at the University of Bristol. Together with his co-authors of the paper in this volume he has studied bias in election results in Britain since 1950 – they have a major paper on their earlier findings in the first volume (1999) of the *British Journal of Politics and International Relations*.

Richard S. Katz is Professor of Political Science at the Johns Hopkins University. He is the author of *Democracy and Elections* (Oxford, 1997) and *A Theory of Parties and Electoral Systems* (Johns Hopkins, 1980) and co-editor/co-author of *Party Organizations: A Data Handbook* (Sage, 1992) and *How Parties Organize* (Sage, 1994).

Iain MacAllister is a graduate of the University of Glasgow and Strathclyde University. After working at the University of Bristol on various ESRC-funded projects related to the 1997 general election he is now working at the Department of Politics and International Relations at Lancaster University on the 1999 Scottish Parliament elections.

Helen Margetts is Senior Lecturer in the School of Public Policy at University College London. She has worked on electoral reform issues in Britain and comparatively since 1992, and with Patrick Dunleavy and Stuart Weir published *Replaying the General Election of 1992* (LSE Public Policy Group), *Making Votes Count* (Democratic Audie, 1997) and *The Politico's Guide to Electoral Reform in Britain* (Politicos, 1998). In addition to electoral studies, her other recent work focuses on public policy issues, including *Information Technology in Government* (Routledge, 1998).

James Mitchell is Professor of Politics at the University of Sheffield. He has published widely on Scottish politics and is currently writing a text on devolution as well as working more generally on aspects of regionalism in Europe.

Charles Pattie is a senior lecturer in Geography at the University of Sheffield and a frequent contributor to political science journals on various aspects of electoral geography. He has recently been involved in a cooperative book-length study of the 1997 Scottish devolution referendum.

David Rossiter is a Research Associate School of Geographical Sciences at the University of Bristol. He recently published (with Ron Johnston and

Charles Pattie) a major study of redistricting in the UK – *The Boundary Commissions: Redrawing the UK's Map of Parliamentary Constituencies* (Manchester University Press).

Andrew Russell is Lecturer in Government at the University of Manchester. His research interests include spatial variation in economic perceptions, party politics in Britain and psephology.

David Seawright lectures in politics at the University of Lincolnshire and Humberside. He is the author of *An Important Matter of Principle* (Ashgate) and is co-editor of *Britain For and Against Europe: British Politics and the Question of European Integration* (Oxford University Press).

Roger M. Scully is a lecturer in European Politics at Brunel University, having recently completed Doctoral studies at the Ohio State University. His major research interests are in the areas of legislative politics and the European Union. His previous work has been published in the *British Journal of Political Science*, *European Journal of Political Research*, *Legislative Studies Quarterly*, and the *Journal of Legislative Studies*, as well as in several book chapters. He is a founder member of the multi-national European Parliament Research Group.

Marianne C. Stewart is Professor, School of Social Sciences, University of Texas at Dallas. Her research interests concern the impact of economic evaluations and party leader images on voting behaviour and party identification in Canada, Great Britain and the United States. She has published in journals such as the *American Political Science Review*, the *American Journal of Political Science*, the *European Journal of Political Economy*, the *European Journal of Political Research*, and the *Journal of Politics*.

Helena Tunstall graduated from the University of Manchester and the London School of Economics. She is now undertaking research for a PhD on aspects of child mortality from accidents in the School of Geographical Sciences at the University of Bristol, having previously worked there on several ESRC-funded projects in electoral geography.

Mark Weinstein is a lecturer in Social Science Research Methods and IT at Nottingham Trent University. He is currently working on a study examining youth participation in British political parties and new social movements, and has published in this area.

Paul Whiteley is Professor of Politics at the University of Sheffield. His current research focuses on the causes and consequences of party activism, political participation in Britain and other mature democracies, and the political economy of party support. He has published several books, and his articles have appeared in journals such as the *British Journal of Political Science*, the *European Journal of Political Research*, the *Journal of Politics*, the *Political Research Quarterly*, and *Political Studies*.

Dominic Wring is a lecturer in the Department of Social Sciences at Loughborough University. His recent research has been focused on the development of political communication in Britain, and a book based on this work entitled *Marketing the Labour Party* is being published by Macmillan.

ABSTRACTS OF ARTICLES

Electoral Reform and Its Discontents
Richard S. Katz

Given the poor track record of prognosticators about the effects of recent electoral reforms in Italy, Japan, Israel and New Zealand, there are reasons to be sceptical about predictions concerning possible reforms in Britain. Problems of prediction stem from three general classes of factors: the mechanical and semi-mechanical, the strategic and the ontological. Applying our knowledge of the mechanical effects of electoral institutions requires knowledge of many details that often are unknowable at the time. Applying our understanding of the strategic imperatives created by electoral institutions is weakened both by the limited knowledge in the hands of those actors who are presumed to act strategically and by our limited knowledge of the goals that they actually will pursue. Understandings of democracy are not necessarily shared universally, yet they influence both choices about behaviour and evaluations of results.

New Labour's Landslide and Electoral Bias: An Exploration of Why the 1997 UK General Election Result Differed from the Previous 13
Ron Johnston, Charles Pattie, David Rossiter, Danny Dorling, Iain MacAllister and Helena Tunstall

The British election system is well known for producing disproportional results: most parties get different percentages of House of Commons seats than they do of the votes cast. It is also prone to produce biased results, whereby two parties with the same percentage of the votes get different percentages of the seats: on our measure used of this, the 1997 result was the most biased (favouring the Labour Party) in the last half-century. Previous analyses of that bias identified six geographical components involved in its production. This article explores those components further using graphical methods, employing three categorizations of votes – wasted, effective and surplus – to suggest why the 1997 outcome was so biased. Labour's focused geographical campaign then improved its ability to translate votes into seats very substantially: it significantly reduced its ratios of both wasted votes to seats lost and surplus votes to seats won, and so achieved a geographically much more efficient distribution of support than before, whereas too many of the Conservative Party's votes were cast in the wrong places.

Reforming the Westminster Electoral System: Evaluating the Jenkins Commission Proposals
Helen Margetts and Patrick Dunleavy
The Jenkins Commission has recommended an innovative AV Plus system as the alternative to plurality rule to be offered in an electoral systems referendum. Eighty-five per cent of MPs would be elected in local constituencies somewhat larger than at present, and the remainder in 80 top areas. We show how the Commission came to its finished scheme, and evaluate its likely effects using detailed simulations of the 1997 and 1992 general elections. We compare the systems' implications in terms of deviation from proportionality and the better territorial representation of parties' vote bases. AV Plus represents a considerable advance on plurality rule, but in 1997 conditions would secure only 'broad' proportionality, in particular performing worse than the straightforward AMS alternative using the same local:top up ratios and top up areas proposed by Lord Alexander. However, in 1992 conditions AV Plus performs reasonably proportionally, and almost as well as AMS.

Party Policy and Electoral Reform: A Survey of Developments, Motives and Prospects
Matt Cole
It is commonly argued by both academic analysts and other commentators that parties' policies on electoral reform are decided upon the basis of their self-interest. However, by this criterion, some parties appear to be acting against their interests. This article explores the nature of the main parties' policies on electoral reform and the current state of opinion in the parties, and tries to establish a framework of key determinants which explains the apparent contradiction between party interest and policy.

New Labour's New Partisans: The Dynamics of Party Identification in Britain since 1992
Harold D. Clarke, Marianne C. Stewart and Paul Whiteley
This article uses survey data gathered in two national survey research projects conducted in the 1990s to investigate the stability of party identification in contemporary Britain. Time series analyses reveal substantial aggregate-level instability in party identification, with the Labour Party gaining a sizeable number of new partisans at the expense of the Conservatives. Binary and multinomial logit analyses of panel survey data indicate that individual-level movements in party identification have been prompted by voters' party and party leader images, as well as by their economic and social policy evaluations, and their attitudes towards Britain's role in the European Union. Mixed Markov Latent Class (MMLC) analyses

confirm the presence of a large number of unstable identifiers in the 1990s. Additional MMLC analyses indicate that this situation is not novel; large-scale partisan instability also characterized the British electorate in the 1960s.

'Independents', 'Switchers' and Voting for Third Parties in Britain, 1979-92
David W. F. Huang

It is frequently assumed that the increase in electoral support for third parties in Britain after 1970 was a consequence of a decline in party identification and an increase in vote switching, which themselves were symptoms of dealignment. Initial analysis of BES data shows that 'Independents' were not more likely to vote for third parties. On the other hand, vote switchers were more likely to do so even when a variety of other factors is taken into account. More detailed analysis finds that 'Independents' were more likely than Labour or Conservative identifiers to vote for third parties. Nonetheless vote switchers provide such parties with a larger pool of potential supporters.

Improving the Measurement of Party Identification in Britain
John Bartle

This article points out a paradox: most political scientists apparently subscribe to a party identification model of voting behaviour and yet there is widespread concern about how that concept is currently measured. In particular there are doubts about whether the traditional measure captures the long-term nature of party identification. The article presents evidence from an experiment, carried out by the Gallup Organization, which compares the traditional measure with a new one. The results suggest that the traditional measure of party identification overstates the level of identification and leads to an exaggerated impression of the relationship between this variable and vote. The article ends with an appeal for more research into the measurement of party identification.

Settled Will or Divided Society? Voting in the 1997 Scottish and Welsh Devolution Referendums
Charles Pattie, David Denver, James Mitchell and Hugh Bochel

Although they were both concerned with devolution, the contexts of the 1997 referendums in Scotland and Wales were significantly different. In particular Scottish national identity is stronger and more widespread than is Welsh identity and the desire for constitutional change has been weaker in Wales than in Scotland. The narrow victory for devolution in Wales contrasted sharply with the decisive result in Scotland. Analysis of survey data shows that in Scotland voters' sense of partisan and national identity largely explain voting patterns and the large 'Yes' majority. In Wales, on the other hand, while party was significant, sense of national identity did not affect voting very strongly.

The Absence of War? New Labour in Parliament
Philip Cowley
The article details and analyses the rebellions by Labour MPs that have occurred since the election of the Blair government. Labour MPs are currently rebelling infrequently, both in absolute terms and in comparison to most of the recent parliaments, although there is nothing exceptional about their behaviour when compared to all post-war parliaments. When they do rebel, however, they are doing so in respectable numbers. Given that first sessions of parliaments are traditionally quiet there is the clear potential for further rebellion. The newly-elected MPs are the most loyal, with the newly-elected women even more loyal than the newly-elected men. And there are few surprise names among those who choose to rebel, especially those who choose to rebel frequently: most could be (and, indeed, were) identified by their behaviour in the last parliament.

MPs and Europe: Enthusiasm, Circumspection or Outright Scepticism?
David Baker, Andrew Gamble and David Seawright
This article empirically tests the views of the contemporary British parliamentary elites on Europe. It draws on the results of an ESRC survey sent to all 659 MPs in mid-1998, and builds on the results of the two previous ESRC surveys examining Conservative and Labour MP's views on European integration. The new survey examines the views of the large influx of new Labour MPs, widely believed to be very pro-European, as well as testing whether the remaining Conservative MPs are as eurosceptic as is commonly assumed. Both major parties have significant minorities opposed to the party line on Europe, especially on issues which deal with fundamental questions of national sovereignty and interdependence; there also appears to be a clear shift in attitudes in both the earlier Conservative and Labour cohorts.

Nowhere to Run...? British MEPs and the Euro
Roger M. Scully
Economic and Monetary Union (EMU) has become one of the most divisive issues in contemporary British politics. When Members of the European Parliament (MEPs) were asked to approve the go-ahead for EMU in May 1998, this raised potential difficulties for British representatives, who were

being asked to take a stance on an issue of great domestic sensitivity. Drawing upon both quantitative and qualitative data, this article examines why British MEPs voted in the way they did on this issue, and discusses what the vote tells us about current European debates within the major British parties and about national parties' relations with their increasingly important European representatives.

Young People and Contemporary Politics: Committed Scepticism or Engaged Cynicism?

Dominic Wring, Matt Henn and Mark Weinstein

Conventional wisdom holds that young people in Britain are alienated from the political process. Moreover, some have suggested that there is a 'historic political disconnection' of youth from *formal* politics and political institutions, with this group more likely to participate in *new* politics formations. In response to these developments some have talked about there being a crisis of legitimacy which should be met by initiatives to increase citizenship and engender a reinvigorated democratic culture. This article presents the results of a regional survey of first-time voters and their attitudes to politics and the democratic process. It aims to reveal the level of engagement that youth have with formal politics in Britain. Specifically, the research addresses the historical interface between young people and political parties, and whether there is a crisis of democratic legitimacy in terms of their attitudes toward politics. As a methodological innovation, the survey focuses exclusively on 'attainers', first-time voters who have only limited experience of formal politics.

Electoral Reform and Its Discontents

Richard S. Katz

When Dieter Nohlen's observation that 'fundamental changes [in electoral systems] are rare and arise only in extraordinary historical situations' was written (1984: 218), it fitted the facts of post-Second World War history quite well. The only 'fundamental change' had been that in France associated with the collapse of the 4th Republic. In recent years, however, there have been fundamental changes in Israel, Italy, Japan and New Zealand, not to mention the reform and un-reform in France between 1986 and 1988, and the reforms and re-reforms, that have been taking place in eastern and central Europe. Moreover, with a variety of alternatives to first-past-the-post (FPTP) being introduced into Great Britain for both sub-national and European elections (PR-STV is already in use in Northern Ireland), and with the report of the Jenkins Commission, far-reaching electoral reform at the national level is more clearly on the British political agenda than at any time in recent memory. In this context, it makes sense to look at the experience of other countries that have reformed their electoral systems, and to ask what lessons might be applied to the current discussions in Britain.

In this article, I have two related objectives. The first is to consider the problems that arise in anticipating the consequences of electoral reforms, and to ask why the track record of prognosticators concerning electoral reform is so poor? The second is to emphasize that there are good reasons to be sceptical about the projections of the likely reception and consequences of the possible reforms that have already been mooted in the British case, and also about those that are sure to be generated by all sides if the reform process continues. With regard to both objectives, I look not only at the possible empirical consequences of reform (impact on the translation of vote shares into seat shares, impact on the format of the party system, etc.) but also at the evaluative consequences, asking in particular why the initial evaluations of electoral reforms appear virtually always to be disappointment (see Reed, 1998). In addressing these questions, I argue that there are several interrelated, but possibly contradictory, paths from changes in electoral institutions to changes first in the electoral behaviour of voters, politicians and parties, and second in the structure of democratic politics more generally, and that, as a result, political engineering through electoral reform is not as simple as it may appear (see Katz, 1998). More specifically, I argue that there are three general classes of factors – 'mechanical and semi-mechanical', 'strategic', and 'ontological' – that need to be taken into account in predicting or explaining the behavioural consequences of institutional change, and moreover that the third especially must also be considered in predicting or explaining the evaluations made of reforms.

Recent Electoral Reforms

In this article, I focus on the four established democracies that have made major changes in their national electoral arrangements in the 1990s. Italy has replaced its almost pure PR system with one in which 75 per cent of deputies and senators are elected in FPTP contests; New Zealand has replaced its FPTP system with one that closely approximates the German system (at least with respect to the partisan distribution of seats, effectively PR); Japan has replaced the single non-transferable vote in medium-sized districts with a system of concurrent FPTP and list PR elections; Israel has introduced a direct vote for prime minister, separate from the vote for members of the Knesset. So far (late 1998) the Israelis, Japanese, and New Zealanders each have had one general election under their new systems, while the Italians have had two. Although it is dangerous to speculate about the objectives of political reformers, since claims about objectives may be made for strategic rather than informational purposes and reforms as actually adopted are often the result of compromises among actors with differing objectives, one is on relatively secure ground in concluding that in all four cases the outcome, at least so far, has not been what the reformers expected or desired.

Briefly, the Israeli reform was supposed to improve governability by reducing 'extreme multipartism, ideological polarization, virtual electoral deadlock, difficulties in forming coalition governments and frequent cabinet crises' (Hazan and Rahat, 1998). The result was to further fragment the Knesset, reducing the number of members representing the two major parties (Labour and Likud) from 76 to 56 (out of a total of 120) while increasing the number of MKs representing sectorial interests (including both the Jewish theocratic parties and the Arab parties) from 21 to 39 and producing a situation in which the prime minister, while personally more secure in office, is less able to govern effectively.

The reform in New Zealand was intended to improve majority rule, by ensuring both that a government with a majority in the House of Commons would have the support of a majority of the electorate as well, and that the leaders of parties in government could be constrained by their own caucuses in the House (Royal Commission on the Electoral System, 1986).[1] The result was the formation of a coalition by parties with the votes of 47.2 per cent of the electorate (party votes), less than a majority, but substantially more than the 35.1 per cent of the vote received by the government party in 1993. Whether this was an improvement in majoritarian democracy appears more questionable. Certainly, recent reports suggest widespread popular dissatisfaction, particularly with the pivotal role played by New Zealand. First in determining which of the two major parties would head the government (Vowles, 1997: 461).

In Japan, the reform was supposed to create a credible alternative to LDP hegemony, reduce the role of factions within the LDP, and reduce the importance of pork-barrel politics and money in Japanese political life (Takabatake, 1993). The result so far has been a restoration of the LDP to power coupled with some reduction (by some accounts temporary) in the influence of factions and cash (Christensen, 1996; Cox *et al.*, forthcoming).

The Italian reform was supposed to 'unblock' the political system by increasing the stability of governments and the transparency of their connection to electoral choice, as well as increasing the accountability of both parties and of individual MPs to their electorates (Katz, 1996). The results to date have been mixed. For the first time, the 1996 election confronted the electorate with a clear choice of alternative coalitions, and the election produced the first example of *alternanza* in post-war Italy. On the other hand, the number of parties in parliament has increased, a minority government was installed that seemed simply to survive from crisis to crisis (until it finally fell less than halfway through the parliament's five-year term), and the blockage that prevented serious reform before 1993 appears to have re-emerged with the collapse of the Bicameral Commission on institutional reform. So far, the conclusion would be 'big change in the electoral arena, little if any change in the governmental arena' (Bardi, 1997).

From Electoral Reform to Political Reform

Electoral reform can have an impact on a political system in a number of ways. The most obvious is to alter the distribution of parliamentary seats, and hence the relative importance, or even persistence, of the various parties. If the changes are sufficiently extreme, one may even see a fundamental change in the nature of the party system, as for example from a two-party to a multi-party format. Following Duverger (1954), this may be called the 'mechanical' effect. It is this mechanical effect that is foregrounded in projections that pass the distribution of votes in an actual election through the lens of an alternative electoral system to ask what the outcome would have been had that alternative system been in place. At least for heuristic purposes, one may also identify what might be called a 'semi-mechanical' factor – effects that are taken to flow from the use of a particular electoral system without sorting out the process through which they are brought about, as for example the unadorned claim that FPTP election will generate majority governments, or that it will be easier for voters to dismiss an unsatisfactory government – 'they just throw the rascals out and replace them with a new government' (Blais and Massicote, 1996: 73). Perhaps the most common and important example of a semi-mechanical argument is the invocation of Duverger's Law – that 'the plurality rule tends to produce a two-party system' (Duverger, 1986) – as if it were a scientific statement of necessary and sufficient conditions for two-party politics.

As Duverger and Downs (1957) emphasized, not just the translation of votes into seats, but the translation of individual preferences into formal votes as well, may be affected by a change in the electoral system. Knowing that a new system changes the likelihood that a vote for a party will be rewarded in the size of the parliamentary representation of that party, some voters will change their votes so as to make them more effective. In the specific case of voters who prefer a party that is in third place in their constituencies deserting that party under the FPTP system, this is Duverger's 'psychological' factor, but as Gibbard (1973) and Satterthwaite (1975) show (see also, Ordeshook, 1986: 82–86), the possibility of analogous behaviour is potentially relevant in any democratic electoral system. The psychological factor is included in more sophisticated projections that either employ survey data about more complete preference structures than can be expressed at the ballot box, or present survey respondents with ballots for hypothetical elections under alternative electoral systems (see, for example, Bowler and Farrell, 1996; Dunleavy *et al.*, 1992, 1997).

Parties and politicians may also adapt in the face of altered constraints and opportunities. A party may conclude alliances or mutual stand-down agreements while in other circumstances it would compete individually; the party may adopt a catch-all strategy while in other circumstances it would adopt a strategy of mobilizing a more narrowly defined clientele (Katz, 1980). In other words, while the translation of preferences into votes reflects the strategic choices of voters, the set of competitors about which voters are allowed to express preferences reflects the strategic choices of the parties and candidates. It is more difficult to include the consequences of this aspect of the general 'strategic' factor in projections, since they depend on negotiating skill as well as 'objective' conditions, but, as will be shown below, they can be crucial.

Finally, one can speculate about what might be called an 'ontological' factor. Differing electoral systems reflect differing conceptions of democracy and democratic values and therefore ask politicians and voters alike to think about elections, and their place in them, differently. While the strategic factor refers to changes in behaviour brought about in order to achieve the actor's (whether party, candidate, or voter) presumably fixed objectives (electoral victory, preferred policies), the ontological factor refers to the possibility that the very definition of those objectives may be altered. One should note that in suggesting that the consequences of an electoral reform depend on values, I intend to qualify, but not to reverse the usual logic that assumes the choice of an electoral reform to be a consequence of value preferences. The argument here is that while an electoral system may be chosen because its expected results are valued, the likelihood that those expectations will be realized depends in part on the normative understandings of those who will give them life.

It is generally recognized – and will not be disputed here – that institutional changes are likely to have enduring behavioural consequences. It is also generally recognized that those consequences may not appear immediately. There is a process of learning and adjustment during which political actors adapt to the new situation; in the electoral sphere, it is often argued that it is not until the second or third election under a new system that its ultimate effects can be seen. To the extent that this is true, it is still too early to reach firm conclusions about the outcomes of the reforms enumerated above. Nonetheless, what I will argue in the rest of this article – based largely on these limited experiences – is that there are sound reasons to doubt whether the effects of reform expected by the reformers will ever be achieved, and moreover that their expectations were unrealistic in understandable ways in the first place.

The Mechanical and Semi-Mechanical Factor

Clearly the most tractable effects are the mechanical. Indeed, in the most straightforward cases, estimating these effects is little more than a clerical exercise of applying a different formula to the same set of data. In most cases, however, and particularly when projections concern a reform whose details have not yet been fixed, assumptions concerning how those details will be worked out are required before even a projection that assumes no behavioural change can be made. While the need to make assumptions hardly distinguishes this exercise from any other scientific research, it is worth underscoring both the centrality and the fragility of these assumptions in this context.

The most important assumption required before an alternative electoral formula can be 'applied' concerns how the territory will be divided into electoral districts. For some potential reforms (involving changes between FPTP, two-ballot majority, and alternative vote, for example) one can assume that the districts would remain unchanged, although even this is an assumption rather than a certainty. When the proposal involves a shift in the number of districts into which a territory is to be divided, even within the single- or multi-member categories, more overt (although no more arbitrary) assumptions are required. As the extensive literature on gerrymandering has long shown, the outcome of elections in such systems is readily subject to manipulation through the redrawing of district lines (see, for example, Musgrove, 1977; Cain, 1985; Johnston, 1986). Without impugning the motives of those drawing district boundaries, the location of district boundaries makes a difference and any projection of likely outcomes will be sensitive to the assumptions made about those boundaries. Further, where PR formulas are to be applied in situations of low effective district magnitude, projections will also be sensitive to the particular number of seats per constituency assumed (Mair, 1986: 300–306).

Interpretations of the consequences of district magnitude, and of differing PR formulas, most often focus on their impact on their treatment of small parties. When conducted in the abstract, these discussions naturally ignore the problems raised by the geographic distribution of small party votes. As with the problem of drawing district lines, this can be crucial to determining actual outcomes. In the case of the Italian reform, for example, it was widely believed that the small parties would do better in the election of the Chamber of Deputies than they would do in the election of the Senate. For the Chamber, there were to be 155 PR compensation seats that would be awarded nationally, with a statutory (and therefore also an effective) threshold of 4 per cent. In the election of the Senate, however, while there would be no statutory threshold and a slightly more favourable electoral formula, the compensation seats would be awarded at the regional level with a maximum district magnitude of 12 (effective threshold of roughly 6 per cent) and more generally with magnitudes under 7 (effective thresholds of 10 per cent or more). In fact, however, in both 1994 and 1996 it proved easier for some parties to cross the higher threshold in a single region than the lower threshold nationally, and they won their only seats in parliament as PR seats in the Senate.

A second common tacit assumption is that the specific reform about which the analyst is speculating is the only one that will be made. In reality, however, whether as a result of explicit compromises or for other reasons, reforms often do not come singly. For example, the imposition of a statutory threshold or the dropping of *apparentement* may accompany the introduction of a more proportional PR formula. Failure to take these collateral changes into account will potentially bias any projections.

This then points to what might be called a 'semi-mechanical fallacy' of directly applying findings based on elections held in one set of countries to project the consequences of adopting the institutions used in those countries elsewhere. This is equivalent to the ecological fallacy in that it arises from inaccurately assuming that some covariances (in a never fully articulated model) are zero (Alker, 1969). Examples would include estimates of the impact of PR on the representation of women that ignore the fact that much of the observed 'PR-effect' is actually a 'Nordic-effect' (Rule, 1987); or that estimate the impact of electoral thresholds without taking account of the fact that these are not randomly distributed among countries, but rather often were introduced in response to specific circumstances.

The problems that arise under the 'mechanical and semi-mechanical' factor heading thus fall into three general types. The first stems from the often unavoidable inaccuracy of unavoidable assumptions. The second, and more easily avoidable, stems from applying models, or estimating outcomes, at an excessively high level of aggregation. The third stems from omitted variable bias; while it is often easy to anticipate that biases of this type may affect projections of the consequences of a reform, it is far more difficult to correct for those biases.

The Strategic Factor

If a simple-minded application of Duverger's Law is a prime example of the semi-mechanical factor, a more sophisticated reading represents a prime example of the strategic factor, in as much as Duverger (and others) support their claim – and try to account for the numerous exceptions such as Canada and India – by appeal to the strategic exigencies confronting voters and parties.

When the 1993 Italian electoral reform was being drafted, the retention of a quota of 25 per cent of the seats to be awarded by proportional representation was widely seen as a concession to the small parties. The presumption, based on a direct application of Duverger's Law, was that the FPTP seats would impose a strong pressure towards a national two-party system, but that the proportional quota would allow at least the strongest of the smaller parties to survive (and therefore convince them to support the reform in parliament where their votes were essential if the reform were to be passed). In fact, the result was quite different. The number of parties in parliament increased, and that increase, as well as the continued strength of the older small parties, was based primarily on seats won in the FPTP districts rather than in the PR portion of the election.

The reason for this result is entirely consistent with the strategic logic of the Duverger argument, but suggests that it was misapplied. In particular, to understand the Italian outcome one must look at the strategic position of the parties rather than of the voters. It was clear to everyone within each of the coalitions contesting the election that the cost of splitting their FPTP votes among several candidates would be very high. But the incentives for the big and small parties within each coalition were different. For the leaders of one of the big parties, the prize was government power, and the prerequisite was a majority for their coalition – but the value of this prize did not depend on marginal differences in the strength of their party within its coalition. For the small parties, the prize was, first, survival as participants in parliament and, second, marginal influence within their coalition – for them, number of seats was important, but being in the majority rather than the minority coalition was less so. The result was that the small parties were in a strong position to negotiate more than 'their share' of safe-seat nominations in exchange for not splitting their coalition's vote in other constituencies. The more general point is that one does not start from scratch with the adoption of a new electoral system, but with existing party organizations and also with sitting members of parliament, able to exploit the opportunities created by the reform.

TABLE 1
SEATS WON BY PARTY AND CONSTITUENCY TYPE,
ITALIAN CHAMBER OF DEPUTIES, 1994 AND 1996

Party/List	1996		1994	
	FPTP seats	PR seats	FPTP seats	PR seats
PDS	145	26	72	37
Forza Italia	86	37	74	25
Alleanza Nazionale	65	28	87	22
Lega Nord	39	20	107	10
Rifondazione Comunista	15	20	27	12
POP-SVP-PRI-UD-Prodi	71	4		
CCD-CDU	18	12	22	7
Lista Dini	18	8		
Lista Valle d'Aosta	1		1	0
Greens	16		11	0
Southern League	1		1	0
PSI			14	0
Rete			6	0
Alleanza Democratico			18	0
Cristiano-Sociali			5	0
Rinascita Socialista			1	0
Independent Left			10	0
PPI			4	29
Patto Segni			0	13
UDC			4	0
Polo Liberal-Democratico			2	0
Riformatori			6	0
SVP			3	0
Other			5	0

As Table 1 shows for the Chamber of Deputies, the tendency of small parties to do better in the FPTP seats than in the PR seats, while markedly stronger in 1994, continued in 1996. The table also appears to show the kind of consolidation that Cox (1997) would lead one to expect. There are, however, two reasons to believe that the 1996 result may be fairly close to the limits of consolidation to be expected. First, there is great regional variation in the strength of the parties, suggesting that even if there were convergence on two-party competition in each FPTP constituency, they would not be the same two parties in the north, in the centre, and in the south. Second, even the appearance of consolidation is in one sense misleading; the Chamber elected in 1996 actually resolved itself into one *more* parliamentary group than was present in the 1994 Chamber, as well as a *larger* mixed group. Finally on this point, as shown in Table 2, the significance of FPTP constituencies for the representation of small parties and independents also is evident in the 1996 Japanese result.

TABLE 2
SEATS WON BY ELECTION TYPE,
JAPANESE GENERAL ELECTION, 20 OCTOBER 1996

Party	FPTP seats	PR seats
Liberal Democratic Party	169	70
Shinshin-to (New Frontier Party)	96	60
Democratic Party	17	35
Japan Communist Party	2	24
Social Democratic Party of Japan	4	11
Sakigake (Forerunner) Party	2	0
Min-kai-ren (Democratic Reform Union)	1	0
Independents	9	0

A second contribution to the mis-predictions regarding the strength of small parties and their relative strength in the Chamber of Deputies and Senate (beyond the mis-prediction regarding PR thresholds) stemmed from the failure to take account of the strategic consequences of an additional difference between the two electoral systems. In the Chamber election, each voter had two ballots, one for a PR list choice and the other for a single-member district candidate choice; in the Senate election there was only one ballot, with list totals computed by summing the votes of each party's candidates. Thus, in order to maximize its list vote a party had to have a candidate in every single-member Senate district, but this was not the case for the Chamber. As a result, in 1994 there was an average of over 40 per cent more candidates per district in the Senate race, meaning that a far smaller percentage of the vote was required for victory. (In 1994, 27.8 per cent of the Chamber single-member districts were won by a candidate with less than 40 per cent of the vote, while for the Senate the figure was 61.6 per cent (Bartolini and D'Alimonte, 1994).) In 1996, the disparity had become even greater; while the average number of candidates per district fell by some 26 per cent for the Chamber election, for the Senate it actually increased, so that there were more than twice as many candidates per district (see Table 3).

TABLE 3
CANDIDATES PER FPTP DISTRICT, ITALY 1994 AND 1996

Year	Chamber	Senate
1994	4.5	6.4
1996	3.3	6.9

The increase in the average number of candidates per Senate district, in particular, points to an additional reason to temper predictions about the consequences of particular reforms – specifically in this case predictions about the degree to which the electoral system for the Italian Chamber of Deputies will lead to a more consolidated party system in that chamber. Parties generally compete in many electoral arenas, and these arenas are not completely insulated from one another. Nominating candidates and running a campaign in an arena in which a party has no chance of success may be rewarded in another arena, through increased credibility ('serious' parties run candidates everywhere), visibility, experience or activist enthusiasm. It having been demonstrated that having an FPTP candidate increases a party's PR vote in the same district (Cox and Schoppa, 1998), for example, it could be seen as strategically sound for a Japanese party to nominate candidates even in FPTP districts in which those candidacies risk throwing the FPTP race to the less preferred of the two locally strong parties.

As with the mechanical and semi-mechanical factors, the lessons regarding the strategic factor are relatively clear. First, it is essential to be clear about whose strategy is being considered (voters' or candidates' or parties'), and about what their objectives are. Second, one must be clear about the strategic positions and relative bargaining strengths of the actors involved. Third, one must be cognisant of spillover effects from one arena to another. Overall, this suggests that while 'rational choice' or 'economic' analysis may be a valuable heuristic, and may contribute to intuitively pleasing *post hoc* explanations, once the 'game' under consideration involves 'players' with multiple objectives, and once trade-offs and spillovers from one aspect of a complex game to another are recognized as being important, its capacity to generate accurate predictions may be quite limited.

The Ontological Factor

The problems of possibly competing objectives raise what I call the ontological factor. This factor is important in two respects. On one hand, the way in which individuals and parties understand the meaning of elections and their roles in them contributes to their definition of objectives, and hence to their choices regarding strategies and behaviour. In this respect, attention to the ontological factor contributes to more accurate prediction, or at least to fuller understanding of the inability to predict. On the other hand, the same understandings about the meaning of elections form one basis for evaluations of electoral reforms, so that attention to the ontological factor contributes to understanding of dissatisfaction with reforms once they are adopted.

The ontology of elections can be addressed in part by identifying some key questions. The first concerns the role of elections in the choice and legitimation of governments. On one hand, the point of an election may be for the people to directly choose their government, even if it is from a very restricted set of options and with a high likelihood that the government actually will be chosen by a minority of voters. On the other hand, elections may allow the people to choose parties to negotiate for them in the formation of a government, possibly with a high likelihood that the government will have the support of parties that together have the support of a majority of the voters, but with little popular input into which of the several possible governments that might be formed will actually result.

The 'elections-as-choice-of government' model generally is more appropriate to a presidential system than to parliamentary government, and indeed reform proposals aimed at increasing the transparency of the popular choice of governments in parliamentary regimes are often labelled as 'presidentialist' or 'semi-presidentialist'. That the equation need not be perfect, however, is illustrated by the Finnish presidential electoral system, especially before the introduction of direct election, in which the same process of inter-party negotiation that generates coalition cabinets might be used in the presidential electoral college, or in the British and pre-reform New Zealand systems, in which the predominance of two parties makes (made) the parliamentary election a direct choice of government as well.

Both in statistical terms, and in their 'inherent logics', these two models are also associated with quite different electoral arrangements. The transparency of the first model is clearly associated with the FPTP system, but the popular majoritarianism of the second is associated with PR (Katz, 1997: 164–6; Milnor, 1969). Although all electoral systems tend to 'manufacture' majorities, this tendency is particularly strong in FPTP systems (Rae, 1967: 74–7); indeed, this is often advanced as one of the

advantages of the FPTP system. Conversely, the implication is that under
the logic of a FPTP election, parties that do not have a serious chance of
forming a government – either alone or in a pre-announced coalition – are
less legitimate (indeed, by some definitions, less 'real' as parties), and that
electors ought not to vote for them, even if they have a substantial chance
of winning in a particular district.[2]

As a matter of practical politics, the difference between these two views
became abundantly clear in Italy in December 1994/January 1995, when the
Lega Nord withdrew from the coalition formed by Silvio Berlusconi after
the 1994 general election. Berlusconi claimed that the election had been
fought as a contest between two alternative heads of government, and hence
that the only legitimate options were a new government with himself as
prime minister or new elections. The erstwhile opposition parties, on the
other hand, claimed that notwithstanding the prominence of electoral
alliances, the election had been a normal parliamentary election, and hence
that any government that could command a parliamentary majority was as
legitimate as any other (Katz, 1996). That is, differing understandings of the
meaning of the 1994 election corresponded to differing assessments of
acceptable behaviour in January 1995; notwithstanding claims that the
'logic' of the Italian political system had been changed, the old
understandings prevailed in 1995, and again in 1998 with the fall of the
government 'elected by the people' in 1996.[3]

One can also see this problem reflected in the complaints raised about
the reformed system in New Zealand, and more generally in arguments that
PR is undesirable because it gives 'too much' influence to small parties,
allowing a party like New Zealand First, with under 14 per cent of the vote,
to determine which of the bigger parties will govern. But how much
influence is too much influence? If one starts from the presidentialist,
majoritarian, direct choice of government, position, which is the mind-set
dictated by New Zealanders' experience, it makes some sense to feel that
the voters have lost influence. From the parliamentary, proportional,
mediated choice of government perspective however, to complain of the
excessive power of a small party is not much different from saying that
western voters in the United States or Canada are 'disenfranchised' because
the overall national result may have been determined before they cast their
votes. On one hand, the power of the small party comes about only because
the voters did not give either of the larger parties a majority. The small party,
however, represents the voters who would have decided which of the larger
parties got a majority had there been only those two choices, and so, by the
logic of parliamentary government, it is quite appropriate that the
representatives of those voters should make the decision in their name. On
the other hand, one must remember that in this scenario there are not two

possible coalitions but three; the small party is the arbiter of government formation only because the two larger parties choose not to form a grand coalition themselves.[4]

This is not to suggest that one of these interpretations is right and the other wrong, but rather that they correspond to different logics, which in turn correspond to different institutions. Conversely, the evaluative problem arises when citizens do not recognize that a change in institutions entails a change in logic and thus in the evaluative standard that ought to be applied. The unrealistic desire to have it both ways was reflected in the Italian *legge truffa* (in force in 1953 and promising 380 of 590 parliamentary seats to any alliance winning 50 per cent of the popular vote) and other proposals to reward alliances, and in the often expressed preference for PR systems that encourage parties to announce their coalition plans in advance of an election.

A second set of questions concerns the nature of electoral choice, and the connection between decisions in the constituencies and the national decision/outcome of an election. The FPTP system (or really the first two or three or four-past-the-post system) derives from the fourteenth and fifteenth centuries when the English kings summoned knights of the shire and burgesses of the boroughs to meet in Parliament. Obviously, the situation then was different in myriad ways from that in contemporary democracies, but two differences are particularly important with regard to the current discussions regarding electoral reform.[5] First, the members chosen were sent to Parliament to represent corporate communities, rather than individual people, or even groups of people presumed to have a common interest. This was particularly obvious in the case of boroughs electing members under a corporation franchise, but was fundamentally true for the knights of the shire as well. Second, Parliament neither governed nor chose a government; the Commons consented to taxation and petitioned for redress of grievances (Neale, 1949: 383). These differences translate into two questions about the current role of representatives: Are they to define their constituencies (not necessarily in a geographic sense) as corporate entities and represent them with the special knowledge that can only come from 'being one of them' (a politics of presence) or are they to define their constituencies as some set of individuals who agree with them, or hope to benefit from their election, and represent these individuals by advancing the ideas or interests that were the basis of their electoral platforms (a politics of interest or ideas)? (See Phillips, 1995.) Are they to represent the interests of, and secure advantages for, their constituents or to contribute to the determination of national policy and the formation of a national government?

The first of these distinctions had a particular bearing on the new Israeli system. As mentioned above, the fragmentation of parliamentary representation that accompanied direct election of the prime minister worked particularly to the advantage of those parties primarily representing identity rather than policy. Thinking through the underlying logic helps to explain why the Israeli system had the result of weakening the major parties and thus also the governing capacity of the prime minister. On one hand, just as in the case of the single-member Italian districts, the winner-take-all nature of the prime ministerial contest greatly strengthened the bargaining power of the minor parties. In particular, the organizational capacity of those parties meant that prime ministerial candidates were forced to make long series of specific concessions and promises to particular parties. On the other hand, in separating the PR parliamentary election from the choice of prime minister, the reform encouraged both voters and parties to think in terms of communal representation rather than government policy.

One potential advantage of a presidential system is that, by separating the choice of government from the choice of (local) representative, it softens the conflict implicit in the question of whether parliamentary representation is properly a local process or a local contribution to a national process. It still leaves the related question of whether the choice of representative is a choice among local candidates as individual persons or a choice among candidates as local manifestations of their national parties. In parliamentary systems, of course, the distinction between representation for a constituency's interests and representation of a constituency in seeking the national interest is unmitigated.

That this distinction can (and does) lead to two quite different senses of strategic voting has been demonstrated by Kathleen Bawn (1993, 1998) in analysing differences between the votes for candidates in single-member districts and the votes for party lists cast in elections for the German Bundestag. Previous analyses (see Fisher, 1973) have assumed that rationality means contributing to the election of MPs of the parties more rather than less to the voter's liking, and have taken the two ballots of the German electoral system to be two parallel elections creating the ideal circumstance to test for Duverger's 'psychological factor'.[6] Bawn, in contrast, suggests that the logics of the two systems are different, and precisely because the district votes rarely have any impact on the final partisan distribution of seats, electors are free to reflect these different logics in their votes. In particular, she suggests that a rational voter, seeing the FPTP election as the choice of representative of the district as a whole, might prefer an MP connected to the governing majority, even if that elector would prefer the other major party to be in power.

The distinction between thinking about representatives as individuals versus thinking about them as partisans was, in effect, explicitly ignored in the debate surrounding the Italian reform. Proponents of single-member constituencies argued, pointing to the UK, that the resulting two-party system would allow voters a direct choice between alternative governments; they also argued, now pointing to the US, that single-member constituencies would allow each district's voters to hold their representative individually accountable to them and to base their voting decisions on the individual positions and characters of the candidates without regard to the fetters of party and ideology. That the result might instead be US-style party coherence, and UK-style individual accountability was ignored. Even short of this, the basic incompatibility of local independence and coherent national choice is bound to result in dissatisfaction.

Attention to the distinction between personal and partisan representation also contributes to understanding dissatisfaction in Japan with their new system. According to Reed (1998), much of that dissatisfaction stemmed from the election to PR seats of candidates who had been defeated in their FPTP constituencies with far fewer votes than other FPTP candidates who were not elected. (A similar complaint was raised in Estonia after the 1992 election held under a system like that used in Finland.[7] The problem was that a candidate of one party might be elected with far fewer votes than the candidate of another party who was not elected. This could happen whenever some other candidate of the first party attracted enough votes to increase that party's number of seats.) As Reed (1998) observes, the problem is the application of a standard appropriate to elections that are 'about individual candidates, not about support for party platforms' to evaluation of a system that is precisely oriented towards support for parties. PR assumes that voters are thinking primarily in terms of party; even with open list systems, the intraparty vote is regarded as secondary, and as a decision internal to the party's electorate, so that votes cast for the parliamentary candidates of two different parties are no more comparable than the votes cast for two candidates in different constituencies or for two different offices. With the 'purer' closed list system, the choice of individuals belongs entirely to the party, and personal voting strength in a parallel FPTP election is no more relevant than personal voting strength in the previous election. FPTP, and even more the old Japanese system of SNTV, assumes that voters are oriented towards individuals, with party secondary. In this case, for the candidate with fewer personal votes to be in parliament while the candidate with more is excluded is a serious anomaly. Similarly, if individual representation of an individual constituency is viewed as central, the inability of voters to dismiss a particular individual is a serious shortcoming; if representation is about contribution to a national decision, then the ability of the voters to alter the balance among the parties is the only thing that counts – with the assumption that the party itself will get rid of representatives who fail to toe the party line.

The lessons regarding the ontological factor are more difficult to articulate than those for the mechanical or strategic factors, because the factor itself is more subjective; meaning is constructed in the mind rather than being determined logically by institutions. The impact of ontological considerations may be crucial, nonetheless, especially with regard to evaluations of the results of electoral reforms. One lesson is that political actors have multiple objectives; while changes in electoral institutions may be designed to open opportunities to pursue one set of objectives, political actors may pursue another. In part, this suggests that 'political culture' plays an important part in determining the political consequences of electoral systems; the same institutions may be associated with quite different outcomes if the actors pursue a different mix of objectives. In part, it is a reminder that even within a single 'culture', the mix of objectives to be pursued remains a choice made by individual actors. A second lesson is that the normative expectations and evaluative standards applied to a reformed electoral system are likely to change more slowly than the strategic imperatives and mechanical results stimulated by the reforms; the result can be both an apparent failure to act strategically, and discontent with the results when actors are strategic.

Conclusion

The conclusion to be drawn from this analysis is one of caution in predicting the consequences of electoral reforms. First, while we know a good deal about the mechanical effects of electoral institutions, applying this knowledge to generate predictions requires knowledge of many details that often are unknowable at the time. Second, while we have some understanding of the strategic imperatives created by electoral institutions, our ability to apply these insights is restricted not only by the limited knowledge in the hands of those actors who are presumed to act strategically but also by our limited knowledge of the goals they actually will pursue. Third, while we have models of democracy that dictate how institutions and actors should behave, these are not necessarily shared universally, yet they influence both choices about behaviour and evaluations of results. Overall, political behaviour is not simply the consequence of adaptation to the environment – it is not a case of change the environment and political actors will mechanistically fall into line. It also reflects the ability of political actors to shape the environment, and to find 'wiggle room' within it, so as to pursue their multiple private and public objectives.

NOTES

1. This interpretation of the objectives of the reform differs significantly from that of Lijphart (1987), who interprets the Royal Commission report as a rejection of majoritarian democracy

and an endorsement of a more consensual form. On this difference of interpretation, see Katz (1997: 302–308).

2. This relates to the debate about whether one should look for the two-party system predicted by Duverger's law at the national level (Rae, 1967; Riker, 1986) or at the constituency level (Katz, 1980; Cox, 1997).

3. It must be recognized, however, that there was a strong correspondence between the arguments advanced concerning democratic principles and the political self-interest of the actors involved. On the idea that the logic of the system had been changed, see the literature on 'the end of the first republic', for example, Pasquino (1994); Mershon and Pasquino (1995).

4. Even from the viewpoint of the parliamentary/proportional logic, however, one might complain that in equating the three possible coalitions, one is asserting equal influence to the three parties, notwithstanding marked differences in their voting strength. For a working out of the idea that this is indeed the correct interpretation, see Banzhaf (1965).

5. A third point that might be mentioned is that part of the attraction of multi-member constituencies was that they allowed compromise instead of competition in the selection of members.

6. In fact, the use of the German case to test for the 'psychological factor' is flawed in at least three respects. (1) Because, as Bawn and others point out, the partisan distribution of seats in the Bundestag is determined almost entirely by the list votes, one could argue that casting a district vote in accordance with Duverger's Law represents a misunderstanding, rather than a sophisticated exploitation, of the electoral system. (2) Any voter who was sufficiently sophisticated for strategic voting to be plausible would have realized that most of the minor German parties had no hope of clearing the 5 per cent threshold; thus list votes cast for those parties were just as much 'wasted' votes as district votes would have been. (3) For the larger minor parties (FDP and Greens) with a chance of winning seats, strategic desertion of the small party in the FPTP contest is confused with strategic voting *for* the minor party in the PR contest by supporters of its larger ally, anxious to assure that the minor party reached 5 per cent, and hence contributed to the bloc's overall parliamentary strength (Roberts, 1988).

7. While votes are cast for individual candidates, these are aggregated into party totals, with seats allocated first to parties by PR, and then to each party's candidates in the order of their individual votes.

REFERENCES

Alker, Hayward R., Jr. (1969) 'A Typology of Ecological Fallacies', in Mattei Dogan and Stein Rokkan (eds) *Social Ecology,* pp.69–86. Cambridge: MIT Press.

Banzhaf, J.F. (1965) 'Weighted Voting Doesn't Work: A Mathematical Analysis', *Rutgers Law Review* 19: 329–30.

Bardi, Luciano (1997) 'Change in the Italian Party System', in Mark Donovan (ed.) *Italy*, Vol.II, pp.321–34. Dartmouth: Ashgate.

Bartolini, Stefano and Roberto D'Alimonte (1994) 'La competizione maggoritaria: le origini elettorale del parlamento diviso', *Rivista Italiana di Scienze Politica* 24: 631–86.

Bawn, Kathleen (1993) 'The Logic of Institutional Preferences: German Electoral Law as a Social Choice Outcome', *American Journal of Political Science* 34: 965–89.

Bawn, Kathleen (1998) 'Voter Responses to Electoral Complexity: Ticket Splitting, Rational Voters and Representation in the Federal Republic of Germany'. Paper presented at the 1998 Annual Meeting of the Midwest Political Science Association, Chicago.

Blais, André and Louis Massicote (1996) 'Electoral Systems', in Lawrence LeDuc *et al.* (eds) *Comparing Democracies: Elections and Voting in Global Perspective*, pp.49–81. Thousand Oaks: Sage.

Bowler, Shawn and David Farrell (1996) 'Voter Strategies Under Preferential Electoral Systems: A Single Transferable Vote Mock Ballot Survey of London Voters' in Colin Rallings, David M. Farrell, David Denver and David Broughton (eds) *British Elections and Parties Yearbook 1995*, pp.14–32. London: Frank Cass.

Cain, Bruce E. (1985) 'Assessing the Partisan Effects of Redistricting', *American Political Science Review* 79: 320–33.

Christensen, Raymond V. (1996) 'The New Japanese Election System', *Pacific Affairs* 69: 49–70.

Cox, Gary W., Francis Rosenbluth and Michael Thies (forthcoming) 'Electoral Reform and the Fate of Factions: The Case of Japan's LDP', *British Journal of Political Science*.

Cox, Gary W. (1997) *Making Votes Count: Strategic Coordination in the World's Electoral Systems,* Cambridge: Cambridge University Press.

Cox, Karen and Leonard Schoppa (1998) 'The Consequences of 'Sticky Voting' in Mixed Member Electoral Systems'. Paper presented at the 1998 Annual Meeting of the American Political Science Association, Boston.

Downs, Anthony (1957) *An Economic Theory of Democracy*, New York: Harper & Row.

Dunleavy, Patrick, Helen Margetts and Stuart Weir (1992) 'Replaying the 1992 General Election: How Britain Would Have Voted Under Alternative Electoral Systems', LSE Public Policy Paper No.3.

Dunleavy, Patrick, Helen Margetts, Brendan O'Duffy and Stuart Weir (1997) *Making Votes Count*, Democratic Audit paper No.11.

Duverger, Maurice (1986) 'Duverger's Law: 40 Years Later', in Bernard Grofman and Arend Lijphart (eds) *Electoral Laws and Their Political Consequences*, pp.69–84. New York: Agathon.

Duverger, Maurice (1954) *Political Parties*, New York: John Wiley.

Fisher, Stephen (1973) 'The Wasted Vote Thesis: West German Evidence', *Comparative Politics* 5: 293–99.

Gibbard, A. (1973) 'Manipulation of Voting Schemes: A General Result', *Econometrica* 41: 587–601.

Hazan, Reuven Y. and Gabriel Rahat (1998) 'Disjointed Electoral Reform: Unintended Consequences vis-a-vis Representation'. Paper presented at the ECPR Joint Sessions of Workshops, University of Warwick.

Johnston, R. J. (1986) 'Constituency Redistribution in Britain: Recent Issues' in Bernard Grofman and Arend Lijphart (eds) *Electoral Laws and Their Political Consequences*, pp.277–88. New York: Agathon.

Katz, Richard S. (1997) *Democracy and Elections*, New York: Oxford University Press.

Katz, Richard S. (1996) 'Electoral Reform and the Transformation of Party Politics in Italy', *Party Politics* 2: 31–53.

Katz, Richard S. (1998) 'Electoral Reform is not as Simple as it Looks', *Inroads* 7: 65–72.

Katz, Richard S. (1980) *A Theory of Parties and Electoral Systems*, Baltimore: Johns Hopkins University Press.

Lijphart, Arend (1987) 'The Demise of the Last Westminster System? Comments on the Report of New Zealand's Royal Commission on the Electoral System', *Electoral Studies* 6: 97–103.

Mair, Peter (1986) 'Districting Choices Under the Single-Transferable Vote' in Bernard Grofman and Arend Lijphart (eds) *Electoral Laws and Their Political Consequences,* pp.289–308. New York: Agathon.

Mershon, Carol and Gianfranco Pasquino (eds) (1995) *Italian Politics: Ending the First Republic*, Boulder: Westview.

Milnor, Andrew J. (1969) *Elections and Political Stability*, Boston: Little Brown.

Musgrove, Philip (1977) *The General Theory of Gerrymandering*, Sage Professional Papers in American Politics, vol.3, no.34, Beverly Hills: Sage.

Neale, John E. (1949) *The Elizabethan House of Commons*, London: Jonathan Cape.

Nohlen, Dieter (1984) 'Changes and Choices in Electoral Systems', in Arend Lijphart and Bernard Grofman (eds) *Choosing an Electoral System: Issues and Alternatives*, pp.217–24. New York: Praeger.

Ordeshook, Peter C. (1986) *Game Theory and Political Theory*, Cambridge: Cambridge University Press.

Pasquino, Gianfranco (1994) 'The Birth of the "Second Republic"', *Journal of Democracy* 5: 107–13.

Phillips, Anne (1995) *The Politics of Presence*, Oxford: Clarendon Press.

Rae, Douglas W. (1967) *The Political Consequences of Electoral Laws*, New Haven: Yale University Press.

Reed, Steven (1998). 'The Effects of Electoral Reform in Japan'. Paper presented at the 1998 Annual Meeting of the American Political Science Association, Boston.

Riker, William H. (1986) 'Duverger's Law Revisited', in Bernard Grofman and Arend Lijphart (eds) *Electoral Laws and Their Political Consequences*, pp.19–42, New York: Agathon.

Roberts, Geoffrey (1988) 'The Second-Vote Campaign Strategy of the West German Free Democratic Party', *European Journal of Political Research* 16: 317–37.

Royal Commission on the Electoral System (1986) *Report of the Royal Commission on the Electoral System: Towards a Better Democracy*, Wellington: V.R. Ward, Government Printer.

Rule, Wilma (1987) 'Electoral Systems, Contextual Factors and Women's Opportunity for Election to Parliament in Twenty-Three Democracies', *Western Political Quarterly* 40: 477–98.

Satterthwaite, M.A. (1975) 'Strategy-Proofness and Arrow's Conditions: Existence and Correspondence Theorems for Voting Procedures and Social Welfare Functions', *Journal of Economic Theory* 10: 1–7.

Takabatake, M. (1993) 'July Revolution', *Japan Quarterly* 40: 387–94.

Vowles, Jack (1997) 'New Zealand', *European Journal of Political Research* 32: 451–61.

New Labour's Landslide and Electoral Bias: An Exploration of Differences between the 1997 UK Election Result and the Previous Thirteen

Ron Johnston, Charles Pattie, David Rossiter,
Danny Dorling, Iain MacAllister and Helena Tunstall

The deficiencies of the first-past-the-post electoral system with regard to proportional representation are well-known and have been detailed in a range of studies (e.g. Rae, 1971; Taagepera and Shugart, 1989; Lijphart, 1994; Dunleavy and Margetts, 1997). Parties with large percentages of the votes cast tend to win even larger percentages of the Parliamentary seats, and the party with most votes usually gets a majority of the seats even though it may not get much more than 40 per cent of the votes. Consequently, small parties (other than those whose support is concentrated in relatively few constituencies) are proportionally under-represented. The 1997 British general election was no different in this respect from the 13 previous contests held under the same system for defining constituencies (the series began with the 1950 general election: Rossiter, Johnston and Pattie, 1999), but it did differ from them in other ways. Labour got a much larger share of the seats than either it or its main rival had previously achieved with either Labour's 1997 or any larger share of the votes, and the Conservatives got a much smaller share of the seats than either party had done previously with that share of the votes.

Why was this? Why was 1997 so different? In this article we explore the reasons for the distinctiveness of the 1997 result, focusing on visual presentations of data to develop the argument.

Disproportionality, Seats: Votes Ratios, and Bias

A variety of measures of the *disproportionality* of an election result has been suggested. Among the most popular is the Loosemore-Hanby index (equivalent to the index of dissimilarity: Loosemore and Hanby, 1971), which has been championed recently by Dunleavy and Margetts as a readily-interpreted measure of the overall differences between parties' shares of the votes cast and seats allocated (Dunleavy and Margetts, 1997). On this, Great Britain has one of the most disproportional electoral systems among western liberal democracies,[1] and 1997 was little different from the previous six elections. As Figure 1a shows, the level of disproportionality more than doubled between the 1970 and 1974 (February) elections: the Liberals, the SNP and Plaid Cymru substantially increased their vote shares between those two contests without commensurate increases in their allocations of seats (especially so in the case of the Liberals). Since then, the index has remained much higher than it was in the 1950s and 1960s because of the continued relative popularity of those third parties in terms of votes but their inability to win a similar share of the Parliamentary seats. The 1997 election outcome was typical of this situation, but no more: it was slightly more disproportional than 1992, but less than 1983.

If there was no significant change in the overall disproportionality of the 1997 general election result, there certainly was in the treatment of the separate parties. This is indicated in Figure 1b, which shows the *seats:votes ratios* for the Conservative, Labour and Liberal parties over the period 1950–97. For much of that time, the ratios for the first two parties followed similar trajectories. Most were above 1.0, indicating that both parties received higher percentages of the seats than of the votes (the exceptions were 1951, 1955 and 1959 for Labour and 1966 – just – for the Conservatives). In addition, until 1983 the two parties' ratios were not very dissimilar (with exceptions in 1959, when the Conservative ratio was much higher than Labour's, and 1966, when the converse held). The Conservative victories in 1983 and 1987 treated that party much better than Labour on this index, however, though even then Labour's ratio was close to 1.2, indicating that it won nearly 20 per cent more of the seats than of the votes. The two ratios converged on 1.2 in 1992, and then diverged very widely in 1997, with Labour's ratio being over 1.4 while the Conservatives' fell below 1.0 for only the second time (with 31.5 per cent of the votes but only 25 per cent of the seats). At the same time, the Liberal Democrats' ratio doubled: its vote share fell slightly between 1992 and 1997 but its number of seats more than doubled.

In terms of seats:votes ratios, therefore, the 1997 election result was very different from what went before: although the overall measure of disproportionality was similar to that of previous elections, the treatment of the separate parties was not – a feature of the 1997 result not brought out by the Loosemore-Hanby index. This distinctness of the 1997 result is further illustrated by another index, that of *electoral bias*. Devised by Brookes (1959, 1960), this index portrays the differences between two parties in their seat-winning performances with similar percentages of the vote share. We use it here to compare how many seats the Conservative and Labour parties would have won if they had achieved parity in their vote shares. Assuming a uniform shift in their performance across all constituencies, so that overall each wins the same percentage of the votes, the bias measure is simply the difference in the number of seats that the two parties would have won: a positive index indicates a bias towards Labour whereas a negative one indicates a pro-Conservative bias.

As Norris (1997) showed, such a uniform shift of the two 1997 vote distributions, so that each party had 37.9 per cent of the votes cast overall, would have seen the Labour Party with an 82-seat lead over the Conservatives – seats:votes ratios of 1.38 and 1.08 respectively. This was by far the largest bias produced by the electoral system over the 14 post-1945 elections (Figure 1c). It was also the only large pro-Labour bias. The 1997 general election once again stands out from its predecessors because of its differential treatment of the two main parties.

FIGURE 1a
TRENDS IN THE OUTCOMES OF BRITISH GENERAL ELECTIONS, 1950–97:
DISPROPORTIONALITY

The Brookes bias measure has two advantages over other indices of such differential treatment of parties in the operation of the electoral system: it uses a readily-appreciated metric (the number of seats difference between the two parties' performances); and it can be decomposed into component parts, reflecting the operation of various factors. Six such factors have been identified in our recent use of this index (Rossiter, Johnston and Pattie, 1997b; Johnston, Rossiter and Pattie, 1999; Rossiter et al., 1999; Johnston et al., 1998a, 1998b):

FIGURE 1b
TRENDS IN THE OUTCOMES OF BRITISH GENERAL ELECTIONS, 1950–97:
SEATS: VOTES RATIOS

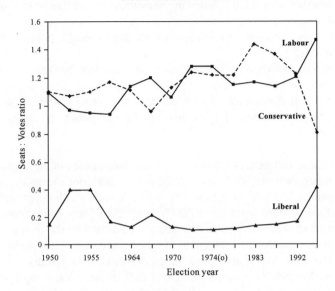

FIGURE 1c
TRENDS IN THE OUTCOMES OF BRITISH GENERAL ELECTIONS, 1950–97:
ELECTORAL BIAS

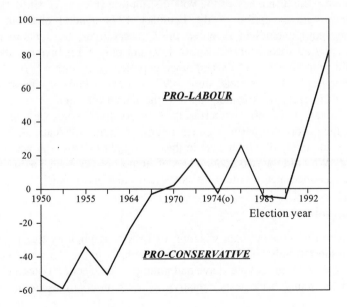

- Differences between countries (England, Scotland and Wales) in the average size of their constituency electorates;
- Differences within each country in the average size of their constituency electorates;
- Differences between constituencies in the average percentage of abstentions;
- Differences between constituencies in the average percentage of the votes won by other parties;
- Differences in the characteristics of constituencies won by other parties; and
- Differences between the parties in the efficiency of their vote distributions.

If any of these differences favour one of the two parties being compared over the other, then they contribute to the overall bias. For example, a party which is strong in a part of the country with relatively small constituencies is likely to win more seats per 100,000 votes than one whose strength is concentrated in areas with relatively large constituencies: the former party gets a better return for its votes than the latter (and as a consequence gets both a larger seats:votes ratio and a biased outcome in its favour).

In an earlier paper we traced the size of each of these components of the bias measure over the period 1950–97 and showed that all but one (the fourth) increasingly favoured Labour (Johnston *et al.*, 1999). We also showed that the major change between 1992 and 1997 was in the sixth component – the efficiency of the vote distribution (Figure 2). Until 1997, with the single exception of the February 1974 general election, the efficiency component had favoured the Conservatives, on a number of occasions by 20 seats or more. But in 1997 not only did it favour Labour, but it did so to an extent (42 seats) never experienced by either party since 1950. The implication is clear: until 1997 the Labour Party's support was not as efficiently distributed across the constituencies as was the Conservatives'. In benefit:cost terms, the Conservatives' votes were located so that they won the party a better return, in terms of seats, than did Labour's, too many of which were in the 'wrong places'. So why was 1997 different? Why did the two geographies of support produce such a different outcome, as illustrated by our seats:votes ratios and bias index?

Types of Votes

It is part of the 'conventional wisdom' of British psephology that Labour has been substantially disadvantaged in the operation of the electoral system because too many of its votes have had no impact on election outcomes: it has had too many 'safe seats', relative to the Conservatives, with large

FIGURE 2
CHANGES IN THE BIAS COMPONENTS, 1992–97

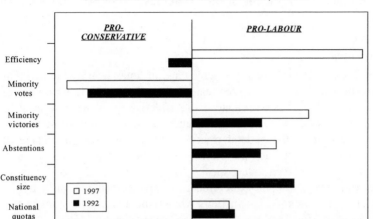

majorities where many votes have been 'wasted' because they make no contribution to the party's seat-winning goals. In part this is undoubtedly true, though Labour's safe seats provided an important bulwark when its vote share dropped substantially in 1983 but its seats:votes ratio remained relatively high (well above 1.0). This clearly did not happen for the Conservatives in 1997. When its vote share fell by more than 10 percentage points, its seats share fell much more, producing a seats:votes ratio of only 0.8: the Conservatives didn't have enough safe seats and 'wasted votes' in 1992 to provide the protection of their seats:votes ratio which the geography of Labour's support provided in the 1980s.

So does the explanation for what happened in 1997 lie in the changing geographies of the two parties' vote-winning? To explore this, we use a threefold classification of each party's votes:

- *Effective*: those which are instrumental in winning a seat;
- *Surplus*: those which are additional to the number needed to win a seat; and
- *Wasted*: those that are won in constituencies that the party loses, and so play no part in the winning of seats.

Thus in a constituency where 50,000 votes are cast – 28,000 for party A and 22,000 for party B – then the distribution of the vote types is:

	Party A	Party B
Effective	22,001	0
Surplus	5,999	0
Wasted	0	22,000

Of party A's 28,000 votes, 22,001 are effective – they are needed to defeat party B – and the remaining 5,999 are surplus. All of party B's votes are wasted.

Overall trends

Figure 3 shows the trends in the percentage of votes won by the two main parties in each of those three categories. Over the full period, the Conservative Party has won many more effective votes, even when it has lost the contest, than has Labour (Figure 3a: in this and all subsequent figures we portray the general trend in the relevant statistics using the moving average, with each point on the trend being the average of the 50 per cent of all observed values closest to it). In 1950 and 1964, when the parties were very close, they got almost the same percentages of their votes in the effective category; and in 1966, when Labour won a large majority of the seats, its effective percentage was several points higher than the Conservatives'. This was not repeated at Labour's 1974 victories, however, and the period from 1970 until 1992 was marked by a divergence between the two, with Labour's effective percentage falling to only 30 in 1987 while for the Conservatives it was over 45 in both 1983 and 1987.

The 1997 election saw a massive turn-round, however, which the moving average trend dampens down. Labour achieved its second highest effective percentage ever (though still less than the Conservative figure for any previous election except 1966 and lower than its own achievement then) whereas the Conservative percentage fell to the lowest experienced by either party, including the Labour performances of 1983 and 1987, when it obtained lower vote percentages than the Tories did in 1997.

The other two graphs in Figure 3 enlarge on these findings. With regard to wasted votes, the moving average trend lines show little difference between the two until 1970, with the winning party losing the smaller of the two percentages (Figure 3b). In the 1980s, the average Conservative wasted percentage fell to less than 30 while Labour's increased to the high 40s, with the gap between the two then closing slightly in 1992. And then in 1997 not only did the position of the two parties reverse but they recorded both the highest (over 60: Conservative) and lowest (21: Labour) percentages of wasted votes over the full period. To complete, Figure 3c shows the trends in the percentages of votes that were surplus. With the exceptions of 1966 and 1983, the gap between the two parties was not very wide until 1997: this last election was very different, however, with Labour recording the highest percentage (42) and Conservative the lowest (11) of surplus votes.

FIGURE 3a
TRENDS IN TYPES OF VOTES WON BY THE CONSERVATIVE AND LABOUR
PARTIES, 1950–97:
PERCENTAGE OF VOTES THAT WERE EFFECTIVE

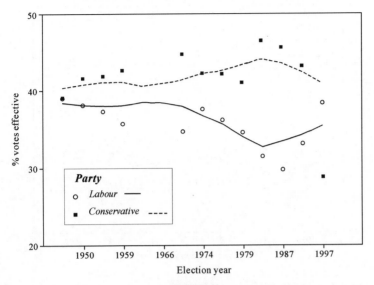

FIGURE 3b
TRENDS IN THE TYPES OF VOTES WON BY THE CONSERVATIVE AND LABOUR
PARTIES, 1950–97:
PERCENTAGE OF VOTES THAT WERE WASTED

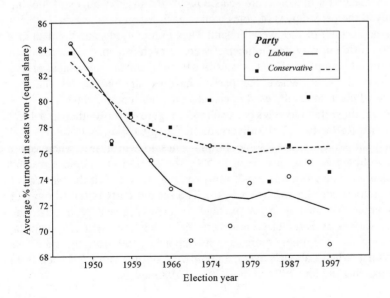

FIGURE 3c
TRENDS IN THE TYPES OF VOTES WON BY THE CONSRVATIVE AND LABOUR
PARTIES, 1950–97:
PERCENTAGE OF VOTES THAT WERE SURPLUS

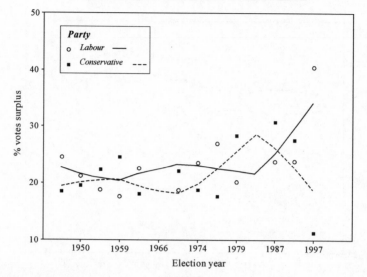

Ratios of vote types to seats

The trends shown in Figure 3 provide further evidence of how different the 1997 general election was from the 13 preceding general elections in terms of the translation of votes into seats. One of the disadvantages of looking simply at the percentages of votes won in each category, however, is that it takes no account of the overall result. Thus Figure 4 presents the data in a slightly different way: the number of votes in each category is expressed in a ratio to the number of seats won (for effective and surplus votes) or lost (for wasted votes) where the parties have equal vote shares (i.e. the simulated election results used to calculate the bias coefficients).

Regarding effective votes per seats won, Figure 4a shows that after 1959 the trends for the two parties diverged: on average by the end of the period it took the Conservatives some 17,000 votes to win a seat whereas for Labour the figure was only about 13,500. The 1997 election does not stand out as a residual from this trend, however, nor does it with the pattern for surplus votes per seat won (Figure 4b). The Labour Party obtained more of such votes (i.e. had a larger average majority per seat won) than the Conservatives at every election except 1970 and from then on,[2] with the exception of 1979, many more than its opponent. 1997 saw the gap close somewhat, when Labour's average number of surplus votes fell back from its peaks in 1987 and 1992 to its 1979 and 1983 levels.

FIGURE 4a
TRENDS IN THE RATIOS OF VOTES WON, AT THE EQUAL SHARE POSITION:
EFFECTIVE VOTES PER SEAT WON

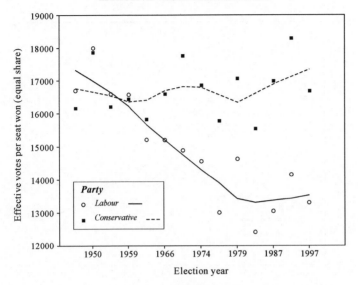

Election year

FIGURE 4b
TRENDS IN THE RATIOS OF VOTES WON, AT THE EQUAL SHARE POSITION:
SURPLUS VOTES PER SEAT WON

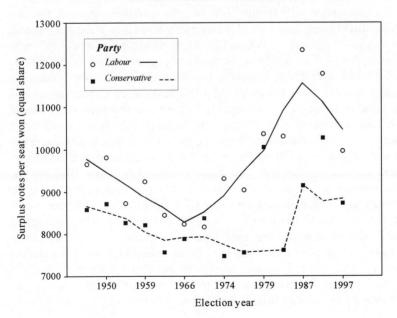

Election year

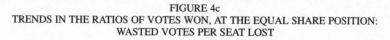

FIGURE 4c
TRENDS IN THE RATIOS OF VOTES WON, AT THE EQUAL SHARE POSITION:
WASTED VOTES PER SEAT LOST

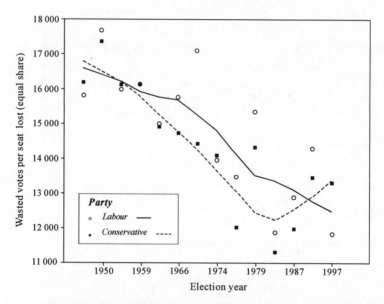

It was only in the pattern of wasted votes per seats lost that 1997 produced a major shift (Figure 4c). For the first five elections, the two parties differed very little indeed in how many votes they wasted in the seats that they lost – between 15,000 and 17,500 each. From then until 1992 (with the exception of February 1974) there was often a wide gap between the two parties which operated to Labour's disadvantage: in 1970, for example, it wasted over 2,000 more votes per seat lost than did the Conservatives – in part because the election was fought in very old constituencies (see Note 2), with Labour wasting a lot of votes in the large suburban constituencies where the Conservatives won. Although the gap remained at 1,000 votes or more from October 1974 on, the trends for the two parties converged after 1983, because on average the Labour ratio fell while that for the Conservatives rose. And in 1997 their relative positions were altered: the Labour Party wasted on average about 1,500 fewer votes in the seats that it lost than did the Conservatives – a major difference to which we return below. (If we contrast the two 'extreme elections', in 1970 Labour performed reasonably well in many of the constituencies where it lost, thus piling up a lot of wasted votes: in 1997, however, it did relatively badly in the seats where it lost, wasting more than 5,000 fewer votes per constituency on average than it did 27 years previously.)

In terms of maximizing the returns from its vote-winning efforts, as reflected either in its seats:votes ratio or the bias coefficient, a party will want to maximize its effective vote share while minimizing both the number of surplus votes it gets where it wins and its wasted votes where it loses: it wants to win well, but not too well, in the first group of seats and to lose badly in the second. There is a paradox with both, of course. If you win well, but not too well, in a constituency, there is a strong chance that you will lose it at a subsequent election if there is an overall swing against you; and if you lose badly, then your chances of winning the seat next time are reduced. A 'happy balance' has to be struck but, given that many seats – perhaps up to one-quarter of the total – are either 'very safe' or 'hopeless' for at least one of the parties, in those at least there is little point in either 'stacking up' more surplus votes or striving to win over a few more wasted votes.

From Vote Types to Bias

The general picture provided by Figures 3 and 4 suggests that over the full period 1950–97 there has been a general trend in the geography of support which has increasingly favoured the Labour Party, with 1997 either an accentuation of that trend or – notably in the pattern of wasted votes – a deviant case. In this section we briefly explore this long-term trend, followed by more detailed consideration of the apparently 'special case' of 1997.

The long-term trends

Our previous analyses of the changing biases over the period 1950–1997 have suggested that most of the six components have increasingly favoured Labour (Rossitor et al., 1999). The reasons for this can be summarized by three characteristics of the constituencies that would have been won by the two main parties with equal vote shares: their size (number of electors); their average turnout; and the performance of other parties.

Figure 5a shows that after the 1959 election there was a divergence between the two parties in the average size of the seats that they won, with the gap widening to almost 10,000 electors by the 1992 contest. The reasons for this are well known: the removal of the pro-rural bias by the Boundary Commissions after 1955; Labour's growing strength in Scotland and Wales, where seats are on average much smaller than in England, from the 1960s on (the difference was some 15,000 voters by 1997); and Labour's concentration of support in all three countries in the older urban and industrial areas, which have experienced population decline (Johnston et al., 1998b). The last of these is especially noteworthy as the constituencies 'age': the gaps between the two parties shown in Figure 5a are smaller at the first election after each of the last three Boundary Commission Reviews (in 1974, 1983 and 1992) than at subsequent contests, because those exercises always result in a reduction in the inter-constituency variation in electorates (Rossiter, Johnston and Pattie, 1999).

The second trend that also shows a divergence between the two parties after 1959 is in the average turnout in the seats that the two parties would have won (Figure 5b). Turnout has fallen substantially at British general elections since the 1950s, with 1997 producing the lowest figure at just over 71 per cent.[3] It has fallen most in Labour-won seats, as the two moving-average trend lines show, and the gap between the two parties in 1992 and 1997 was particularly large. Labour thus benefits – in terms of its seats:votes ratio and bias coefficient – from low turnouts in the seats that it wins: more votes for it there would be very unlikely to gain it further Parliamentary representation.

Finally, what of the performance of the 'third parties' (the Liberal Democrats and their predecessors over the full period, the Scottish Nationalists and Plaid Cymru since 1970, and others which have had small successes, such as the Greens and, in 1997, the Referendum Party)? Figure 5c shows that, with one exception (October 1974), these parties have always performed better in the seats won by the Conservatives, which has been to that party's advantage since the number of votes needed for victory in close three- and four-party contests is usually smaller than the position where the 'third parties' perform badly: 1997 was no different from the general trend.

FIGURE 5a
TRENDS IN THE CHARACTERISTICS OF SEATS THAT WOULD HAVE BEEN WON BY
LABOUR AND CONSERVATIVE PARTIES, 1950–1997:
AVERAGE ELECTORATE IN SEATS WON

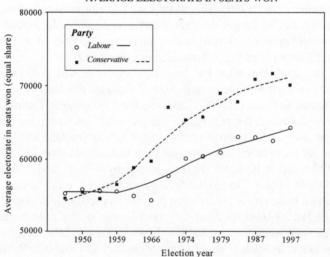

FIGURE 5b
TRENDS IN CHARACTERISTICS OF SEATS THAT WOULD HAVE BEEN WON BY
LABOUR AND CONSERVATIVE PARTIES, 1950–1997:
AVERAGE TURNOUT IN SEATS WON

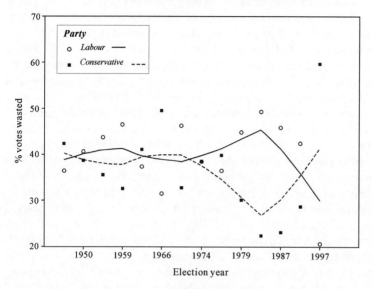

FIGURE 5c
TRENDS IN THE CHARACTERISTICS OF SEATS THAT WOULD HAVE BEEN WON BY
LABOUR AND CONSERVATIVE PARTIES, 1950–1997:
AVERAGE VOTE FOR THIRD PARTIES

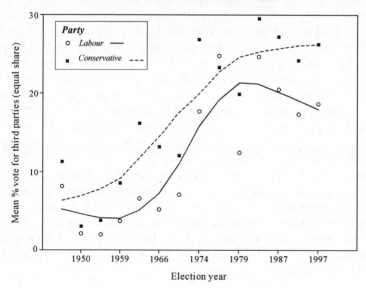

And 1997?

Of the three long-term trends in constituency characteristics explored above, therefore, two favoured the Labour Party but only one – the fall in turnout – appears to account for the major shifts in seats:votes ratio and bias coefficient that occurred in 1997.[4] So what was particular about 1997?

It is widely accepted that one of the main features of the 1997 contest was not only the professionalism of the campaigns run by Labour and the Liberal Democrats (especially the former) but also their geographical specificity. Although the 'conventional wisdom' of psephologists and other commentators has been that constituency campaigning is almost irrelevant to the election outcome there, and that only the national campaign matters, an increasing volume of research evidence using a range of indicators has shown otherwise: the greater the intensity of a party's campaign in a constituency, all other things being held equal, the better its relative performance (Denver and Hands, 1997). In 1997, Labour built on its appreciation that this was the case with a very focused and targeted campaign, which concentrated on 100 constituencies in the two years preceding the election (Denver *et al.*, 1998) and was followed by high levels of spending during the six weeks of the 'campaign proper' (Johnston, Pattie and MacAllister, 1999): together with a similar, though less extensive, spatially-focused campaign by the Liberal Democrats, this contributed substantially to the challengers' success then.[5]

The success of these campaigns is shown by the geography of the outcome (Figure 6). The Conservative share fell by an average of 11.4 percentage points between 1992 and 1997: it fell by much less in those seats where its 1992 overall share was relatively small, however (Figure 6a).[6] As a consequence, not only did it increase its tally of wasted votes by losing a large number of seats to its challengers but also its number of wasted votes did not fall substantially in many of the constituencies it failed to win in 1992. This accounts for not only the substantial increase in its percentage of votes wasted (Figure 3b) but also in its average number of wasted votes per seat lost (Figure 4c). Linton and Southcott's (1998) data for selected constituencies suggest that this is a continuation of a trend that increasingly distinguishes the Conservative and Labour parties: whereas Labour's vote percentage has declined very substantially over the period in those seats now 'hopeless' for the party, from over 40 per cent on average in 1951 to around 10 per cent in 1997 (they cite the Isle of Wight, Wiltshire North, Cheltenham, and Newbury as exemplars), the Conservatives have retained a similar percentage of the vote in their 'hopeless seats' throughout the period (the example cited is Hemsworth, where the party gained 18 per cent in both 1951 and 1997).[7]

FIGURE 6a
VARIATIONS IN PARTY PERFORMANCE, 1992–97:
ABSOLUTE CHANGE IN SHARE OF VOTES CAST: CONSERVATIVE

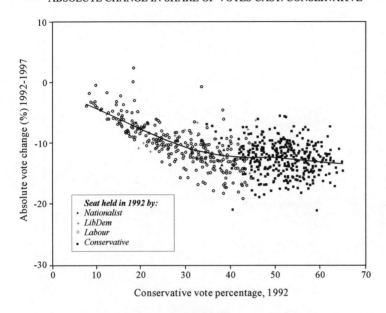

Conservative vote percentage, 1992

FIGURE 6b
VARIATIONS IN PARTY PERFORMANCE, 1992–97:
ABSOLUTE CHANGE IN SHARE OF THE VOTES CAST: LABOUR

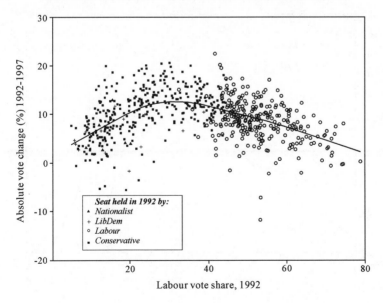

Labour vote share, 1992

FIGURE 6c
VARIATIONS IN PARTY PERFORMANCE, 1992–97:
ABSOLUTE CHANGE IN SHARE OF THE VOTES CAST: LIBERAL DEMOCRAT

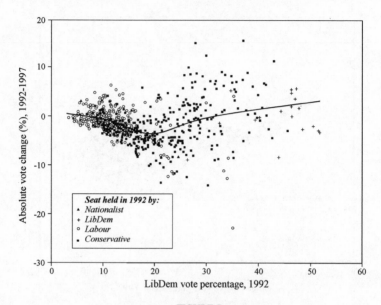

FIGURE 7
FREQUENCY BY DISTRIBUTIONS OF THE CONSERVATIVE VOTE SHARE, BY
CONSTITUENCY, 1992 AND 1997

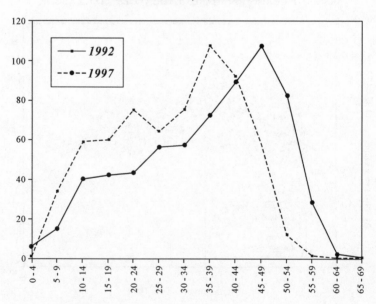

The consequence of this is shown by the frequency distributions for the Conservative vote share at the two elections (Figure 7). Between 1992 and 1997 the distribution shifted leftwards, as expected given the reduction in the Conservative vote share overall; the mode moved down two categories (from 45–49 per cent of the votes cast to 35–39) and the right-hand portion of the distribution appears to have shifted en bloc. But on the left-hand side there is a second mode, at 20–24 per cent of the vote share, which is much more pronounced than that at 25–29 per cent five years previously. The Conservatives' relative success at retaining support in constituencies where they had no significant chance of winning in 1997 – presumably in part at least because Labour and the Liberal Democrats did not campaign hard there (as shown in Johnston, Pattie and MacAllister, 1999) – meant that the party won many more wasted votes than Labour had done at previous contests: where Labour lost in 1997 it lost badly, with benefits shown in its seats:votes ratio, but where the Tories lost they did relatively well, and got no Parliamentary return for the extra votes!

Whereas the Conservatives piled up more wasted votes in 1997, however, Labour and the Liberal Democrats did not. Labour's share of the poll increased by 9.6 percentage points overall between 1992 and 1997, but with very considerable variation about this average (Figure 6b). In its safe seats and also those where its chances of victory were slight it performed at well below its national average, thus winning most votes in the centre of the distribution (i.e. the constituencies which it held by relatively small margins plus those where it occupied a close second place before the 1997 poll). Labour neither 'piled up' excessive numbers of surplus votes in its safe seats nor worked hard to get more wasted votes where it had no chance of victory: it garnered votes where they mattered most, hence the very large increase in its effective percentage (Figure 3) and the substantial fall in both its number of wasted votes per seat lost and surplus votes per seat won (Figure 4).

For the Liberal Democrats, too, the result of the campaign was that it performed best where it was most important to do so. Their overall share fell slightly between 1992 and 1997, but they performed better than that in the small number of constituencies that they were defending (Figure 6c) and also in many of the others where their 1992 share was above 30 per cent and they had a chance of victory.

Tactical voting and campaign intensity

These graphical analyses provide strong evidence that the changing performance of the Conservative and Labour parties in 1997 relative to previous elections was a result of not only the overall shift in support from the former to the latter but also a geography to that shift which saw Labour perform best where it most needed votes: its much improved seats:votes ratio in 1997 reflected a more efficient vote distribution, consequent on its lack of attention to winning-over more support where the additional votes would be either wasted or surplus. The Conservatives, on the other hand, not only lost vote share overall but lost it most where it mattered most, to a greater extent (it is assumed here) than ever before: its very low seats:votes ratio in 1997, and the shift in the efficiency component of the bias index between 1992 and 1997 reflects that, and especially on the Tories' much greater harvest of wasted votes per seat lost.

Circumstantial evidence suggests that these changed geographies were strongly influenced by the spatially-focused nature of the Labour and Liberal Democrat campaigns at the 1997 election. One aspect of their campaigning which has attracted much attention since is the volume of tactical voting, and whether this led to many more Conservative defeats than might otherwise have been the case because there were substantial switches to the second-placed party, not only from former Conservative supporters and those who did not vote in 1992 but also between the two main challengers (Labour and Liberal Democrat). Several attempts have been made to measure the volume of such tactical voting (e.g. Berrington, 1997; Johnston et al., 1997; McAllister, 1997; Evans et al., 1998), with the latter group concluding that 'in 1997 more people voted tactically in order to try to defeat their local Conservative candidate than did so in 1992' (p.77).

Figure 8 illustrates the consequence of this in Conservative-held seats. The ratio of the two challenger parties' 1992 vote share is the independent variable (transformed to a logarithmic scale) and the relevant party's changed vote share between the two elections is the dependent. Labour's vote share clearly increased much more where it was better placed to contest Conservative incumbency (i.e. a log ratio greater than 0.0), with the exceptions of a small number of constituencies where it was in third place (i.e. a log ratio below 0.0) but performed better than its opponent (Figure 8a). The Liberal Democrats' share increased much more, on average, where they were in second place (a ratio of less than 0.0 on the independent variable), with a number of very substantial increases (Figure 8b). Their performance was poorest in those seats where Labour's 1992 share was only slightly larger than their own (log ratios around 0.0): where Labour had a very strong second place (i.e. a ratio of 0.5 or more) the Liberal Democrat performance was somewhat better (another piece of evidence that Labour did not build up large blocks of surplus votes).

FIGURE 8a
THE EVIDENCE FOR TACTICAL VOTING: CHANGE IN LABOUR SHARE OF THE VOTE
1992–97, ACCORDING TO THE (LOG OF) THE RATIO OF THEIR VOTE SHARES IN 1992

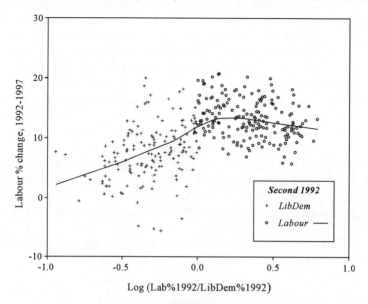

FIGURE 8b
THE EVIDENCE FOR TACTICAL VOTING: CHANGE IN LIBERAL DEMOCRAT SHARE
OF THE VOTE, 1992–97, ACCORDING TO THE (LOG OF) THE RATIO OF THEIR VOTE
SHARES IN 1992

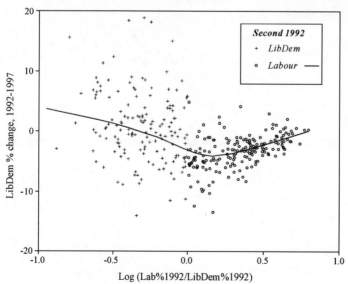

Further evidence of the important role of tactical voting is provided by our estimates of the flow-of-the-vote between the two parties between 1992 and 1997. (The estimation of flow-of-the-vote matrices follows procedures detailed elsewhere: Johnston *et al.*, 1988.) For each constituency, we have an estimate of the flow of support from Labour to Liberal Democrat between 1992 and 1997, and also of the flow in the other direction: the ratio of these indicates the magnitude and direction of tactical voting – a ratio exceeding 1.0 indicates a net flow to Labour whereas a ratio below 1.0 indicates a net flow to the Liberal Democrats. Graphs (not reproduced here) show that where Labour was in second place (or a close third) the net flow was towards it, whereas the Liberal Democrats were the main beneficiaries where they were lying second. To relate this to campaign intensity, our independent variable is the ratio of the amount spent on the campaign, as a percentage of the maximum, by the two parties. (Again, this is using standard methods: Johnston, Pattie and MacAllister, 1999.) The two ratios are logged and regressed in Figure 9 (for Conservative-held seats only), which provides strong circumstantial evidence that tactical voting which favoured one party rather than another increased the more that the former party outspent its opponent.

FIGURE 9
THE RELATIONSHIP BETWEEN SPENDING AND TACTICAL VOTING FLOWS,
1992–97

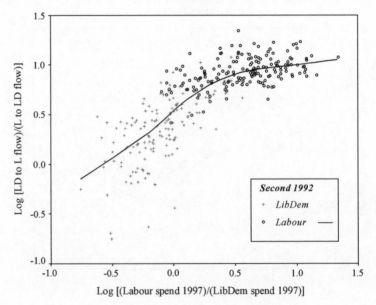

Finally we turn to an issue which has intrigued a number of commentators. Although the Labour Party concentrated much of its effort on its 100 key seats, most of which the Conservatives held by a margin of ten percentage points or less, it actually increased its share of the vote more in the seats where it was 10–20 points behind than it did in the key seats (Curtice and Steed, 1997). This led to doubts that Labour's focused campaign really worked, and suggestions that other factors must have been more influential (Crewe, 1997). Our explanation for this apparent anomaly is that it reflects the relative intensity of the challengers' campaigns in the individual constituencies. Labour outspent the Liberal Democrats in most of the constituencies that the Conservatives held by a margin of more than 10 percentage points, and the greater the degree of outspending (i.e. a log ratio in excess of 0.0) the larger the increase in Labour's vote share and the greater the probability that Labour defeated the Conservative who was defending the seat (Figure 10a). In effect, Labour did so well in those seats where the gap between it and the Conservatives was wide because it out-campaigned the third-placed party. The Liberal Democrats lost support in the great majority of those seats (Figure 10b) but increased their vote share very significantly (by 10 percentage points or more) in a small number of those where they outspent Labour – and they won in 16 of those contests.

FIGURE 10a
CHANGES IN VOTE SHARE, 1992–97, FOR LABOUR IN CONSERVATIVE-HELD SEATS BY A MARGIN OF 10 PERCENTAGE POINTS OR MORE, ACCORDING TO THE RATIO OF THE TWO PARTIES' SPENDING ON THE 1997 CAMPAIGN AND VICTORY IN 1997

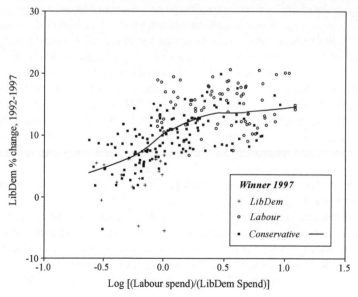

FIGURE 10b
CHANGES IN VOTE SHARE, 1992–97, FOR LIBERAL DEMOCRAT IN CONSERVATIVE-
HELD SEATS BY A MARGIN OF 10 PERCENTAGE POINTS OR MORE, ACCORDING
TO THE RATIO OF THE TWO PARTIES' SPENDING ON THE 1997 CAMPAIGN AND
VICTORY IN 1997

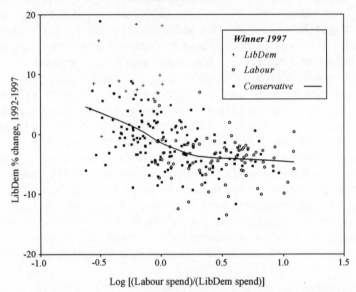

Log [(Labour spend)/(LibDem spend)]

The message is clear: tactical voting, and its relationship to constituency campaign intensity, not only contributed to the overall Conservative defeat but also was a contributor to Labour's much more efficient vote distribution in 1997. In Conservative-held seats where one of the challengers had a good chance of victory, the flow of tactical votes to it increased its chances of success, and thus its store of effective votes, whereas for the other challenger it reduced its possible accumulation of wasted votes. Labour's substantially increased seats:votes ratio in 1997 reflects this: where it was third, it came an even worse third than it would have done without tactical voting and got relatively few wasted votes; where it was second, tactical voting increased its chances of success, which meant more effective votes (and, again, fewer wasted ones). The corollary of this was that the Liberal Democrats, too, achieved a substantial increase in their seats:votes ratio for the same reason (Figure 1b).

The mechanism underpinning this remains unclear, however. In part, the volume of tactical voting undoubtedly reflects the individual decisions made by an increasingly sophisticated electorate. But the clear link between not only the flow of tactical votes within constituencies and the intensity of local campaigns suggests that the parties mobilize some of this either through their direct contacts with electors or simply by the impact of their advertising and other activities locally. The 1997 BES cross-section survey data show no difference between those who reported voting tactically (as analysed by Evans *et al.*, 1998) and those who did not in the probability of their being contacted by canvassers, either at their home or by phone. Voters, it seems, 'go with the flow' in their local milieux: the stronger the evidence that one of the challenger parties is campaigning hard (evidenced, for example, by the number of posters they have displayed in the constituency), the greater the shift of voter support in their favour.[8]

Conclusions

The 1997 general election result produced a landslide for Labour in terms of Parliamentary representation, though its share of the votes cast was not extraordinary, and it saw the Conservatives lose an incommensurate proportion of the seats relative to their vote share (which even so was their lowest ever over the last 50 years). These features are obscured by a summary measure of disproportionality, such as the Loosemore-Hanby index. Two other measures – the seats:votes ratio for each party and the Brookes index of electoral bias – make very clear just how different the 1997 result was from those that preceded it, however.

In this article we have explored the reasons why the 1997 result should have been so different in the allocation of seats relative to votes, using a division of votes won into three categories – effective, surplus and wasted. With these, we have shown both long-term trends that have increasingly favoured Labour over the Conservatives, because of differences between the two in the average size of the constituencies that they have won and in the average turnout there. But these were insufficient to account for the major changes between 1992 and 1997. These were consequences of significant shifts in the geography of vote-winning, which were consistent with the spatially-focused constituency campaigns conducted by the challenger parties in 1997 and accentuated by tactical voting, which meant that the Conservatives substantially increased their number of wasted votes per seat lost whereas Labour very significantly reduced its ratios of both surplus votes to seats won and wasted votes per seat lost. Labour's landslide was a geographical phenomenon, and the parties' performances at the next election will reflect the degree to which they and the British electorate have all learned this lesson.

NOTES

1. Throughout this article we deal only with Great Britain, excluding Northern Ireland with its separate party system.

2. The 1970 election was fought in constituencies defined in the mid-1950s, because of Labour's decision not to implement the 1969 Reviews of constituencies reported by the Boundary Commissions. This meant that there were many small, inner city constituencies in 1970, the vast majority of which were won by Labour with relatively few votes even though in percentage terms many of the majorities were large (see Rossiter, Johnston and Pattie, 1999).
3. As the evidence presented to the Home Affairs Select Committee (1998) on this issue shows, turnout has been especially low at elections where the likely outcome is very clear beforehand. The exact figures are very difficult, if not impossible, to calculate because of difficulties regarding electoral registration which that report also demonstrates.
4. Although the performance of 'third parties' in seats that it won favoured the Conservatives, their increased electoral success told against them, especially in 1997 when they more or less negated the general advantage (Johnston *et al.* 1998b, 1999).
5. So much so that in July 1998 the Labour Party decided to repeat it for the next election, by identifying the 91 seats it needed most effort to hold on to then, and initiating the 'long campaign'.
6. The 1992 vote percentages for each constituency are those calculated by the procedure described in Rossiter, Johnston and Pattie (1997a).
7. An alternative interpretation of some of these trends over recent (post-1979?) elections is the growth of anti-Conservative tactical voting.
8. This is consistent with recent work on the role of conversations in local milieux as an influence on voting decisions (Pattie and Johnston, 1999).

REFERENCES

Berrington, H. (1997) 'The Liberal Democrat Campaign', in P. Norris and N. Gavin (eds), *Britain Votes 1997*, pp.47–60. Oxford: Oxford University Press.

Brookes, R.H. (1959) 'Electoral Distortion in New Zealand', *Australian Journal of Politics and History*, 5: 218–23.

Brookes, R.H. (1960) 'The Analysis of Distorted Representation in Two-party, Single-member Elections', *Political Science*, 12: 158–67.

Crewe, I. (1997) 'Book Review', *New Statesman and Society*, 12.12.1997

Curtice, J. and M. Steed (1997) 'The Results Analysed', in D. Butler and D. Kavanagh, *The British General Election of 1997*, pp.295–325. London: Macmillan.

Denver, D. and G. Hands (1997) *Modern Constituency Electioneering: The 1992 General Election*. London and Portland, OR: Frank Cass.

Denver, D., G. Hands and S. Henig (1998) 'Triumph of Targeting? Constituency Campaigning in the 1997 General Election', in D. Denver, J. Fisher, P. Cowley and C. Pattie (eds) *British Elections and Parties Review Volume 8: The 1997 General Election*, pp.171–90. London and Portland, OR: Frank Cass.

Dunleavy, P. and H. Margetts (1997) 'The electoral system', in P. Norris and N. Gavin (eds), *Britain Votes 1997*, pp.225–41. Oxford: Oxford University Press.

Evans, G., J. Curtice and P. Norris (1998) 'New Labour, New Tactical Voting? The Causes and Consequences of Tactical Voting in the 1997 General Election', in D. Denver, J. Fisher, P. Cowley and C. Pattie (eds) *British Elections and Parties Review Volume 8: The 1997 General Election*, pp.65–79. London and Portland, OR: Frank Cass.

Home Affairs Committee (1998) *Fourth Report: Electoral Law and Administration*. Cm 768-I, 768-II. London: HMSO

Johnston, R.J., C.J. Pattie and G. Allsopp (1988) *A Nation Dividing? The Electoral Map of Great Britain 1979–1987*. London and Portland, OR: Longman.

Johnston, R.J., C.J. Pattie and I. MacAllister (1999) 'The Funding of Constituency Party General Election Campaigns in Great Britain', *Environment and Planning C: Government and Policy*, 17.

Johnston, R.J., C.J., Pattie, I. MacAllister, D.J. Rossiter, D.F.L. Dorling and H. Tunstall (1997)

'Spatial Variations in Voter Choice: Modelling Tactical Voting at the 1997 General Election in Great Britain', *Geographical and Environmental Modelling*, 1: 153–79.

Johnston, R.J., C.J. Pattie, D.F.L. Dorling, D.J. Rossiter, H. Tunstall and I. MacAllister (1998a) 'New Labour Landslide – Same Old Electoral Geography?', in D. Denver, J. Fisher, P. Cowley and C. Pattie (eds) *British Elections and Parties Review Volume 8: The 1997 General Election*, pp.35–64. London and Portland, OR: Frank Cass.

Johnston, R.J., C.J. Pattie, D.J. Rossiter, D.F.L. Dorling, H. Tunstall and I. MacAllister (1998b) 'Anatomy of a Labour Landslide: The Constituency System and the 1997 General Election', *Parliamentary Affairs*, 51: 131–48.

Johnston, R.J., D.J. Rossiter and C.J. Pattie (1999) 'Integrating and Decomposing the Sources of Partisan Bias: Brookes' Method and the Impact of Redistricting in Great Britain', *Electoral Studies*, 17: 367–78.

Lijphart, A. (1994) *Electoral Systems and Party Systems*. Oxford: Oxford University Press.

Linton, M. and M. Southcott (1998) *Making Votes Count: The Case for Electoral Reform*. London: Profile Books.

Loosemore, J. and V.J. Hanby (1971) 'The Theoretical Limits of Maximum Distortion: Some Analytic Expressions for Electoral Systems', *British Journal of Political Science*, 1: 467–77.

McAllister, I. (1997) 'Regional Voting', in P. Norris and N. Gavin (eds), *Britain Votes 1997*, pp.133–49. Oxford: Oxford University Press.

Norris, P. (1997) 'Anatomy of a Labour landslide', in P. Norris and N. Gavin (eds), *Britain Votes 1997*, pp.1–33. Oxford: Oxford University Press.

Pattie, C.J. and R.J. Johnston (1999) 'Context, Conversation and Conviction: Social Networks and Voting at the 1992 British General Election', *Political Studies*, 47: XXXX

Rae, D.W. (1971) *The Political Consequences of Electoral Laws (second edition)*. New Haven CT: Yale University Press.

Rossiter, D.J., R.J. Johnston and C.J. Pattie (1997a) 'Estimating the Partisan Impact of Redistricting in Great Britain', *British Journal of Political Science*, 27: 319–31.

Rossiter, D.J., R.J. Johnston and C.J. Pattie (1997b) 'Electoral Bias and Redistricting in Great Britain', *British Journal of Political Science*, 27: 466–72.

Rossiter, D.J., R.J. Johnston, and C.J. Pattie, (1999) *The Boundary Commissions: Redrawing the UK's Map of Parliamentary Constituencies*. Manchester: Manchester University Press.

Rossiter, D.J., R.J. Johnston, C.J. Pattie, D.F.L. Dorling, I. MacAllister and H. Tunstall (1999) 'Changing Biases in the Operation of the United Kingdom Electoral System, 1950–1997', *British Journal of Politics and International Affairs*, 1: 133–64.

Taagepera, R. and M. Shugart (1989) *Seats and Votes: The Effects and Determinants of Electoral Systems*. New Haven CT: Yale University Press.

Reforming the Westminster Electoral System: Evaluating the Jenkins Commission Proposals

Helen Margetts and Patrick Dunleavy

The method of electing the House of Commons was the 'source code' of plurality rule voting systems worldwide. As the genetic forerunner of all other plurality systems the UK system has been an enormously symbolic and influential case. So the report of the UK government's Independent Commission on the Voting System chaired by Lord Jenkins on 28 October 1998 marked a historic date, the third time in the twentieth century when the source code seemed to be in real danger. The two earlier occasions were the 1917 debates on the representation of the People's Act and a 1931 Labour/Liberal bill, when clear Commons majorities voted for legislation adopting the Alternative Vote (AV) – a change killed off on both occasions by House of Lords opposition (Hart, 1992). The Jenkins Commission's brief was to propose a new method of electing the House of Commons, to be offered in a referendum giving British voters the choice to keep plurality rule or to adopt a single alternative. This initiative was pledged in both the Labour and Liberal Democrat manifestos in 1997 and it formed a central element of the Cook-McLennan pact, which created co-operation arrangements between the two parties. A majority of the Jenkins Commission continued the 1917 and 1931 tradition by recommending a mixed electoral system, known as AV-Plus, under which the vast majority of MPs would be elected by AV in local constituencies and a small minority (a fifth to a sixth) of MPs would be elected in broader top-up areas to give enhanced levels of proportionality. We first briefly recap on the way in which the Commission came to this view, and then explore how the Commission's scheme would work in practice using data from simulations of the 1997 and 1992 general elections. The conclusions briefly evaluate the extent to which the proposed system meets the criteria set for the Jenkins Commission and consider how likely the scheme is to be implemented in its original form.

The Commission's Method of Working

The Blair government gave the Commission a brief of choosing one, and only one, alternative to plurality rule elections that satisfied four criteria: extending voter choice; achieving 'broad' proportionality; maintaining the existing constituency links of MPs; and providing for stable government. In his public statements the Commission's highly influential chair, Lord Jenkins has stated that he had three further criteria of his own. The system chosen should be 'intellectually acceptable'. It should represent 'a significant change' from the existing system. And it should have a 'reasonable chance of coming about politically' (Lord Jenkins in the LSE Democratic Audit Seminar, 20 November 1998).

No electoral system could maximize performance on all four formal criteria simultaneously, let alone the full seven; rather, different electoral systems will satisfy them to differing degrees. And for all of them, there are controversial questions of measurement. The Commission first simplified their choice by deciding upon acceptable or unacceptable limits for each criterion, before moving on to restrict the choice of available systems, and finally designing a finished system

Setting limits on the four main criteria

To improve voter choice, a change from plurality rule (called FPTP for 'first past the post' in the Commission document) was evidently necessary: 'One thing that FPTP assuredly does not do is to allow the elector to exercise a free choice in both the selection of a constituency representative and the determination of the government of the country' (Jenkins, 1998: 8). Given that plurality rule allows voters only to choose to support a single candidate for one party, and that each party chooses the candidate specified, it is difficult to see how any electoral system apart from List PR with a closed list could offer less voter choice.

The link between MPs and a single geographical constituency is one of the most frequently quoted reasons for maintaining the current system. Apart from the Alternative Vote or Supplementary Vote, any other voting system is bound to require larger constituencies. So by paragraph 91 of the report, the Commission had concluded that it could 'only discharge its duty of providing the electorate with a valid alternative choice to FPTP and come nearest to meeting its four criteria by accepting some modification of the one constituency/one member pattern.' Otherwise it could make no contribution at all to the requirements of broad proportionality and 'an extension of voter choice'. However, to respect the requirement to maintain the constituency link, they endeavoured to make this modification as 'limited as is reasonably effective'.

'Stable government' in the sense of single-party majority administrations is another much cited advantage of plurality rule elections, and any system which comes closer to 'broad proportionality' is likely to reduce the likelihood of majority governments forming. The Commission's limiting move here was that it would be unacceptable to create a 'coalition habit' – that is, a situation where every election almost necessarily resulted in a coalition, as in contemporary Germany. In addition, the background political feasibility condition (Jenkins' 'reasonable chance of coming about' criterion) emerged here. The Commission recognized that any alternative electoral systems that would not have delivered an outright Labour majority in the 1997 election (or a Conservative majority in 1983) would be almost impossible to sell to Labour MPs.

Finally, the question of 'broad proportionality' was the most controversial of the Commission's criteria. There are many ways of measuring proportionality, but the most widely accepted and intuitively understandable is the deviation from proportionality (DV) score (Taagepera and Shugart, 1989:105). DV is calculated by subtracting the percentage of seats a party gained in the Commons from its percentage vote share to give a deviation for each party, adding up the moduli of these deviations and then dividing by 2. This calculation gives a score of 21% for the 1997 general election under plurality rule. The minimum score possible is theoretically zero, although no real electoral system in practice would obtain this ideal because of the presence of small minority parties that gain no seats. Such parties accounted for 4.4% of the mainland British vote in the 1997 general election. The maximum possible DV score is not even theoretically 100. Instead it may for all practical purposes be regarded as $(100 - V_1)$ where V_1 is the largest party's share of the vote. It is possible to simply compute an adjusted deviation from proportionality (ADV) score that shows how far a liberal democracy is to being maximally disproportional while still remaining a democracy, by expressing the normal DV score as a percentage of $(100 - V_1)$. For 1997 the ADV score = (21.1*100) / (100-44.4) = 38%, showing that Britain was two fifths of the way to being maximally disproportional. Britain's DV and ADV scores since the early 1970s in general elections, European elections and local elections have been consistently amongst the largest recorded amongst liberal democracies worldwide.

For a UK system to be considered 'fully proportional', it should obtain a DV score of around 4 to 8 per cent, the level commonly achieved both by proportional representation systems across Western Europe and by the USA's perfect two-party plurality rule system. DV scores of this level were only briefly recorded in Britain during the two-party era of the 1950s. The kind of DV score that could be described as 'broadly proportional' will obviously lie somewhere between the top end of the fully proportional range (7–8%) and some substantial improvement on actual British plurality rule DV scores, such as around half the actual average level, and this zone was certainly what the Commission was seeking.

Lord Jenkins and the other Commission members were also particularly determined to avoid one element of plurality rule's unfairness, the creation of 'electoral deserts' where a party wins no or virtually no MPs across a whole region of the country despite piling up hundreds of thousands or million of votes there. The national DV figure is normally artificially lowered by the offsetting of pro-Conservative deviations in the South East against pro-Labour deviations in Scotland and the North. In 1992 the national DV score was just 17.4%, but citizens in most regions experienced far higher levels of disproportionality. Across the whole of south-east England outside London, the Conservatives won 97% of seats in 1992 on the basis of 55% of the votes, leaving all the other parties virtually unrepresented. So the DV for the South-East was 43%, and the ADV score was a staggering 93%, just about as high as it is possible to get inside a liberal democracy. Similar effects also occurred in several regions in 1997 because of plurality rule's tendency to discriminate heavily against parties whose support falls below about a third. In 11 out of the 18 regions we used in our 1997 election analysis, the Conservatives fell badly below the 33% mark, and obtained no seats in Scotland or Wales, and almost none in all the English conurbations outside London. The Commission was resolved to remove the 'electoral deserts' problem and end the 'geographically divisive' effects of plurality rule, commenting that: 'Such apartheid in electoral outcomes is a heavy count against the system which produces it. It is a new form of Disraeli's two nations'.

Eliminating alternatives

Two majoritarian systems were early candidates for the Commission's attention, the Alternative Vote (AV), which is used in Australia, and the Supplementary Vote (SV), which is to be used to elect the London Mayor (see Dunleavy and Margetts, 1998a). Their attractions lay in keeping intact existing constituencies but securing a major change from the 1997 plurality rule outcome, when 47% of MPs were elected without majority support in their local constituencies. But majoritarian systems are not proportional systems and in some circumstances they may generate even higher DV scores than plurality rule elections. In 1992 both AV and SV would have operated slightly more proportionally, but in 1997 both systems would have increased Labour's majority, cut Conservative representation even further and yielded a DV score of 23.5 instead of 21 under plurality rule (Dunleavy, Margetts, O'Duffy and Weir, 1997). Once this finding became public it became impossible for the Commission to see AV or SV alone as 'broadly proportional'. Nor could these systems meet Lord Jenkins' informal criterion of being a substantial improvement on plurality rule, since even under 1992 conditions they would have made only a marginal difference to parties' representation in the Commons.

List systems of proportional representation were also rejected early in the Commission's deliberations because the large multi-member constituencies involved must work against maintaining a constituency link. Nor could List PR extend voter choice, since people get only a single vote, even if an open list method is used which allows voters to indicate their preferred candidate instead of a party slate. List PR would also increase the likelihood of permanent coalition government. From their public meetings and discussions, all members of the Commission also became convinced that the British electorate would never accept a list system.

The Commission also considered the Single Transferable Vote (STV), for which the Electoral Reform Society organized a vigorous campaign at the Commission's public meetings. Lord Jenkins and his colleagues none the less gave three main reasons for rejecting STV. First, they felt that the size of constituencies necessary to run STV elections (generally requiring between four and six member seat) would weaken the constituency link for all MPs. Second, STV involves candidates of the same party competing against each other, which might encourage factionalism within parties and within government. Third, it was ruled out because it satisfied one of the Commission's criteria too much. The final report criticizes STV as offering too much voter choice, which should not be 'a caricature of an over-zealous American breakfast waiter'.

These successive restrictions (reflecting the four criteria) therefore lead the Commission towards adopting a mixed system. The main mixed system, the 'classic' version of the Additional Member System used in Germany and New Zealand, with 50% locally elected MPs and 50% top-up seats, was never seriously under consideration. It went against the Commission's stated wish not to impose a 'coalition habit' on the country and even in 1997 conditions it would not have produced a Labour majority (Dunleavy, Margetts, O'Duffy and Weir, 1997a; 1998). Instead, the Commission was pushed towards the 'British AMS' solutions already developed in Scotland, Wales and Greater London. Here, a majority of representatives in a mixed system are elected in single member local constituencies, with the balance elected in relatively localized top-up areas, using a two vote system, and a d'Hondt system for allocating top-up seats, and retaining relatively high thresholds (Dunleavy and Margetts, 1999, Table 1). But although the Commission came close to following these existing systems in the end it went for a novel system in key respects.

Designing a finished system

One member of the Commission, Lord Alexander, did advocate adoption of a British AMS solution, with a very high proportion of locally elected MPs (on which he agreed with his fellow Commissioners). His 'Note of

Reservation' at the end of the report dismissed some of the Commission's arguments in favour of AV for electing local seats and outlined reasons why in his view AV could not satisfy the conditions 'to be sound in principle, easy to understand and above all capable of commanding the enduring respect of the electorate' (Jenkins, 1998: 53).

Instead of a British AMS system, however, Lord Jenkins and his three other colleagues made a key innovation by suggesting a completely new system which uses the Alternative Vote as the first stage of a mixed system, has a very high proportion (80 to 85%) of MPs elected in single-member constituencies, and yet includes a substantial minority of top-up MPs to enhance proportionality. This compromise outcome called AV Plus was first researched in a systematic way in the spring of 1998 (Dunleavy, Margetts and Weir, 1998a). The results of this study showed both that British voters could easily understand and operate such a system, and that using either AMS or AV Plus (or SV Plus) schemes with high proportions of local seats could all produce much more proportional outcomes than had previously been thought. There is evidence that at Easter 1998 Lord Jenkins talked over the Commission's interim ideas with Tony Blair, and at that time recommended proceeding with a mixed system where two thirds of MPs would be elected in single member seats and one third in top-up areas. However, the Prime Minister reportedly rejected this possibility, following advice from Peter Mandelson and Number 10 staffs that systems with more constituency MPs were feasible, and warnings that the PLP would not accept so radical a change. Instead he asked Lord Jenkins to look again at systems which preserved a larger number of single-member constituencies.

By July 1998 the majority view of the Commission had settled on using an AV Plus or SV Plus system and had narrowed the proportions of locally elected to top-up members to three options – a central case of 82.5% local and 17.5% top up MPs, plus 80:20 and 85:15 options. Voter choice would be extended because in electing local members people would number candidates 1, 2, 3, 4 in order of their preferences. Under AV if a candidate gets a majority of first preference votes, he or she is elected. Otherwise, the bottom-placed candidate is eliminated and his or her second preference votes are distributed among the other candidates to ascertain if someone now has a majority. This process continues by eliminating candidates from the bottom until one candidate secures a simple majority of votes, a key legitimacy improvement on plurality rule. The Commission also felt that AV would free citizens from having to face the common 'tactical' choice between supporting their first preference candidate/party or instead voting for a lower-ranked but still acceptable candidate with a chance of winning the seat. People can vote in a sincere order of preference, knowing that their second and third preference votes may still count towards the local result if their first preference candidate is knocked out.

In addition, the Commission argued that the choice of AV would be valuable in promoting stable government because it would encourage likely coalition partners to announce their engagement in advance, and parties would campaign to attract both first and second votes. In the 1990 Australian lower house election, for example, Labor advertising acknowledged that many voters would probably give their first preference vote to the Australian Democrats or to another minor party, and appealed for the second preferences of these voters. This tactic was 'widely credited with winning the election for Labor' and described by some commentators as 'one of the most blatant attempts to manipulate the preferential voting system' (Bean, 1997, p.106).

The second vote for top-up MPs also helps voters to avoid tactical voting dilemmas between their top choice in the local constituency and the most effective vote at the top-up area level, and again it extends voter choice – opening up the possibility of split-ticket voting. The Commission argued that the 'party vote' at the top-up area level should use an open list system, giving people a choice of ticking an individual candidate on each party's list.

By July 1998 the Commission had also decided not to adopt national or regional areas as the basis for the top-up areas, but instead to follow the British AMS pattern of relatively localized top-up areas. In Scotland and Wales the AMS systems use Euro-constituency areas for top-up purposes, and for the Greater London Assembly there is a city-wide top-up area. The Commission decided to use counties as top-up areas in provincial England, because of their strong historic existence and voters ability to identify with them, and they initially planned to draw up new equivalent-sized areas both for metropolitan zones in England and for Scotland and Wales. They had also settled on around 75 top-up areas in total and planned that the number of top-up MPs should range between one and four depending on the size of the top-up area.

In August 1998 we were requested by the Commission staff to evaluate their then proposals and generate firm data on the possible effects of the different systems. We pointed out to the Commission staff opportunities for simplifying their scheme by dividing the four largest counties (Kent, Essex, Lancashire and Hampshire) into two parts each, thereby ensuring that all top-up areas would have either one or two top-up MPs. This step simplifies the size range of top-up areas and very importantly avoids creating too large a variation between top-up areas in the threshold levels at which parties would win seats, a feature otherwise likely to have a severely distorting effect on party behaviour. We also suggested using the same top-up areas in

Scotland and Wales as for the Scottish Parliament and Welsh National Assembly, on the grounds that co-operation between the Westminster MPs and devolved representatives would be maximized, and because voters would have far greater chance of recognizing the same top-up areas. We then devised with Commission staff illustrative top-up area boundaries for the English metropolitan areas and for London – which were included in the final report. At a late stage we also outlined options for top-up areas in Northern Ireland, from which the Commission chose a two-seat solution in late September 1998.

We evaluated a number of rules for allocating top-up seats between the component countries of the UK, and between top-up areas, and devised a system (subsequently accepted) which could be easily varied with the proportion of top-up MPs finally chosen by the government. The allocation rule is: (i) Calculate the number of top-up MPs needed in each component country of the UK (England, Scotland, Wales and Northern Ireland) to maintain a constant ratio of top-up to total MPs, (20, 17.5 or 15% according to which scheme is adopted); (ii) assign one top-up seat to each top-up area in each country; (iii) assign a further one top-up seat to each of the most populous top-up areas in each country, ranked in descending order of their population size (measured by number of electors) until all available top-up seats for that county have been allocated.

When all these proposals were accepted by the Commission their final scheme included 80 top-up areas – 65 in England, eight in Scotland, five in Wales and two in Northern Ireland. With the Commission's central top-up ratio of 17.5%, 44 of these areas would have a single top-up MP and the remaining 36 would each elect two top-up MPs. The choice of locally identifiable top-up areas was a significant innovation. It is designed by the Commission both to reduce central party control of the choice of top-up candidates and their place on the party lists, and to provide both local accountability and a broad local link for between 98 and 132 top-up MPs (depending on the local:top-up ratio eventually adopted). The Commission felt that extending the constituency system so far as possible to cover top-up MPs also would make the AV Plus system more easily assimilable into the British culture. It would also avoid regionally elected top-up MPs acting as a 'flock of unattached birds clouding the sky and wheeling under central party directions' (Jenkins Report: 40), which was Lord Jenkins' view of the German electoral system.

Under the Commission's central case the 27 top-up areas in England with most electors are assigned two top-up seats each, plus the five most populous areas in Scotland and the two most populous Welsh areas. The size of the Commission's top-up areas in terms of population size is shown in Table 1, and essentially varies between 0.3 and 0.8 million people, with a peak of 21 areas between 500,000 and 600,000 electors, tapering off fairly symmetrically to either side. The mean number of electors per top-up area is 546,000 across Britain, and the more robust median is 520,000 (for more information, see Dunleavy and Margetts, 1998: 10). The mean figure in England is slightly larger at 560,000 people, while the means for Scotland and Wales are considerably lower at 493,000 and 440,000 people respectively.

TABLE 1
THE DISTRIBUTION OF TOP-UP AREAS BY SIZE OF ELECTORATE
IN THE JENKINS COMMISSION PROPOSALS

Electors per top-up area	No. of top-up areas
Below 300,000 people	1
300,000 to 399,000 people	11
400,000 to 499,000 people	19
500,000 to 599,000 people	21
600,000 to 699,000 people	11
700,000 to 799,000 people	13
Over 800,000 people	2

The resulting 80 areas (with two exceptions) all contain at least five current Westminster constituencies and no more than 11 constituencies. The most common total of MPs for each area would be eight (which is also the median size). The distribution around the median is fairly symmetric, except for a small bulge of 12 areas with 11 MPs each. Because of the emphasis on maintaining historic areas there is a single historic county in the scheme (Northumberland) with only four seats, including one top-up MP; and another county (Staffordshire) with 12 seats in total, including two top-up MPs.

Having decided on the basic elements of the scheme, the Commission decided to present the government with three alternatives of the same basic scheme, varying only in the ratios of constituency to top-up MPs. The central case (17.5% top-up) included 112 top-up seats in Great Britain, and the 20% scheme had 128 and the 15% scheme 96 top-up MPs (allocated as outlined above). The three options use the same structure of areas. The Commission left the precise top-up ratio open in this way due to the inevitably long period before any alternative system might plausibly be implemented. Many other electoral changes will have taken place before then, and the Commissioners felt that such a decision should be made by Parliament in light of current conditions. Their report includes data provided from our analysis to show how the three schemes would have operated under the quite different electoral conditions of 1992 and 1997.

Simulating the Effects of AV-Plus

We first explain the basic methods used to simulate the outcomes which would have resulted had the 1997 and 1992 elections been held under the Jenkins Commission's AV Plus system (or the AMS version recommended in Lord Alexander's minority report), and then present some key comparative results.

Methods

There are considerable methodological challenges to overcome in simulating elections under mixed systems, especially where the ratio of local to top-up MPs deviates from 50:50. Calculating the result of a 'classic' AMS scheme, with half local seats and half top-up seats, can be almost completely realistic. Existing Westminster constituencies are paired together, and their results calculated from the actual election results. Top-up area vote shares are then calculated for groups of seats, and top-up MPs are allocated across the parties using the d'Hondt method. To calculate results with other proportions of top-up and local seats is much more difficult and for the Commission's scheme we adopted the following approach:

Stage 1. We defined a set of local seats for 'classic' AMS within the Commission's 78 top-up areas, and projected an outcome in terms of both local and top-up seats for each such area. We tried to pair socially similar constituencies and to preserve so far as possible a diversity of party representation in the paired local seats. Note that the AMS pairings used here are quite different from those used in Dunleavy, Margetts, O'Duffy and Weir (1997a) where paired seats only had to fit into between 11 and 18 broad regions.

Stage 2. We established the difference between each party's local seats in the 100% local scheme (that is, the general election constituencies) and in the 50:50 scheme described above. From there we computed a marginal increment (or decrease) in local seats which each party in each top-up area would receive, as the proportion of local seats in that area grows from 50 to 100% in single percentage steps.

Stage 3. A small additional complication is that the percentage of all seats in each top-up area varies considerably in the Commission's schema, depending on the number of MPs per area and the point where the limits of two top-up seats is placed. With 17.5% top-up MPs nationally the share of top-up MPs in differently sized top-up areas actually varies from 12.5 to 22%. With 20% top-ups, the range is from 14 to 25%; and with 15% top-up MPs, from 11 to 20%. For the actual proportion of local seats in each individual top-up area under the Commission's scheme we then interpolated a local seats projection for that scheme. An essential assumption here is that there is a linear relationship between changes in the proportion of local seats used under various AMS or AV Plus schemes and in the seats won by parties. If this relationship is not in fact completely linear, some distortions will arise in our estimates.

Stage 4. In a number of cases the model makes conflicting arithmetical predictions of the number of seats that would be won by two different parties in a single top-up area – for instance, requiring that two parties win the same local seat. These cases have to be resolved judgementally, making reference to the geographic pattern and extent of party support in that top-up area in the base election year, and the fit between these variables and the likely AMS or AV Plus constituencies under the Commission's scheme in that top-up area.

Stage 5. Having estimated local seat outcomes under the Commission's scheme, we then allocated the one or two top-up seats in each area using the d'Hondt allocation rule (already legislated for use in the Scottish Parliament, the Welsh Assembly and the European Parliament elections). This method is slightly different from our previous work (such as Dunleavy, Margetts, O'Duffy and Weir, 1997) which allocated top-up seats using a generic 'minimising DV' allocation rule. The distinctive impact of the d'Hondt rule is relatively restricted, however, because there are so few top-up seats in each area, and these seats normally go to very conspicuously under-represented parties. Note that the impact of the top-up seat allocations still tends to correct for any substantial biases in estimating local seats distributions – because in the end AMS seats must get as close to matching vote shares as the number of available top-up MPs allows.

Stage 6. Our procedures for simulating AV-Plus outcomes are essentially the same as for a Jenkins version with AMS, but with one significant difference. We used data from surveys of 9,200 people in 1992 and 8,400 people in 1997 on how people filled in AV ballot papers across the regions of Great Britain – 13 regions in 1992 and 18 in 1997 (see Dunleavy, Margetts, O'Duffy and Weir, 1997). With these regional results we could run AV contests for the existing Westminster constituencies, and for our paired constituencies. In each case we used the second and subsequent preference rankings of voters for party A in region Z to model the second and subsequent preferences of party A voters in each constituency (or paired constituency) within region Z. But of course we used the general election votes to set the number of party A supporters in each constituency in the first place. The 100% and 50% local seats outcomes under AV thus obtained were then substituted in the simulation, instead of the plurality-rule results used with AMS.

Key outcomes of the Jenkins system

The most distinctive and important decision that the Commission made was to combine a very high ratio of locally elected MPs with very small top-up areas. An obvious first question is the extent to which the use of the 78 top-up areas in mainland Britain reduced the proportionality of their schemes, compared with either using larger regions or using the component countries of Britain (England, Scotland and Wales) as the units for allocating top-up MPs. Our initial expectation was that larger regions would generate lower DV scores, because they would mass more top-up seats together and be better able to adjust for misrepresentations of parties in constituency seats. In our previous published work we have computed DV scores for AMS and SV Plus/AV Plus schemes with 83% local members and 17% top-up MPs. This mix is very close to the Commission's central mix (which is 82.4% local MPs and 17.6% top-up MPs). In response to an earlier request from a member of the Commission we also computed how an 83:17 mix would work if top-up MPs were allocated for England, Scotland and Wales, and reached DV scores for 1997 and 1992. Table 2 puts this information together.

TABLE 2
THE DISPROPORTIONALITY OF SIMILAR AMS AND AV PLUS SCHEMES WITH TOP-UP MPS
ALLOCATED AT DIFFERENT SPATIAL LEVELS, IN MAINLAND BRITAIN

	1997 election		1992 election	
DV SCORES	AV Plus	AMS	AV Plus	AMS
17% top-up MPs allocated at national level in England, Scotland and Wales	12.5	9.5	3.8	3.7
17% top-up MPs allocated regionally	13.3	10.8	8.2	8.2
17.5% top-up MPs allocated in 78 areas	12.9	10.8	8.7	8.3

Notes: The bottom row shows the Commission's central variant. The number of regions used in
1997 was 18, and it was 11 in 1992.

This table needs to be interpreted a little cautiously, because the extra 0.5% top-up MPs in the bottom row may slightly flatter the Commission's scheme. Nonetheless the conclusions seems clear-cut. Under both 1997 and 1992 conditions the Commission's scheme is as proportional as allocation of top-up seats in wider regions. Under 1997 conditions the Commission's scheme for AV Plus is also as proportional as national list allocation of top-up MPs, and it is only slightly less proportional for an AMS scheme. Under 1992 conditions national list allocation would be radically more proportional than either the Commission's scheme or the regional area allocations of top-up MPs. These findings are important and counter-intuitive. They show that with an 83:17 local/top-up mix for MPs the Commission's schemes cannot be made more proportional by allocating top-up MPs in larger regional areas, and cannot be improved on at all except by using national lists allocations and then only under 1992 conditions.

Table 2 includes data for both the majority recommendation of an AV Plus system and for the minority report argument for a 'British AMS' variant of the same scheme. The bottom row shows that in 1997 the AV Plus variant was over 2 percentage points worse in DV score terms, but that under 1992 conditions there would be a much smaller differential. Table 3 below shows the impacts of the two alternatives more comprehensively, not just in DV score terms but also looking at the impacts of AV Plus versus AMS on the representation of the three major nationwide political parties. The Commission also provided for three possible mixes of local to top-up seats, and Table 3 also shows how these different combinations would affect national outcomes.

The most important conclusion to be drawn from these comparative tables concerns the DV penalty involved in using AV Plus (or the alternative SV Plus system) compared with AMS. Under 1997 conditions this penalty ranged from an additional 1.7 to 2.5 percentage points (assessed on completely matched seats allocations), but under 1992 conditions its range was only from 0.2 to 0.5 percentage points. The variation in DV levels was more consistent between the three schemes with differing numbers of top-up seats. Using 127 seats instead of 100 seats would improve DV by 2.8 percentage points in 1997 under AMS, and 2 points under AV Plus; in 1992 conditions the improvement produced by the 27 extra top-up seats would be 1.4 points under AMS, and 1.2 points under AV Plus.

In terms of the impacts on party representation there is a clear distinction between the 1997 and 1992 elections, with AV Plus giving both Labour and the Liberal Democrats substantial gains at the Conservatives' expense compared with AMS in 1997 conditions, but virtually no change between the two systems in 1992 conditions. We have shown elsewhere that there was a major shift in the second preferences of Liberal Democrats away from even-handedness between Labour and the Tories in 1992 to a heavy pro-Labour preponderance in 1997, along with a slower warming of Labour supporters towards giving the Liberal Democrats a second preference vote in 1997 (Dunleavy, Margetts, O'Duffy and Weir, 1997). In 1997 in constituencies where the Liberal Democrats ran third, Labour was advantaged and the Tories lost out – an effect apparent both in actual Westminster constituency contests rerun under SV or AV and in our paired AMS constituencies. In areas where the Liberal Democrats ran second, they could generally rely on attracting the bulk of third-placed candidates' second preferences, whether from Conservative or Labour supporters. Detailed analysis shows that the Conservatives were relatively isolated from all other parties' supporters in 1997 on multiple possible indicators of voters' orientations (Dunleavy and Margetts, 1998c; see also Thurner and Pappi, 1999).

TABLE 3

SUMMARY TABLE OF HOW DV SCORES AND THE REPRESENTATION OF THE THREE MAJOR PARTIES VARY ACROSS THE COMMISSION'S SCHEMES (MAINLAND BRITAIN)

	1997 election		1992 election	
A. DV SCORES	AV Plus	AMS	AV Plus	AMS
96 or 100 top-up seats (15%)	14.6	12.2	9.2	9.0
112 or 113 top-up seats (17.5%)	12.9	10.8	8.9	8.3
128 or 127 top-up seats (20%)	11.6	9.4	8.0	7.6

	1997 election		1992 election	
B. LABOUR SEATS	AV Plus	AMS	AV Plus	AMS
96 or 100 top-up seats (15%)	378	363	244	242
112 or 113 top-up seats (17.5%)	367	354	240	236
128 or 127 top-up seats (20%)	359	345	240	239

	1997 election		1992 election	
C. CONSERVATIVE SEATS	AV Plus	AMS	AV Plus	AMS
96 or 100 top-up seats (15%)	160	191	315	316
112 or 113 top-up seats (17.5%)	167	194	316	317
128 or 127 top-up seats (20%)	175	198	309	310

	1997 election		1992 election	
D. LIBERAL DEMOCRAT SEATS	AV Plus	AMS	AV Plus	AMS
96 or 100 top-up seats (15%)	89	71	71	71
112 or 113 top-up seats (17.5%)	92	77	74	75
128 or 127 top-up seats (20%)	91	82	81	79

Notes: The AV Plus and AMS comparisons were carried out for the Jenkins Commission using slightly different allocations of top-up seats, as the seat allocation rules were updated in the course of the research.

Table 3 also shows the impacts of the different mixes of local to top-up members included in the Commission's report. As expected under 1997 conditions, the scheme allocating a fifth of MPs by top-up seats is the most proportional, its DV score at just over 11% – almost halving the DV score in the actual general election. By contrast a scheme with only 15% top-up MPs has a DV score three percentage points higher. These 1997 effects occur in both AV Plus and AMS versions of the Commission's plan – the more restricted the top-up seats the more Labour benefits at the other parties' expense. However, when we consider the 1992 results although the same basic patterning of effects is apparent, the differences between the schemes are muted in both AV Plus and AMS. Essentially all the AV Plus schemes in 1997 would be well above the fully proportional DV range of around 4 to 8%, but in 1992 conditions at least the scheme with one fifth of top-up MPs would operate proportionally under either AV Plus or AMS.

Looking in more detail at how AV Plus would have worked in 1997 Table 4 shows how the Commission's central scheme (with 17.5% top-up seats) would have worked out across the old government standard regions. It also shows how the parties would have fared in terms of winning local or top-up seats, and the resulting regional DV scores. Labour would have gained virtually all their seats under AV Plus at the local level, the 357 local seats in Great Britain being enough to secure an overall majority in the House of Commons (where the winning post is 330 seats). The Conservatives would still be under-represented, gaining almost the same total of seats (167) as they did in the actual general election (165), while the Liberal Democrats would double their seat count from 46 actual seats in 1997 to 92 MPs under AV-Plus. In terms of broadening the spatial basis of parties' support Table 4 also shows that the Commission's scheme would be effective in avoiding electoral deserts via the top-up seats. The Conservatives would have five or more MPs in every region, and the Liberal Democrats three or more seats, except in the North.

Table 5 shows the essential differences between the Commission majority's AV Plus scheme and the minority recommendation of AMS within the same top-up areas and ratios of local to top-up MPs. In 1997 conditions the Conservatives would win 45 more local seats under straight AMS than under AV Plus, and would go on to win 27 more seats overall than the majority Commission scheme, avoiding any significant under-representation. The Tory gains under AMS would come chiefly from the Liberal Democrats whose local seats would almost halve, and whose total seats would be 15 less, but Labour would also lose a net 13 seats. In 1992 conditions the difference between the two systems in overall seat shares is trivial for all parties, but the Tories would win ten more local seats under AMS, again chiefly at the Liberal Democrats' expense.

Turning to the local level impacts of the Jenkins Commission scheme within the 78 mainland top-up areas, the proposed reform would indeed go a long way towards eliminating 'electoral deserts'. Both the Conservative and Labour would gain an MP in all the top-up areas in 1997, except for three top-up areas in central Scotland where the Tories would win no seat, and one top-up area (Somerset) where Labour would go unrepresented. The Liberal Democrats would have no MP in 25 top-up areas, mostly in Labour heartland territory. All eight of Glasgow's local seats would still go to Labour, with the SNP claiming the two top-up seats. On 1997 patterns the SNP would gain an MP in four out of eight top-up areas in Scotland, while Plaid Cymru would win seats in two out of five top-up areas in Wales.

TABLE 4
SEATS WON UNDER AV-PLUS WITH 17.5% TOP-UP SEATS IN A RE-RUN 1997 ELECTION (GREAT BRITAIN)

	Local Seats					Top-up Seats					All Seats						
	Con	Lab	LD	Nat	Other	Con	Lab	LD	Nat	Other	Con	Lab	LD	Nat	Other	Total	DV
South East	50	32	14	0	0	6	7	8	0	0	56	39	22	0	0	117	7.9
East Anglia	6	10	2	0	0	2	1	1	0	0	8	11	3	0	0	22	11.7
East Midlands	10	25	1	0	0	4	1	3	0	0	14	26	4	0	0	44	11.3
North West	5	47	3	0	1	10	0	4	0	0	15	47	7	0	1	70	12.9
Wales	0	28	3	3	0	5	0	1	0	0	5	28	4	3	0	40	15.3
London	7	48	5	0	0	11	0	3	0	0	18	48	8	0	0	74	15.4
North	1	28	1	0	0	6	0	0	0	0	7	28	1	0	0	36	16.9
West Midlands	7	39	3	0	0	9	0	1	0	0	16	39	4	0	0	59	18.3
South West	3	14	25	0	0	9	0	0	0	0	12	14	25	0	0	51	18.8
Yorks & Humb'side	4	39	3	0	0	7	1	2	0	0	11	40	5	0	0	56	19.5
Scotland	0	49	9	6	0	5	0	0	5	0	5	47	9	11	0	72	19.7
GREAT BRITAIN	93	357	69	9	1	74	10	23	5	0	167	367	92	14	1	641	12.9
Compare:																	
1992																	
GREAT BRITAIN	277	223	24	5	0	39	17	50	6	0	316	240	74	11	0	641	8.7

TABLE 5
SEATS WON UNDER AMS WITH 17.6% TOP-UP SEATS IN A RE-RUN 1997 ELECTION (GREAT BRITAIN)

	Local Seats					Top-up Seats					All Seats						
	Con	Lab	LD	Nat	Other	Con	Lab	LD	Nat	Other	Con	Lab	LD	Nat	Other	Total	DV
England	138	270	28	0	1	43	9	40	0	0	181	279	68	0	1	529	9.6
Scotland	0	45	8	4	0	7	0	0	8	0	7	45	8	12	0	72	17.0
Wales	0	30	1	3	0	6	0	0	0	0	6	30	1	3	0	40	20.3
Great Britain	138	345	37	7	1	56	9	40	8	0	194	354	77	15	1	641	8.3
Compare:																	
1992																	
Great Britain	287	221	16	5	0	30	15	59	8	0	317	236	75	13	0	641	8.3

Looking more closely at the impacts of AV Plus at the top-up area level Figure 1 shows the patterning DV scores. With only 5 to 11 seats to allocate in each top-up area, seat allocations are inherently bound to be quite coarse-grained in their fit to vote-shares at this level. Seen in this light the results are impressive with a median DV score of 16.5, and the middle mass of the date located between 11 and 21%. Thus three quarters of top-up areas would have local DV scores under AV Plus below the national DV score achieved in the real 1997 general election. There are four upper outliers clearly visible in Figure 1: two are Labour dominated areas (Bradford and Scotland West), but two are unusual areas (Dorset and Somerset) where the operations of AV in local seats works strongly to deprive the Conservatives of any local seats despite their substantial vote shares, and benefits the Liberal Democrats. These apparently anomalous results are quite likely to recur under AV in British conditions, however.

We can also measure the extent to which the Jenkins Commission proposals would broaden out the presence of parties at the top-up area level by examining the 'effective number of parties' (ENP) index. The ENP score is computed as 1 divided by the sum of the squared decimal seats shares of the parties (see Taagepera and Shugart, 1989, Ch.8). Figure 2 shows the ENP scores for the 78 mainland top-up areas on the vertical axis, charted against the Labour share of the vote on the horizontal axis. There is clear inverse relationship in the main block of data, but there are some important outliers (shown boxed on the left lower side of the chart) where Tory or Liberal Democrat predominance reduces the ENP score radically despite Labour's surge in 1997. (Again the two bottom left scores are for Somerset and Dorset, reflecting the particular impact of AV local elections there). The median ENP score shown is just over 2, and the middle mass of observations stretches from 1.6 to 2.6. Only in 16 mainly Labour one-party areas is the ENP score below 1.5, and in no case does it dip below 1.2

The 'relative reduction in parties' (RRP) measure is calculated by subtracting the ENP score for seats from that for votes, dividing this difference by the ENP score for votes, and expressing the result as a percentage. It measures the extent to which an electoral system cuts back the number of parties represented in Parliament compared with the number of parties that citizens have voted for (Taagepera and Shugart, 1989, pp.209, 273). Table 6 shows that the AV Plus results even in the small top-up areas are much better than the results we have previously established for the plurality rule system in the 1997 election across much larger regions – where we should expect to see a much greater capacity for a mix of parties to win seats (Dunleavy and Margetts, 1997). The middle mass of the data for the AV Plus top-areas in fact lies below the level of lower quartile for the regions under plurality rule.

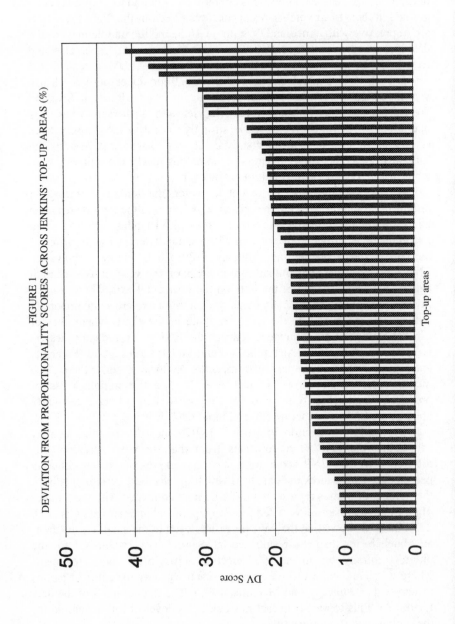

FIGURE 1
DEVIATION FROM PROPORTIONALITY SCORES ACROSS JENKINS' TOP-UP AREAS (%)

FIGURE 2
HOW THE ENP SCORES VARY WITH LABOUR'S VOTE ACROSS
THE JENKINS TOP-UP AREAS

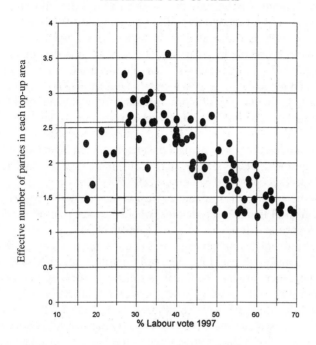

TABLE 6
RELATIVE REDUCTION IN PARTIES (%) IN 78 JENKINS COMMISSION TOP-UP AREAS IN
BRITAIN UNDER AV PLUS, COMPARED WITH 18 REGIONS UNDER PLURALITY RULE AT
THE1997 ELECTION

	AV Plus 78 top-up areas	Plurality rule 18 regions
Top observation	57	62
Upper quartile	34	49
Median	27	40
Lower quartile	17	34
Lowest observation	6	12

In other respects, however, the Jenkins Commission scheme makes less difference, especially in its degree of friendliness towards small or new parties. We noted above that existing British AMS systems all embody high thresholds for parties to qualify for a seat. There are two thresholds to consider. The *inclusion threshold* level for one seat indicates the lowest possible total of votes from which a party could secure representation. For the Jenkins scheme it is set by the equation 1/(M+p-1) where M stands for the district magnitude (in this case the total number of MPs allocated within a top-up area) and p for the number of parties (Rokkan, 1968). Because the top-up MP or MPs are allocated in a compensatory way M can range between 5 and 11, and the larger it is the more likely it is that small parties will gain seats. The *exclusion threshold* is the maximum number of votes that a party can get and still receive a certain number of seats. Again for the d'Hondt formula (but not for all other formulae) the exclusion level for zero seats is the highest vote which a party could get and still have no seats in the House of Commons. It is set by the equation (S+1)/(M+1), where S denotes the number of seats being considered and M again denotes the district magnitude (Rae, Hanby and Loosemore, 1971; for a fuller discussion see Taagepera and Shugart, 1989: 274–5).

Table 7 shows the inclusion and exclusion thresholds for securing zero or one seat in an 11 member top-up area, where the local seats allocation has operated proportionately and where the number of parties in contention is four or five or six. (The number of parties in contention, of course, does not affect the exclusion threshold,). The way to interpret this table for a situation where there are four parties is as follows: if party A wins less than 7.1% support they will not win a seat; between 7.1 and 8.3% support party A may win either one seat or no seats; between 8.3 and 14.2% the party is bound to win one seat; above that level the party may win either one or two seats. The bottom of Table 7 shows the same votes in absolute number terms, assuming a top-up area of mean size and a 70% turnout rate. The conclusion to be drawn from both parts of Table 7 is that even in highly favourable circumstances (a large top-up area with the maximum number of seats and a basically proportional pattern of wins in local seats) it will be pretty hard for any new or small party to win seats in Westminster. Of course, the absolute number of votes indicated in the bottom part of the table only has to be assembled across 11 current constituencies, but it is still a considerable number. Far right racist parties are highly unlikely to enjoy any greater success under the Jenkins scheme than under plurality rule – but so too are the Greens or other new parties. Finally we should note that where local seats are *not* proportionally allocated, the main opposition party or parties will normally win the top-up seats on much higher vote shares than those shown in Table 7, so excluding any smaller parties from contention.

Conclusions

In choosing a mixed electoral system, the Independent Commission strengthened the momentum already created by British AMS and placed

TABLE 7
INCLUSION AND EXCLUSION THRESHOLDS FOR A TOP-UP AREA WITH 11 SEATS IN
PERCENTAGES OF THE VOTE, ASSUMING BASICALLY PROPORTIONAL LOCAL SEATS
ALLOCATIONS

	To win:	Inclusion thresholds with:			Exclusion Threshold
		4 parties	5 parties	6 parties	
% Vote shares	0 seats	0.0	0.0	0.0	8.3
needed	1 seat	7.1	6.7	6.3	16.7
	2 seats	14.2	13.3	12.5	
Number of	0 seats	0	0	0	31,700
votes needed	1 seat	27,200	25,600	24,100	63,500
	2 seats	54,300	51,200	48,200	

Notes: The inclusion threshold shows the minimum vote share needed to win each number of seats; the exclusion threshold shows the maximum vote share with which that number of seats can still be won. The lower part of the Table assumes the constituency has the mean top-up area number of electors and a 70% turnout rate. Cell entries there are rounded to the nearest hundred.

House of Commons elections squarely within the 'trend towards mixed electoral systems' emerging in the contemporary world, both in plurality-rule countries and countries with proportional representation systems (Dunleavy and Margetts, 1995: 10). This trend is neither 'necessary' nor 'invariant', but neither is it coincidental. The Commission clearly sought to combine the accountability strengths of plurality rule or AV in single-member constituencies with the offsetting proportional qualities of a list element. The limited additional proportionality achieved via top-up MPs may seem inadequate, but it is certainly a greater change than the Alternative Vote alone. Yet at the time of the publication of the Plant report in 1992, some commentators encouraged Liberal Democrat activists to accept AV as the system which 'may well be the maximum reform they can realistically hope to achieve' (Kellner, 1997: 113; see also Linton and Southcott, 1998: 97–105).

The limitations of the Jenkins scheme mainly reflect the fact that it has been developed in response to a brief constructed by a party unsure of its own view of reform. Finding a system that represents a compromise between reform and non-reform will not necessarily unite the Labour Party behind it. The initial reaction to the Jenkins scheme was hostile at the October 1998 Labour conference, even before the report was published, and following its launch Blair kicked the next critical consideration of Labour's stance back to the October 2000 conference. The timing of an electoral system referendum was implicitly pushed back to perhaps the next general election at the earliest, or perhaps to the next parliament. A great deal now hinges upon the development of Labour's co-operation with the Liberal Democrats, and upon some 'confuser' issues – such as the reform of the House of Lords to include some or all directly elected members, on which a Royal Commission is due to report in December 1999. The possible future trajectories involved here are too complex and conjectural at the time of writing (April 1999) to pursue further here. At the least the reactions to the Jenkins report demonstrate that the Commission did not exaggerate the difficulties in persuading a majority of the PLP to accept even holding an electoral reform referendum.

However, there is evidence to suggest that often when countries change their electoral systems, it is not due to a fervent and united desire of major parties for reform. In Japan and New Zealand for example, the reform of the voting system was implemented despite 'substantial continuity in political elites' control of power'. In Italy, the electoral reforms introduced in 1993 were 'forced on dominant party elites' and were 'the product neither of a rational process of institutional engineering nor even of conflicting party strategies' (Donovan, 1995: 47). In New Zealand few thought that a referendum process put in motion by ambivalent major parties would lead to change (Vowles, 1995). We have suggested elsewhere (Dunleavy and Margetts, 1995: 23–4) that a small overlap can exist between the 'indifference curves' of the Labour and Liberal Democrat parties if Labour's optimum point on electoral reform moves to accept greater proportionality (as it seems to have done) and if the Liberal Democrats' optimum point shifts towards governability considerations, as it has ever since the negotiation of the Cook-McLennan concordat on constitutional issues in March 1997. But the overlap area created is a small one, and the possibility for change remains conjectural.

In terms of the Jenkins Commission's formal criteria the AV Plus scheme succeeds strikingly well in maintaining constituency links for both local MPs and top-up area MPs It has the happy results for the 'stable government' criterion of probably producing single party majority governments in clear-cut elections (like 1983, 1987 and 1997), and almost certainly coalition governments in more close-run contests (such as 1992, 1974 and probably also in 1979). In terms of extending voter choice the system gives voters the chance to express multiple preferences in local contests, and to 'split ticket' vote if they wish to in their top-up vote. Our analysis of split ticket voting shows that if the main predicted pattern occurs (favouring the Liberal Democrats) it would either make little difference to the way that AV Plus operates in 1997 conditions, or radically enhance the system's proportionality in 1992 conditions (Dunleavy and Margetts, 1999: 34–5). This outcome contradicts the alarmist conjectures of some commentators (for example, Kellner, 1998). Of course, assessing the split ticket possibilities in an actually existing system may open up important finer-grain pictures (Cox, 1997; Thurner and Pappi, 1998), and lead to some articulation of this picture. Finally in terms of achieving 'broad proportionality' we have shown that both the AV Plus and the AMS variants of the Commission's scheme come close to the full proportionality range of 4 to 8% DV in 1992 conditions. But under 1997 voting patterns both variants could not get very close to this range, and the AV Plus variant clearly performed worse than the AMS version. The Commission saw the DV penalty of AV Plus as compensated for by the system's impact in extending voter choice.

Our hunch would be that the full Jenkins Commission report is unlikely to be put before the electorate in exactly the form that it was published. There are some recommendations that are quite unclear, especially how the top-up element of the election can be run under 'open' lists, where voters may indicate candidates within the list, even though in 56% of the top up areas in the Commission's central variant of its scheme there is only a single top-up MP to be elected. The Commission seem to have envisaged that parties would be compelled to put up (say) two candidates for a single top-up seat, and three candidates for two top-up seats – but the risks here in terms of confusing voters about how the election operates would seem severe. The whole logic of localizing the top-up MPs so that they are elected individually or off lists of two at a maximum is to almost magic the 'list' element of the election out of existence. So insisting also on artificial measures to create 'open lists' here seems perverse. Similarly the complexities of combining numerical voting in local constituencies with 'X' voting at the top-up stage seem to have been discounted with little thought by the Commission, especially since all other British AMS systems operate with just two 'X' votes. Critics of the AV element of the scheme also fastened on the fact that AV weights people's first and fifth preferences as equivalently important in deciding local constituency contests.

The odds must therefore be that if an electoral system referendum is not simply scrubbed by the Labour Party, breaking the clear manifesto pledge made in 1997, then the alternative system to plurality rule put before voters will be a less complex version of the Jenkins proposals. One alternative here would be Lord Alexander's British AMS variant which, we have shown, performed better in proportionality terms under 1997 conditions, and which would fit much more clearly with systems already in use for Scotland, Wales and London. A second alternative would be to use the Supplementary Vote (SV) instead of AV as the voting method for constituency MPs. SV allows voters to mark only two choices, using X voting, and would be simpler to explain, and more consistent with using X voting at the top-up stage. We have shown elsewhere that SV and AV results are virtually always identical under British voting conditions, so that SV Plus will essentially operate in exactly the same ways as AV, but would be simpler to explain and more favourable for the maintenance of major party discipline than would AV Plus. SV will also be used to elect the London Mayor in May 2000 and, in all likelihood, in any other elections of executive mayors which take place in England. So adopting SV Plus instead of AV Plus would help check the criticism of the Jenkins Commission that its scheme adds to a confusing cornucopia of electoral systems in post 1997 Britain.

ACKNOWLEDGEMENTS

This article presents abbreviated results from Dunleavy and Margetts (1998b), while different elements from the same source are also reported in Dunleavy, Margetts and Weir (1998b) and Dunleavy and Margetts, (1999). We are especially grateful to Lord Jenkins of Hillhead, Ros McCool, and Gus Park for their help in structuring this work. These reports are the latest in a series of studies including Dunleavy, Margetts and Weir (1998a), Dunleavy, Margetts, O'Duffy and Weir (1997a and 1997b) and Dunleavy, Margetts and Weir (1992). The research for our 1998 survey was funded by the Joseph Rowntree Charitable Trust. The 1997 survey was funded both by the Economic and Social Research Council (ESRC Award Number N000222253. Award Title: 'Modelling Alternative Electoral Systems in British Conditions in the 1990s') and by the Joseph Rowntree Charitable Trust. The 1992 research was funded by the Joseph Rowntree Reform Trust. We are very grateful to Lord Trevor Smith and to Steve Birkman for their help and support. We thank Richard Katz, Justin Fisher and EPOP members at the 1997 and 1998 conferences for comments and suggestions included here.

REFERENCES

Bean, C. 'Australia's Experience with the Alternative Vote', *Representation* 34:103–10.

Blais, A. and L. Massicott (1996) 'Mixed Electoral Systems: An Overview', *Representation*, 33:115–9.

Cox, G. (1997) *Making Votes Count: Strategic Co-ordination in the World's Electoral Systems,* Cambridge: Cambridge University Press.

Donovan, M. (1995) 'The Politics of Electoral Reform in Italy', *International Political Science Review* 16: 47–65.

Dunleavy, P. and H. Margetts (1994) 'The Experiential Approach to Auditing democracy', in D. Beetham (ed.) *Defining and Measuring Democracy,* pp.152–82. London: Sage.

Dunleavy, P. and H. Margetts (1995) 'Understanding the Dynamics of Electoral Reform', *International Political Science Review,* 16: 9–29

Dunleavy, P. and H. Margetts (1998a) *Report to the Government Office for London: Electing the London Mayor and Assembly,* London: LSE Public Policy Group.

Dunleavy, P. and H. Margetts (1998b) *The Performance of the Commission's Schemes for a New Electoral System: Report to the Independent Commission on the Voting System,* London: LSE Public Policy Group and Birkbeck Public Policy Centre.

Dunleavy, P. and H. Margetts (1998c) 'The Preference Structure of British Voters for Political Parties in the 1990s', Paper to the UK Political Studies Association Conference, University of Keele, 7–9 April 1998.

Dunleavy, P. and H. Margetts (1999) 'Mixed Electoral Systems in Britain and the Jenkins Commission on Electoral Reform', *British Journal of Politics and International Relation* 1: 12–38.

Dunleavy, P., H. Margetts and S. Weir (1998a) *Making Votes Count 2: Special Report on Mixed Voting Systems,* Democratic Audit Paper No. 14, 1997.

Dunleavy, P. H. Margetts and S. Weir (1998b) *The Politico's Guide to Electoral Reform in Britain.* London: Politicos.

Dunleavy, P. H. Margetts, B. O'Duffy and S. Weir (1997) *Making Votes Count: Replaying the 1990s General Elections Under Alternative Electoral Systems,* Democratic Audit Paper No. 11, 1997.

Hart, J. (1992) *Proportional Representation: Critics of the British Electoral System, 1820–1945,* Oxford: Clarendon Press.

Jenkins' Commission (1998), *The Report of the Independent Commission on the Voting System,* London: The Stationary Office.

Kellner, P. (1997) 'Blair's Modest Proposal on Reform', *Representation* 34: 111–3.

Kellner, P. (1998) 'Think Again on Vote Reform – for the Sake of Democracy', *Evening Standard,* 7 September 1998; also BBC2's *Newsnight,* 7 September 1998.

Linton, M. and M. Southcott (1998) *Making Votes Count: The Case for Electoral Reform,* London: Profile Books.

Rae, D., V. Hanby and J. Loosemore (1971) 'Thresholds of Representation and Thresholds of Exclusion: An Analytic Note on Electoral Systems', *Comparative Political Studies* 3: 479–88.

Rokkan, S. (1968) 'Elections: Electoral Systems', *International Encyclopaedia of the Social Sciences,* New York: Crowell-Collier-Macmillan.

Taagepera, R. and M. Shugart (1989) *Seats and Votes: The Effects and Determinants of Electoral Systems,* New Haven: Yale University Press.

Thurner, P.W. and F.U. Pappi (1998) 'Measuring and Explaining Strategic Voting in the German Electoral System', Mannheim: Mannheim Zentrum fur Europaishce Sozialforschung, Arbeitbereich II, Nr.21.

Thurner, P.W. and F.U. Pappi (1999) 'Causes and Effects of Coalition preferences in a Mixed-Member Proportional system', Mannheim: Mannheim Zentrum fur Europaishce Sozialforschung, Arbeitspapiere, Nr.1.

Party Policy and Electoral Reform: A Survey of Developments, Motives and Prospects

Matt Cole

Never wholly separate in your mind the merits of any political question from the men who are concerned in it. You will be told, that if a measure is good, what have you [to] do with the character and views of those who bring it forward. But designing men never separate their plans from their interests... Where two motives, neither of them perfectly justifiable, may be assigned, the worst has the chance of being preferred (Edmund Burke).

Most writing about the course of electoral reform has a deeply pessimistic tone. Most commentators have come to the conclusion arrived at by Anthony Wigram, the former parliamentary candidate and constituency association chairman who established Conservative Action on Electoral Reform (CAER) after the Tories' defeat of February 1974: he told the party conference on 8 October 1975 that 'we have connived in the use of an unfair system because it was thought to be to our political advantage to do so'. After 16 years' service in the cause of Proportional Representation (PR) he wrote wearily to *The Independent* (5 October 1990) that:

Electoral reform can never be achieved under our existing system, because the party that wins an election and has the power to make the change has a vested interest in retaining the system under which it was elected... I have no doubt that had the Conservative Party lost three elections in a row, sentiment would have turned strongly in favour of reform. Equally, I have no doubt that, once we were elected, this sentiment would have evaporated like early-morning mist. The Labour Party will do likewise.

He drew the still more dramatic conclusion that 'the only way reform has ever been achieved is by physical dissent by those persons who suffer disadvantage under the existing system'. Even those more recent analysts who have seen reform rise up the political agenda as never before remain cautious: Ivor

Crewe wrote in *Marxism Today* (October 1991) that 'since PR will deprive at least a third of existing MPs of their seats, one might as well ask turkeys to vote for Christmas'; Robert Blackburn (1992), argued more despondently that 'left to its own devices, Labour will not introduce PR or any other bold measure of democratization'; and Andrew Marr (1995: 29) concluded that 'no subject in politics is more caked in hypocrisy and self-interest than the electoral system, and no reform is harder to envisage than voting reform'.

The report of the Jenkins Commission in October 1998, and reactions to its work, provides a pertinent opportunity to examine this widely held view that self-interest governs the policy and tactics of parties over electoral reform. For the first time since the war the parties have been obliged to present and defend their policies on the subject in a formal and comprehensive – and indeed official – framework. The result has been to bring into question the most simplistic conceptions of policy-making on electoral reform: even a brief survey of the main parties' policies over the last 30 years shows that all are divided; the 'self-interest' which allegedly guides them is a complex and contradictory guide; and this is, moreover, not the only guide to their actions.

Conservatives

Ideologically, and historically, the Conservatives have been both defenders of the traditional features of the constitution, and pragmatic reformers of it when occasion demanded. This was reflected in recent times by the willingness of the party to flirt with electoral reform in the middle 1970s. After four defeats in five elections, one despite the Tories' winning the largest single number of votes, Wigram established CAER to lobby for a pro-PR policy within the party. Initially split between advocates of the Additional Member System (AMS) and the Single Transferable Vote (STV), CAER settled the debate in 1986 in favour of the latter. Under the Labour government of 1974–79 the group prospered modestly if temporarily, reflecting the reformist mood which also bore fruit in the October 1974 manifesto's commitment to a Speaker's Conference on electoral reform, in the debates on constitutional reform at the 1975 and 1978 conferences, and in the sympathetic comments of leading lights such as Gilmour (1977), Hailsham (1978) and latterly Patten (1983). The level of support for CAER at this time is, as with all such groups, difficult to gauge, with reformers' own reports of Commons membership ranging from 41 to 80, or even 100 supposed sympathizers whose names Tim Rathbone claimed to carry in his wallet. Certainly, a third of the parliamentary party voted for PR in the divisions over devolution legislation in the late 1970s, despite the exhortations of the Tory whips.

Nonetheless, the idea of reform (and concern about 'elective dictatorship' more generally) had dropped out of view as an issue by the time Margaret Thatcher took office as Prime Minister. By the mid-1980s CAER was reduced to a shadowy existence, with no full-time office, few publications, and a dwindling band of active supporters. The new parliamentary intakes of 1983 and 1987 included few sympathizers, and leading campaigners such as Sir David Knox, Robin Squire, Ian Gilmour and Tim Rathbone took office, moved on or were electoral casualties. From 1991 onwards, defence of the existing system (as part of the constitutional settlement and the Union) became an article of Majorite faith as a means of uniting the party in pressing circumstances.[1]

So far this looks like ringing confirmation for those who are sceptical about the motives of reformers: a party ill-served by the existing system considered replacing it, until in office, when it dropped PR like a hot brick. However, this is to neglect the finer points of policy change before 1997, and to explain nothing of what has happened since.

First, the very fact of division among the Conservatives proves that self-interest, even if it was the key policy determinant, did not lead clearly in one direction. While some speculated that the Labour Party – and potentially a far-left Labour government – would be able to establish itself in office at length on less than even a plurality of the vote, others saw the results of 1974 as freak occurrences, and argued that in the long term the party's interests were best served by retaining first-past-the-post (FPP). In addition, it should be noted that the turning point in Conservative opinion dates not from the return to office of 1979, but from Thatcher's assumption of the party leadership in 1975. The fact that CAER was halted in its tracks is a reflection not merely of the increasing electoral optimism of the party under her leadership, but also of her personal style, convictions and her factional loyalties. Thatcher not only rejected the intellectual case for PR, but (as other European leaders were soon to discover) abhorred the politics of compromise and negotiation which it usually entails. In addition, CAER was closely associated with the interests of the moderate Conservatives who were ready to engage in compromise with other centrist politicians, and whose influence the new leader was keen to curtail (see Russell, 1978: ch.13). Even if she had accepted PR as an abstract idea, and accommodated the idea of coalition, Thatcher would have been deterred by the new lease of life it might have given party rivals and their ideas. In the transition from Thatcher's to Major's leadership, advocacy of the current system became still more instrumental: it moved from being a badge of loyalty to the leadership faction, to being an amulet of party unity for all groups at a time of deep division. Although Major himself had expressed sympathy for PR in 1979 (*Independent on Sunday,* 16 February 1992) he saw opposition to electoral reform as an effective rallying-point for his distressed troops.

More remarkable to the sceptic is the hardened attitude of the party, and particularly its leadership, following the 1997 election. In contrast to the 1970s, the Conservatives have reacted to under-representation by nailing their colours still faster to the current system. Scarcely a single MP will openly criticize FPP: even CAER can name only one potential sympathizer in the Commons, recently drawn on to the front bench.[2] Loyalty to FPP was made the theme of the Opposition Day debate on 2 June 1998, when not one Conservative defied the party line. In the previous year, the Conservative front bench had tabled amendments to legislation for devolved assemblies in Scotland and Wales promoting FPP even for those parts of the country in which in 1997 the party had been left with no representation for almost a fifth of the vote. The Conservative submission to the (in the words of party briefings) 'rigged' Jenkins Commission rejected all alternatives to FPP, and concluded that no referendum on the electoral system was justified. Although CAER made a separate submission, which was received and circulated among the leadership by Cecil Parkinson, it enjoyed no support from the Conservative MPs in the Commons.

The system of AV+ proposed by Jenkins was immediately condemned by Hague on Channel 4 News (29 October 1998) as 'incredibly complicated... I think it is a dog's breakfast'. Some (though not all) right-wing editorials of 30 October 1998 agreed: the *Daily Mail* thought the proposal 'should be widely debated. And then left to gather dust'. *The Times* thought it 'Too clever by half'; *The Daily Telegraph* described it as 'Rococo and wrong'. *The Sun* quoted Conservative spokesman Liam Fox extensively in a report headed 'You've Got It Wong, Woy'.

This development in policy cannot be explained solely by short-term demands of party representation. At the very least this would argue for a more open debate about PR, and a willingness to accept it in Scotland, Wales and Europe. Notwithstanding the Conservatives are pushing at a closed door under the weight of the government's majority, this does not explain the increased determination with which they are pushing: it is noticeable that, unlike in other areas of constitutional reform such as the Lords, the electoral system is an institution to which the Conservatives will accept no amendment. This is not because the issue is a particular passion of William Hague, who has not taken the high profile in the campaign adopted (and maintained in the Opposition Day debate) by John Major, and who, in a cryptic claim of the CAER submission, 'is reputed to have been a member of CAER' (p.2); rather, the determining factors here are party unity, ideology and consistency.

Advocacy of the current system contrasts government and official opposition policies very effectively, and unites all the existing parliamentary party around convictions they mostly share regardless of the circumstances. Major made full use of this function of unifying and morale boosting during the divisions of the 1992 parliament. More important, however, is the fact that whether the Conservatives wished to consider PR or not, and whether or not it is in their interests to do so, their opposition to it in the years since 1979, and their general resistance to constitutional reform, makes advocacy of change fatal to any public impression of integrity. They are bound by the obligation to pursue an entrenched policy, rather than entirely free to pursue their interests. Current Conservative policy, then, has less to do with immediate interest than a certain sort of inevitability. Only the resistance (and it is the Conservatives' greatest fear) to the introduction of pure Alternative Vote (AV) can be attributed to concern about representation; but since this has never been a serious prospect in policy terms, its damage to their interests is a hypothetical question.

Liberal Democrats

The policy of the Liberal Democrats is the one most commonly accused of barely-clothed self-interest in their support for the introduction of PR. 'The Liberals' (*sic*), assert the Conservative Research Department, 'refuse to admit that they do not win elections because they have failed to produce an attractive political programme: they blame the electoral system'. The attack continues: 'The needs of the nation as a whole have no place in their plans: their sole concern is their own selfish party interest' (Cooke, 1996: 85). Brian Mawhinney claimed on 7 February the same year that supporters of PR 'cover their arguments in the flag of principle, but underneath it all it is about winning a slice of power for parties that have failed to convince the electorate of their case'.

The sceptics often observe that the Liberal Party adopted a policy favouring PR at just that point – 1922 – when it became evident that as the third party in an emerging two-party system, they would be punished by FPP. Liberal prime ministers up to and including Lloyd George in 1918 had passed up the opportunity to reform the voting system to produce proportionality, even as part of wider Reform Acts.

There is currently very little dispute among Liberal Democrats about the best electoral system. Although leading figures (including Jeremy Thorpe and Sir Robin Day, both of whom appeared at the London hearing of the Jenkins Commission) favour a mixture of AV and STV, the majority of the limited contributions from party members received by Maclennan's working party backed the system which has the authority of party policy since the SDP/Liberal merger, a special commission appointed by the Alliance in the 1980s, Liberal policy since 1922, and the endorsement of leading Liberal radicals such as J.S. Mill since the nineteenth century – namely STV. However, although the Liberal Democrats would have fared markedly better under STV, their preference for which was confirmed in their submission to Jenkins, it is – as Dunleavy *et al.* (1997) have shown – not the optimal system in terms of their own interests. STV would have been likely to grant Blair a small overall majority in 1997 by giving Labour the greater benefit of an efficient mutual transfer between Liberal Democrat and Labour candidates. A proportional variant of AMS, on the other hand, would have given the third party the pivotal position in a Commons with no overall control which sceptics argue has so long been the object of Liberal fantasy and which is said to explain their support for reform.

High principle and shallow interest aside, the Liberal Democrats are bound in part by what one of their submission's authors described as 'entrenchment': that is, the need to appear consistent to avoid public embarrassment. Like the Conservatives, they could not at this stage (or for some time) consider advocating an electoral system other than STV after spending so long as its keenest proponents. Paddy Ashdown acknowledged the possibility of accepting a compromise involving AV before the Jenkins Report was published, and had been encouraged in this by others (for example, Kellner, 1997): however, such a compromise would be even less reliable in bringing office to his party.

Many Liberal Democrats have grave misgivings about this strategy precisely because it involves trading off the long-term demand for what they see as 'pure' PR (STV) against the short-term accommodation with Blair, and the medium-term prospect of intermittent office under AV+. Indeed it was on the negative basis of 'the opportunity to break out of the prison of First-Past-the-Post' that Ashdown heartily endorsed the system proposed by Jenkins (BBC News, 29 October 1998). Certainly, Jenkins' proposals do not represent a Liberal Democrat dream: they would offer the prospect of periodic coalition partnership, dependent upon maintaining a cordial relationship with one of the main parties. Liberal Democrats are not entirely agreed as to what their best interests are; but they are even less sure of how much they are prepared to let circumstances force them into compromise, and are burdened with a long history of clear policy on electoral reform.

Labour

Labour is the party most obviously divided over electoral reform. Though Labour governments flirted with the introduction of AV openly under MacDonald and privately under Wilson, opinion in the party prior to 1987 was overwhelmingly against changing the current system. Callaghan was unable to persuade the PLP to support PR for elections to the devolved assemblies or the European Parliament, and the formation of the SDP in 1981 only served to flush out reformers and intensify Labour hostility to a policy that was dismissed by loyalists as a characteristically irrelevant revisionist distraction. The striking contrast of opinions in the Labour Party since 1987 serves only to illustrate that neither principle nor party (nor any other) interest is a clear guide as to what to do next.

The growth of the Labour Campaign for Electoral Reform (LCER) began after Labour's third consecutive defeat. Between 1987 and 1992, LCER recruited leading supporters such as Jeff Rooker and Robin Cook, boosted its membership tenfold to 2,000, and sponsored a growing number of conference resolutions provoking the debate which culminated in the Plant Report and Kinnock's readiness to open its discussions to those outside the party. The experience of repeated defeat – in 1992 under what were thought favourable circumstances – at the hands of a Conservative administration which was introducing radical measures such as the Poll Tax gave the case for PR greatly enhanced credibility with Labour supporters (Wainwright, 1987; Linton and Southcott, 1998). By the 1997 election, Labour was committed to the use of a new electoral system for almost all levels of election except Westminster, for which the manifesto promised a referendum on 'a proportional alternative to the first-past-the-post system'.

As with the Conservatives, the purist sceptic finds ideal material in the outline of events to this point, but has greater difficulty explaining both details and subsequent events. Since the election Labour's active membership has continued to fragment into a kaleidoscope of campaigns.

The LCER has recruited well from among the new parliamentary intake, winning 60 sponsors in the Commons from Labour newcomers, to reach a new record of 122 sponsor MPs. Only six of the 1997 departures were LCER sponsors. The group's political organizer claims 'time is on our side – the drift is in our direction', arguing that there remain around 20 more potential sponsors in the Commons, ten of whom are already known to LCER as sympathizers, and some of whom sign pro-reform Early Day Motions, but will not join an organization to which they cannot devote time. Others await the signal of the leadership before declaring on the issue, or have been discouraged from speaking out on the issue by a hostile constituency party. The LCER also claims that limited resources make it impossible even to canvass all MPs directly for support.

The support for PR in a party still feeling the generous benefits of FPP is explained in a number of ways: a small number of MPs such as Austin Mitchell are conviction reformers, and have always favoured PR; others, such as Lawrie Quinn (Scarborough), hold seats which they know are most vulnerable to a swing under FPP, and are therefore most likely to be receptive to arguments about the system's regional distortions; but most of all there is the lingering desire to avoid the experience of the 1980s, which looms large in the memories of many new MPs. At its strongest, this takes the form of a conscious desire to create a new, non-adversarial, pluralist and decentralized political culture, but even at its most limited, it is a powerful awareness that the grand scale of the 1997 victory was, in Mitchell's words, 'a temporary phase', and while that awareness is 'wasting, it still remains'. However, while LCER claims championship of both party and public, both titles are likewise boasted by the party's proponents of FPP.

The LCER's critics in the party attribute Labour's reform measures to entrenchment. The party had been committed, as a result partly of the need to compete with other parties electorally, to devolution based on PR since the Scottish Constitutional Convention from 1987; to renege on that promise would be implausible. European elections, on the other hand, were affected by pressure for comparable systems across the EU, rather than opinion in the Labour Party. Today, MPs in the 'first-past-the-post' group like Fraser Kemp argue; 'the mood has changed... a lot of support for PR was based on the idea that we couldn't win again'. Kemp argues that if policy on the electoral system for any of these bodies were written today, it might be very different. According to this view, LCER members, who are so divided as to which reform to introduce that their submission to Jenkins did not nominate a preferred option, will soon start to distance themselves from reform and diminish in number.[3] The FPP group has a loose structure, and though its supporters claim it represents the opinion of 'nine-tenths' of the party, its opponents will acknowledge only a minimum of 100 known FPP supporters among Labour MPs. Certainly the group has experienced and varied supporters: its Chair is Stuart Bell, and Dennis Skinner and John Spellar joined forces at the 1998 conference to promote the group's fringe meeting. The AEEU committed £10,000 in August 1998 to the campaign against PR; in the Cabinet, Jack Straw and John Prescott are among the known opponents of reform, and one MP attributed Straw's introduction of a closed list system for European elections to a cynical desire to discredit PR, commending him on 'playing a blinder'. Straw was ready to tour the television studios on the publication of the Jenkins Report pouring cold water upon hopes that the promised referendum would take place before the next general election.

In between these groups is one called 'Keep the Link', whose supporters claim that it is the largest in the PLP, with over 100 Labour MPs, including Cabinet ministers. Its policy position, in the words of one of its members, Martin Salter (Reading), lies 'mid-way between the anoraks and the dinosaurs', rejecting both FPP and any system which does not maintain a link between each constituency and a single MP. In practice, this means supporting variants of AV and SV. The motive for doing this as a Labour MP, in Salter's view, is the likely benefit and greater reliability to be gained from eliminating tactical voting, while retaining the advantages to the public of the identifiable local MP. Moreover, AMS and STV are a direct threat to the current membership of the Commons, and therefore 'there's not a snowball's chance in hell of AMS or STV getting through Parliament'. It is also acknowledged that AV has some appeal outside the group as the 'least disliked' option of FPP and PR supporters, and some Liberal Democrats. Certainly, increasingly strong rumours throughout 1998 suggested that the Prime Minister had accommodated himself to a system based around AV or SV, and his reaction to the Jenkins Report as 'a well-argued and powerful case for the system it recommends' confirmed this approach of non-committal goodwill.

There is a good deal of shared membership between these fluid groups in the Labour Party, and new groups are still emerging, most recently the cross-party Making Votes Count group. Such is the division and volatility of opinion in the Labour Party that no submission was made to the Jenkins Commission until July, some five months after the Commissioners' request for last contributions, and this submission indicated no preferred system. It did, however, observe that not all of the Commission's criteria could be met with in full, and it stressed the importance of the constituent-MP link, and the need to avoid 'permanent coalition' and 'make single party majority government realistically possible' (pp.5, 6). Long-term and short-term interests, including prospects of office, and a continued entente with the Liberal Democrat leadership, have been balanced against the strong convictions of certain backbenchers and Cabinet ministers, and the need to fulfill election pledges. It is less clear with Labour than with the other parties where the scales will eventually rest. Those intimately involved in the debate within the Conservatives and Labour respectively went as far as to say that 'the received wisdom is that no governing party will change the electoral system – but that's a naive view because there's no such thing as a governing party', and even that 'people underestimate the amount of altruism' in the governing party. It is these elements which we must incorporate into any model of policy formulation on the subject of electoral reform.

Factors Determining Party Policy on Electoral Reform

The foregoing demonstrates that party policies on electoral reform cannot be determined by a simplistic equation of party advantage. The simplistic version of the sceptical view does not recognize the following three points.

First, party advantage, whether short- or long-term, is not easily agreed upon. Politicians of different experiences and dispositions are driven in different directions even by pure party selfishness. There is also tension between a party's interest – in respect of its image and identity – in securing votes, in gaining representation, and in retaining office in delicate parliamentary circumstances such as under the Lib-Lab Pact.

Second, other political interests than those of party, sometimes contradictory to those of actors' parties, are also at work: these include conflict between the leadership and backbenchers; factional struggle between left and right; and the interests of MPs with safe or marginal seats.

Lastly, even when utilizing a wide interpretation of political interest, some parties, or at least elements of parties, act against their own interests and in accordance with some sort of consistent principle. If they do not guide party policy, then the conviction activists do at least provide the organizations and support to which other politicians turn when their perception of their own interest requires it.

This much – and the prospect of change it suggests – has been more widely recognized by serious commentators than the introduction above might suggest (Mount, 1993: 267; Norris, 1995; Shell, 1995; Smyth, 1992). Hypocrisy, the saying goes, is the compliment vice pays to virtue, and it is indeed difficult to determine motives from actions; it is therefore futile to seek to attribute levels of nobility or selfishness to particular actions or policies. Is it noble or selfish of Labour pro-reformers to seek to protect the country from another Poll Tax by engineering permanent centre-left coalition? Is current Conservative policy directed at appearing consistent, or preserving a valued system, even at the party's expense? The outcome of the Jenkins Commission and its proposals for the conduct of the referendum are perhaps a familiarly messy compromise, but it was not one caused merely by splitting the difference between party interests. The ultimate outcome of the process will be the result of a constellation of factors, each appearing at different times.

If it is not possible to identify one simple determinant, we can nonetheless seek to chart the landscape of the policy-making process: to establish a sort of framework within which policy-making occurs. The forces involved can be grouped around three themes, each associated with three motives (see Figure 1).

It is the diverse outcomes produced by the tension and contest between these determinants that illustrate the dynamic and at times unpredictable nature of the process. Put simply, parties do not always do what a simple conception of self-interest would suggest they might. Table 1 shows the preferences of each party based upon the criteria of their historical and ideological tradition alone; immediate improvement in their representation on parliament; and the perception of their interests of the chief dissident group in the party.

FIGURE 1
ELECTORAL REFORM POLICY DETERMINANTS

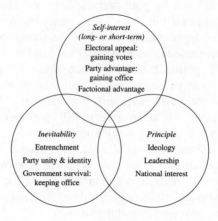

TABLE 1
ELECTORAL REFORM POLICY DETERMINANTS AND OUTCOMES

	History & ideology	Self- interest	Dissident view	Jenkins submission
Conservative	FPP	AMS	STV	FPP
Labour	FPP	AV	Mixed	Mixed
Liberal Democrat	STV	AMS	AV	STV

Each of the three themes identified here would point to a particular policy for each party, often at odds with other motives, so that self-interest cannot explain all of the submissions made by the parties to the Jenkins Commission.

Self-interest
Into this category fall those motives of personal or factional advancement usually attributed to reforming politicians. Even each of these gives rise to fierce dispute among those similarly moved by it, since it may be interpreted in a long- or short-term fashion, and speculation will continue as to how best to secure the said interest.

Electoral appeal. One aim of adopting policies, usually favouring reform, has been to make inroads into, or to halt the rise of, another party's share of the poll. The most obvious recent examples are provided by the Labour Party, warding off nationalism through the Scottish Convention, and appealing to Liberal Democrat voters through Kinnock's offer of broadening the range of groups involved in the Plant enquiry in the 1992 election campaign.[4] However, this strategy was also seen when Heath sought Liberal votes by promising a Speaker's Conference on reform in October 1974.

Party advantage. This is the simplest form of self-service, and the one most often identified by commentators, namely the attempt to secure the introduction or preservation of a system likely to bring the party concerned greater representation, and greater likelihood of office. This might explain the Liberals' enthusiasm for reform ever since 1922; the Conservatives' abandonment of it after 1979; and Blair's interest in AV, and his establishment of the Jenkins Commission, which according to Hugo Young (*Guardian*, 2 December 1997) 'is about...power... His real objective...is to do everything he can to secure the base of his political project for many years ahead'. Even a Labour campaign newsletter cited by Conservative MPs in the Opposition Day debate was indiscreet enough to acknowledge that 'the *realpolitik* reasons for electoral reform' are that 'we can abolish right-wing Tory governments forever'.

Factional advantage. The driving force behind some politicians' views may have been their interests not merely as party members, but as supporters of a specific section of a party. Exemplars would be Gilmour as a moderate in 1977, the few Conservative dissidents in Scotland today, Dennis Skinner's hostility to the Blair-Ashdown project, and, some would say, the Labour leadership in their eagerness to introduce a closed list system in the European elections. In each of these cases, actors served their interests as members of groups within parties, interests that might at times conflict with the broader party interest.

Inevitability
This term is used to refer to situations in which politicians advocate a policy, not because they anticipate advantage from it, but because the consequences of the alternative are so much worse as to leave little choice. It could be argued that such 'inevitability' is in reality a form of self-interest, since the motives associated with it are concerned with the protection of the party, or of some other interest. However, a qualitative difference exists between calculating the optimal electoral system for one's own party and then

manipulating its introduction (which is the form of self-interest commonly attributed to politicians); and acquiescing in a policy which is no more than a *fait accompli*. One entails preference; the other does not.

Entrenchment. This is the effect of precedent created by a party policy argued from a basis of principle over time, but which becomes contradictory to the party's current interests. The price of altering the policy so evidently cynically is higher than that of defending a system less favourable to the party in terms of representation, prohibitively so. This is the situation in which the Conservatives find themselves, as do Labour in the devolved assemblies. Each has given a hostage to fortune and is now faced with the ransom demand.

Party unity and identity. Parties also adopt positions contrary to their immediate interests because to do otherwise might fatally threaten the stability, image or morale of the party. Again, this was partly the anticipated effect of Major's attack upon reform, and of Hague's decision to defend FPP because 'this is a referendum we can win' (*The Times*, 5 September 1998). Similarly, electoral reform was an unpopular issue in the Labour Party while the 'betrayal' of the Social Democrats rankled; yet in the era of 'constructive opposition' and 'modernization', it symbolizes the open, tolerant, reforming image Blair seeks to establish.

Government survival. At times, it is simple parliamentary arithmetic that demands consideration of otherwise unpalatable reforms. This was the situation of the MacDonald government of 1929, of Wilson when he ordered studies of the outcome of the 1964 election under different systems while in negotiation with Grimond, but most obviously under the Lib-Lab Pact. In a less strict numerical fashion, Blair's future success clearly relies upon a reasonably cordial relationship with the Liberal Democrats to avoid vote splitting at the electoral level.

Principle
These are the occasions on which the beliefs of actors in the process appear to have influence, even against their interests, or those of their group.

Ideology. Each party's values, and their development over time, give some direction to their policy in the field. Hague draws on the Conservatives' tradition of discouraging tampering with the constitution except as a means of resolving crises; the Liberals have a long heritage of electoral reform; and the Labour Party has a mixed history, suspicious of constitutional answers to economic and social problems, but also periodically keen to present itself as modern and democratic. These values, so far as they are shared by influential portions of the parties, set the psychological parameters of debate about policy, and affect the language in which reform is discussed.

Leadership. The tone and sometimes the policy of parties change not with interests, but with the beliefs of their leaders. The Conservatives abandoned reform in 1975 because of Thatcher's personal antipathy to pluralism; Kinnock's decision to open the door to reform was pivotal to the success of the LCER; and now, as Austin Mitchell acknowledges, 'a lot depends on how the leadership jumps'.

National interest. Perhaps less discernible and more rare than other factors, the condition of the country is undoubtedly a consideration of at least some actors in the process, whether that is LCER members opposed to Conservative health cuts, or Ian Gilmour's fear (1977) of 'Marxist chains' being imposed upon Britain by a minority-backed Labour government under FPP, we must acknowledge at least the possibility that these were genuine sentiments, especially when expressed by people arguing what was an unpopular case within their own party.

Conclusion

Doubtless it is possible to think of other important determinants not mentioned here. External events, for example, are clearly important, such as the adoption of a mixed-member system in New Zealand, with mixed results, or the pressure for conformity of election systems throughout Europe in electing the European Parliament. What is less easy is the pretence that the development of policy on electoral reform is predictable because it is monocausal. Burke's remarks quoted at the top of this article reflect a characteristic healthy scepticism which remains as relevant today as it was in the era of the French Revolution; but as a systematic explanation of events, they are misleadingly incomplete. Like all monocausalists, those who rely upon a narrow definition of self-interest to predict the future of the electoral system will begin with certainty and end in confusion.

ACKNOWLEDGEMENTS

The author is grateful for the co-operation of six staff of the Liberal Democrats, the Conservative Party, the Jenkins Commission, the LCER, CAER and ERS, and three Labour MPs, all of whom gave extended interviews between 24 July 1998 and 5 August 1998, and from whose comments are taken all quotations not otherwise attributed.

NOTES

1. Major launched his attack at the conference that year, and went on to dismiss PR as 'Paddy's Roundabout' at the Central Council meeting, on 13 and 14 March 1992.
2. Even those Conservatives who criticize the existing system do so in very muted tones. See for example Cormack (1996: 281).
3. One example of such 'drift' cited is Tony Wright's speech in the Opposition Day debate, 2 June 1998, in which he declared: 'I have changed my mind over the years... I had not anticipated that a government could be elected under (FPP) who would move to put in place a series of checks and balances that would reform the political system' (HC Debs, 2 June 1998, c.236).
4. Kinnock also indicated a personal change of heart in a *Labour Party News* interview (October 1991) in which he revealed that the constituent-MP link was the only vital element of any system; on 6 April 1992 he refused to reject the possibility of PR in a 'Granada 500' TV interview.

REFERENCES

Blackburn, R. (1992) 'The Ruins of Westminster', *New Left Review* 191: 12–3.

Cooke, A. B. (ed) (1996) 'The Liberal Democrats: at best confused, at worst duplicitous', *Politics Today*, Conservative Research Department, 12 April.

Cormack, P. (1996) 'Restoring Faith in Parliament', *Journal of Legislative Studies* 2: 277–82.

Dunleavy, P., H. Margetts, B. O'Duffy and S. Weir (1997), *Making Votes Count: Replaying the 1990s General Elections under Alternative Systems*. London: Democratic Audit.

Gilmour, I. (1977) *Inside Right*. London: Hutchinson.

Hailsham, Lord (1978) *Dilemma of Democracy*. London: Collins.

Kellner, P. (1997) 'Getting it in Proportion', *Fabian Review* 109: 5.

Linton, M. and M. Southcott (1998) *Making Votes Count*. London: Profile Books.

Marr, A. (1995) *Ruling Britannia: The Failure and Future of British Democracy*. London: Michael Joseph.

Mount, F. (1993) *The British Constitution Now*. London: Mandarin.

Norris, P. (1995) 'The Politics of Electoral Reform', *International Political Science Review* 16: 65–78.

Patten, C. (1983) *The Tory Case*. London: Longman.

Russel, T. (1978) *The Tory Party*. Harmondsworth: Penguin.

Shell, D. (1995) 'The British Constitution in 1995', *Parliamentary Affairs* 49: 391–9.

Smyth, G. (1992) 'The Pattens, Plant and Paddy: Where the Parties Stand', in G. Smyth (ed.) *Refreshing the Parts*, pp.9–27. London: Lawrence and Wishart.

Wainwright, H. (1987) *Labour: A Tale of Two Parties*. London: Hogarth Press.

New Labour's New Partisans: The Dynamics of Party Identification in Britain since 1992

Harold D. Clarke, Marianne C. Stewart and Paul Whiteley

Since its introduction in the American National Election Studies (ANES) in the 1950s (see Campbell *et al.*, 1954, 1960), the concept of party identification has provoked a host of theoretical and methodological controversies. According to its original social-psychological definition, party identification is an enduring element in the political psychology of party support and, as such, exercises important effects on electoral choice and the contours of party systems. Party identification is an affective attachment with a political party, and typically such an attachment is formed as a result of early-life socialization processes (e.g. Campbell *et al.*, 1960: chs 6–7; Miller, 1991). Because party identifications tend to be stable and to strengthen over time, they act as a powerful long-term force anchoring voting behaviour and party fortunes in successive elections (e.g. Campbell *et al.*, 1966; Converse, 1976).

Starting in the early 1980s, this social psychological conception of party identification has been challenged by scholars who contend that voters' partisan attachments should be seen as summary 'running tallies' of current and past party performance evaluations, with more weight being given to recent, as opposed to earlier, assessments (e.g. Fiorina, 1981: ch.5; see also Achen, 1992; Franklin, 1984, 1992; Franklin and Jackson, 1983). Because party performance evaluations vary over time, individual- and aggregate-level partisan change are continuing possibilities. These critics of the traditional conception of party identification have used panel data gathered by national election surveys conducted in the United States and other countries to show that responses to party identification questions manifest considerable over-time instability. Recently, however, Green and his colleagues (e.g. Schickler and Green, 1997; see also Green and Palmquist, 1990, Green, Palmquist and Schickler, 1993) have claimed that this *observed* instability in individual-level responses to survey questions concerning party identification is an artifact of random measurement error. They contend that once it is purged of measurement error party identification typically is highly stable – just as Campbell and his colleagues asserted nearly a half-century ago.

At the aggregate level, MacKuen, Erikson and Stimson (1989: 1136) have demonstrated that American 'macropartisanship', as measured by a question in monthly Gallup surveys, responds to voters' economic evaluations and presidential approval ratings. This finding, which contradicts the traditional view of party identification as an 'unmoved mover' in the skein of forces affecting electoral choice, has stimulated another heated controversy concerning measurement. Abramson and Ostrom (1991), *inter alia*, have argued that the Gallup party identification question is flawed because it does not ask respondents to think about which party they 'usually' or 'generally' support. Moreover, when party identification is measured using the traditional ANES question, it more nearly resembles the exogenous force hypothesized by advocates of the venerable 'Michigan model'. Abramson and Ostrom's time series analysis shows that party identification is affected only weakly by judgements about the state of the economy and not at all by evaluations of presidential performance. The macropartisanship debate has raged for several now in the United States (e.g. Bishop *et al.*, 1994; Box-Steffensmeier and Smith, 1996; Clarke and Suzuki, 1994; MacKuen *et al.*, 1992). The situation is different in Britain where an absence of time series data has prevented analysts from addressing longstanding disagreements (see Budge, Crewe and Farlie, 1976; Crewe, 1986; Crewe, Sarlvik and Alt, 1977; Heath, Jowell and Curtice, 1985; Heath *et al.*, 1991; Heath and McDonald, 1988; Heath and Pierce, 1992; Sarlvik and Crewe, 1983) concerning the nature and dynamics of party identification.

In this article, we address controversies about party identification in the context of analyzing movements in Labour Party identification over the 1992–98 period. Two research projects initiated in 1992 provide the data for our analyses. The authors have carried out the first of these projects, and it is designed to gauge aggregate movements in party identification. Starting in January 1992, this study has included the standard sequence of party identification questions used in the British Election Studies (BES) in successive monthly Gallup polls.[1] Using the BES party identification battery avoids the dispute over question wording that has bedevilled research on the aggregate dynamics of partisanship in the United States. The second research project has been conducted under the auspices of the CREST organization, and it involves multi-wave national panel surveys of the British electorate. Since these British Election Panel Surveys (BEPS) include the standard BES party identification battery and a wide variety of questions concerning political beliefs, attitudes and opinions, they are useful for studying stability and change in party identification at the individual level.

The Dynamics of Labour Party Identification

Aggregate-level Change

Information on responses to the first question in the BES party identification battery administered in monthly Gallup polls over the January 1992–July 1998 period is displayed in Figures 1–4.[2] Figure 1 shows there is a substantial aggregate dynamic to these responses. Labour Party identification, which stood at 33% in January 1992, moves sharply upward at the time of the September 1992 ERM crisis, and then surpasses Conservative identification in all subsequent months. In April 1997, just prior to the general election, the percentages of Labour and Conservative identifiers were 40% and 28%, respectively. The Labour share has grown in the aftermath of that contest – *circa* July 1998, 47% of the electorate claimed to be Labour identifiers, 28% said they were Conservatives, and 12%, Liberal Democrats.

FIGURE 1
CONSERVATIVE, LABOUR AND LIBERAL DEMOCRAT PARTY IDENTIFICATION,
JANUARY 1992–JULY 1998

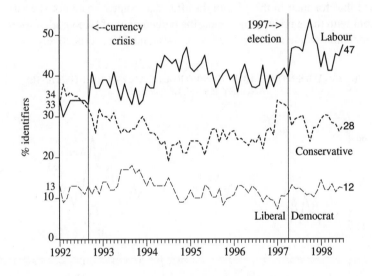

Figures 2, 3 and 4 show the dynamics of the growth in Labour partisanship among social class, age and gender groups in the electorate. In keeping with the party's traditional strength in the working class, Figure 2 indicates that a substantial gap in the percentage of working versus middle or upper class persons identifying with Labour persisted throughout the entire 1992–97 period. Although the upward movements and strong correlation (r = +0.74) between the percentages of upper/middle and working class Labour identifiers in the time series data for these two groups indicates that Labour's partisan share was increasing in both of them, the party's strength in upper and middle classes remains considerably less than in the working class (38% versus 55% in July 1998). Parallel age and gender dynamics also are apparent, with Labour attracting increasing partisan support from both older and younger voters (r = +0.51) and men and women (r = +0.62). Perhaps most interesting are changes in the relative support for Labour offered by these age and gender groups. Applying the Hodrick-Prescott filter (Enders, 1995: 210) to these time series reveals that the underlying trend in Labour partisanship among voters 35 years of age and older surpassed that for younger persons in early 1996, and that the gap between the two age groups has increased after the 1997 election (data not shown). A similar situation obtains for the two gender groups. For much of the period before the 1997 election, the percentage of Labour identifiers was greater among men than women (Figure 4). However, applying the Hodrick-Prescott filter indicates that the underlying trend in Labour partisanship among women turned sharply upward in the run-up to the election, and surpassed that for men in the 15 months after that contest (data not shown). Consistent with these underlying trends, the percentages of Labour identifiers among men and women in July 1998 were 44% and 51%, respectively.

FIGURE 2
LABOUR PARTY IDENTIFICATION, UPPER/MIDDLE AND WORKING CLASSES,
JANUARY 1992–JULY 1998

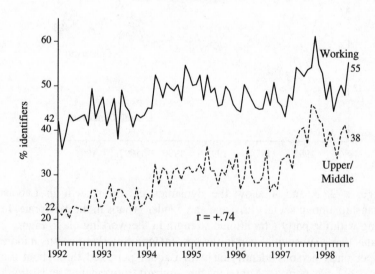

FIGURE 3
LABOUR PARTY IDENTIFICATION, YOUNGER AND OLDER AGE GROUPS,
JANUARY 1992–JULY 1998

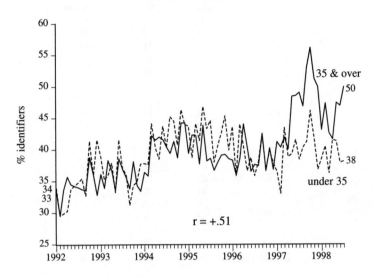

FIGURE 4
LABOUR PARTY IDENTIFICATION, MEN AND WOMEN,
JANUARY 1992–JULY 1998

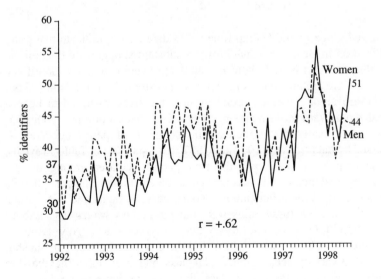

TABLE 1
THE DEMOGRAPHICS OF LABOUR PARTY IDENTIFICATION, 1992 AND 1997

		1992	1997	Difference
Age:	18–24	37	63	+26
	25–34	32	50	+18
	35–44	30	41	+11
	45–54	28	37	+9
	55–64	30	36	+6
	65 and over	30	40	+10
Gender:	Men	32	42	+10
	Women	30	40	+10
Social Class:	A	22	27	+5
	B	22	29	+7
	C1	25	36	+11
	C2	36	49	+13
	D	46	57	+11
	E	54	61	+7
Trade Union	Member	46	58	+12
	Non-Member	26	36	+10
Region:	North	44	54	+10
	Midlands	24	35	+11
	South	23	29	+6
	London	29	40	+11
	Wales	39	53	+14
	Scotland	32	47	+15

Viewed globally, the Gallup time series data clearly indicate that party identification in Britain has manifested a substantial aggregate dynamic in the 1990s, and that New Labour has attracted many new party identifiers. Although there are differences in levels of and strength of trends in Labour partisanship among various social groups, the basic pattern has been a generalized upward movement since 1992. The conclusion that Labour has enjoyed a broadly based increase in its group of party identifiers is buttressed by data from the 1992 and 1997 BEPS panels. As Table 1 reveals, the Labour partisan share over this time period increased among all age, gender, regional and social class groups in the electorate. The party had its greatest growth in identifiers among young persons, Scots and those in the C2 class group, but these gains were but the highest waves in a Labour partisan flood tide. This is not to say that everyone is now 'New Labour'. The figures in Table 1 clearly show that the extent of Labour partisanship continued to vary by age, region, social class, and trade union membership in 1997. In terms of the social class divisions that have undergirded the

British party system for much of the twentieth century (e.g. Butler and Stokes, 1976), the composition of the New Labour partisan cohort remains quite different from those of the Conservatives and Liberal Democrats. The BEPS data indicate that in 1992 44% of Labour's party identifiers were non-manual workers and 56% were manual workers (data not shown). The 1997 numbers were essentially unchanged – 46% and 54%. In sharp contrast, the Conservative and Liberal Democrat party identifier groups retained their traditionally strong middle-class bias, with approximately two thirds of their 1992 and 1997 identifiers falling into the non-manual category.

Individual-level Change

The multi-wave BEPS panel surveys enable one to analyze the dynamics of Labour Party identification at the individual level. Table 2 shows considerable individual-level instability over all of the adjacent two-wave panel surveys conducted between 1992 and 1997, with Labour identifiers consistently exhibiting the least likelihood of deserting their party. This is not surprising given that most important short-term political forces at work favoured Labour and, hence, worked to reinforce, rather than to erode, Labour support. The Labour pattern is very different from those for the Liberal Democrats and the 'other' party identifier groups, as well as for those who state that they do not identify with a party. All of these groups consistently manifest substantial levels of instability with, for example, the Liberal Democrats losing from one-quarter to one-third of their identifiers across all of the adjacent two-wave panels, and fully two-fifths of their 1992 identifiers by 1997. The Conservative pattern is different again, with sizeable losses occurring between 1992 and 1994, and smaller ones thereafter. The large erosion in Tory partisanship in the period shortly after the 1992 election accords well with the aggregate-level trends presented above. It is also consistent with recent time series analyses demonstrating that the September 1992 currency crisis exerted large negative and positive effects, respectively, on the Conservative and Labour partisan shares (Clarke, Stewart and Whiteley, 1997, 1998).

TABLE 2
INSTABILITY OF REPORTED PARTY IDENTIFICATION, 1992–97 BEPS PANELS PERCENTAGES OF
WAVE ONE IDENTIFIERS UNSTABLE ACROSS PANEL

	Con	Lab	Lib-Dem	Nat	Other	None
Panel						
1992–94	28	9	32	26	56	56
1994–95	15	8	36	24	57	51
1995–96	7	8	25	24	71	47
1996–97	10	10	24	18	64	57
1992–97	26	6	39	37	75	71

Regarding *net* inter-party movements between 1992 and 1997, Labour was the recipient of substantial percentages of erstwhile Liberal Democrats (24%), SNP/Plaid Cymru (29%), 'other' party identifiers (50%), and non-identifiers (33%) (see Table 3A). Labour also gained the support of 11% of those who had identified with the Conservatives in 1992. Although this latter group is smaller in percentage terms than the former ones, it is numerically non-trivial because the 1992 Tory Party identifier cohort was much larger than that of any other group but Labour. Thus, as Table 3B shows, 1992 Conservatives constituted the largest single source of new (1997) Labour partisans. In 1997, fully 29% of Labour identifiers in the BEPS panel had not identified with the party five years earlier, and 41% of these new Labour identifiers were 1992 Tories.

TABLE 3
THE DYNAMICS OF PARTY IDENTIFICATION 1992–97 BEPS PANEL

A. Where 1992 Identifiers Went (Column Percentages)

1992 Party Identification

1997 Party Identification	Con	Lab	Lib-Dem	Nat	Other	None
Conservative	74	2	8	0	0	15
Labour	11	94	24	29	50	33
Liberal-Democrat	9	3	61	4	17	18
Nationalist	x	1	1	63	0	3
Other	x	0	2	0	25	2
None	5	x	6	4	8	29

B. Where 1997 Identifiers Came From (Row Percentages)

1992 Party Identification

1997 Party Identification	Con	Lab	Lib-Dem	Nat	Other	None
Conservative	92	2	3	0	0	4
Labour	12	71	8	1	1	7
Liberal-Democrat	27	6	56	1	1	10
Nationalist	9	9	4	65	0	13
Other	20	0	30	0	30	20
None	39	4	14	1	1	41

Note: x = less than 0.5%

The large-scale individual-level dynamics documented by the BEPS panel data are consonant with the much disputed thesis that party identification is a potentially mutable product of voters' reactions to a changing mix of short-term political forces. According to this thesis, observed movements in such panel data are not simply stochastic artifacts of random measurement error, but rather are systematically related to such reactions. Here, we specify a multivariate model of 1997 party identification to investigate these relationships. Predictor variables in the model include several variables measured in the 1997 wave of the BEPS panel. These variables are party images, party leader images, economic evaluations, social policy evaluations, and attitudes towards the European Union (EU).[3] Consonant with the hypothesis advanced by Fiorina (1981) and others that such attitudes and evaluations are employed by voters to update existing partisan attachments, 1992 party identification also is used as a predictor variable.[4] Several demographic variables (age, gender, region, social class, trade union membership) also are included in the model.

Binary logit and multinomial logit procedures (see, e.g. Long, 1997) are used to provide parameter estimates. In the standard binary logit, we employ a dichotomous dependent variable, with 1997 Conservative identifiers scored 1, and all other party identifiers and non-identifiers scored 0. Multinomial logit is a straightforward extension of the binary logit analysis, and it permits one to investigate how a set of predictor variables affects identification with several alternative parties within the framework of a single analysis. In our analysis, we treat identification with the Conservatives as a reference category, and analyse the effects of the predictor variables on moving voters from a Conservative identification to identification with Labour, the Liberal Democrats, or no party. Since few persons indicate that they identified with 'other' parties and highly skewed distributions can create estimation difficulties for multinomial logit estimation, we eliminate the 'other' party identifiers from the analysis.

Table 4 displays the parameter estimates for the binary and multinomial logit analyses. As anticipated, several attitudinal and evaluative variables have significant (and correctly signed) coefficients. Net of controls for prior party identification and demographic characteristics, persons who had positive images of Labour and negative images of the Conservatives and the Liberal Democrats were more likely than others to identify with Labour in 1997 (rather than the Conservatives). Similarly, persons who made negative economic and social policy evaluations, and those who held favourable attitudes towards Britain's membership in the EU were likely to be Labour identifiers. Party leader images do not have consistent effects – Tony Blair's image neither facilitated nor inhibited the adoption of a Labour identification, but a negative image of Prime Minister Major (and both the Gallup and BEPS survey data indicate that a large majority of the electorate were negatively disposed towards him in 1997) enhanced the likelihood of a Labour identification. The binary logit analysis for Conservative identification (see Table 4, column 1) indicates that these several variables also affected Tory partisanship in 1997. In every case, a factor boosting the probability that a voter would identify with Labour lessened the probability of identifying with the Conservatives. Again, the strong anti-Conservative/pro-Labour bias of all of these variables in 1997 is consistent with the aggregate- and individual-levels shifts in party identification documented above.

TABLE 4

LOGIT AND MULTINOMIAL LOGIT MODELS OF 1997 PARTY IDENTIFICATION

		1997 Party Identification		
Predictor Variables	Con	Lab	Lib-Dem	None
1992 Party Identification:				
Conservative	2.46a	-2.46a	-1.86a	-3.20a
Labour	-1.35b	2.46a	0.03	-1.75b
Liberal-Democrat	-0.54	-0.05	1.50a	-1.02c
1997 Party Image:				
Conservative: Moderation	0.86a	-0.94a	-0.97a	-0.49b
Unity/Strong Gov	0.33a	-0.31c	-0.43b	-0.22d
Labour	-0.27c	1.23a	0.05	-0.00
Liberal-Democrat	0.48	-0.38c	0.69a	-0.64a
1997 Party Leader Image:				
Major	0.24d	-0.58a	0.13	-0.10
Blair	-0.00	0.15	-0.19	0.16
Ashdown	-0.25c	0.24c	0.53b	-0.01
Economic Evaluations	0.45a	0.55a	0.41b	0.40c
Social Policy Evaluations	-0.22a	0.28a	0.22b	0.28b
Attitudes Towards EU	-0.47a	0.45a	0.45a	0.54a
Age	0.01	-0.01	0.01	-0.03b
Gender	-0.35c	0.20	0.55c	0.31
Social Class	-0.03	0.20c	-0.00	-0.27c
Trade Union Membership	-1.14a	1.23a	0.99a	1.18a
Region:				
London	0.23	-0.06	-0.25	-0.46
Midlands	0.54c	-0.40	-0.63c	-0.77d
South	0.53c	-1.00a	-0.49d	-0.14
Scotland	-0.16	0.21	-0.18	0.38
Wales	-0.73d	0.81d	0.57	1.01d
Constant	-0.43	-1.53d	-2.07c	0.72
Estimated R^2		.64	.57	
% correctly classified		90.1	79.70	
PRE (Lambda)		.72	.67	

a = p ≤ .001; b = p ≤ .01; c = p ≤ .05; d = p ≤.10; one-tailed test

Note: The analysis of 1997 Conservative party identification is a binary logit (Conservative v. other parties and no party identification). The analysis of Labour, Liberal-Democrat and no party identification is a multinomial logit with Conservative identification as the reference category.

Is party identification really unstable?

The impressive array of aggregate- and individual-level evidence from two large-scale studies conducted in the 1990s strongly indicates that Labour Party identification, in particular, and identification with British political parties, more generally, has been characterized by substantial, and quite predictable, dynamics in recent years. This evidence is consistent with the arguments of Fiorina (1981) and other revisionists who have challenged the conventional wisdom of the Michigan school that party identification is essentially an 'unmoved mover' – one of the most stable elements in public political psychology. As noted above, Green and his associates have attempted reinstate this 'old time religion' by arguing that, net of random measurement error, party identifications appear remarkably stable in the United States, Britain and elsewhere. Green et al. use structural equation models (SEM) of multi-wave panel data to provide empirical support for their argument. But, as Clarke and McCutcheon (1998) have observed, these models suffer from a number of technical problems that render their testimony suspect. Greater analytic leverage on the question of individual-level dynamism in party identification is provided by newly developed mixed Markov latent class (MMLC) modelling procedures (see Clarke and McCutcheon, 1998). Although these procedures require at least four-waves of panel data to estimate all parameters of interest, they permit one to go well beyond what is possible with standard SEMs. In addition to allowing for random measurement error, one may specify mixture models with separate 'mover' and 'stayer' chains. This latter capacity is attractive because it enables one to estimate models that incorporate the intuitively plausible conception of electorates, which across any particular time interval, are composed of groups of stable and unstable party identifiers. MMLC techniques enables one to take account of the presence of these 'stayer' and 'mover' groups, and to estimate how many voters are in each group.

The 1992–97 BEPS and some of the earlier BES national surveys have the requisite four waves of panel data necessary for MMLC modelling. Figure 5 documents that all of these four-wave panels – not only the 1992-94-95-96 and 1994-95-96-97 ones – are characterized by substantial instability in responses to the standard party identification question battery. For example, only 64% of the respondents in the 1992-94-95-96 panel gave stable responses, whereas 23% indicated that they switched their party identifications at least once, and an additional 11% moved one or more times to or from identification and non-identification. Few panelists (2%) indicated that they were consistent non-identifiers. The extent of response instability in the very first four-wave panel (1963-64-66-70) is even greater

– only 61% report identifying with the same party, 28% switch parties, and
a further 10% move between identification and non-identification. Thus, if
survey responses are reliable guides, partisan instability is not novel to the
post-1992 period. But, as Green *et al.* have emphasized, the reliability of the
survey responses is precisely the issue in the debate over the extent of
individual-level instability in party identification.

FIGURE 5
DYNAMICS OF RESPONSES TO FIRST PARTY IDENTIFICATION QUESTION,
BES AND BEPS FOUR-WAVE PANELS

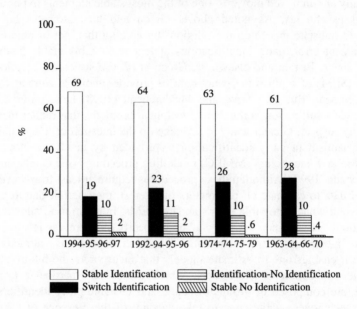

The results of applying MMLC modelling techniques to the 1992-94-95-
96 panel are presented in Table 5. Note first that the MMLC model with
mover and stayer chains has a much better fit than either a classic latent
class model or a single-chain latent Markov model. The classic latent class
model specifies that, controlling for random measurement error, everyone
has a stable party identification, whereas the single-chain Markov model
specifies that everyone has a non-zero probability of moving (again, net of
random measurement error). Thus, in effect, these two rival models to the
MMLC model correspond to what might be called pure 'Michigan' and
'Rochester' (evaluative) conceptions of party identification. The MMLC
model also has a superior fit to these alternatives for the 1994-95-96-97
panel (data not shown). For both of these recent multi-wave panels, the
MMLC models indicate that the proportion of movers is decidedly non-

trivial – 37% for the 1992–96 panel and 34% for the 1994–97 one. These results are consistent with our argument that New Labour recruited new partisans – not just new voters – on the way to its massive victory in the 1997 general election.

TABLE 5

MIXED MARKOV MODEL PARAMETER ESTIMATES FOR PARTY IDENTIFICATION, 1992-94-95-96 BEPS PANEL

	Parameter Movers		Stayers	
Mixture Proportion (π)	.373		.627	
Initial State (δ):				
Conservative	.546		.378	
Labour	.251		.370	
Other	.203		.252	
Response Probabilities (ρ):				
	True		True	
Measure:				
Conservative	.979		.970	
Labour	.844		.996	
Other	.943		.935	

Transition Probabilities (τ) for Movers:		Con	Lab	Other
Conservative:	Wave 1 – Wave 2	.565	.149	.286
	Wave 2 – Wave 3	.741	.048	.211
	Wave 3 – Wave 4	.945	.042	.013
Labour:	Wave 1 – Wave 2	.000	1.000	.000
	Wave 2 – Wave 3	.000	.994	.006
	Wave 3 – Wave 4	.015	.985	.000
Other:	Wave 1 – Wave 2	.000	.673	.327
	Wave 2 – Wave 3	.192	.221	.586
	Wave 3 – Wave 4	.247	.000	.753

Rival Models:

MMLC (Movers and Stayers) χ^2 = 67.02, df = 45, p = .00, BIC = 56.61
Classic Latent Class (All Stayers) χ^2 = 190.48, df = 54, p = .00, BIC = 179.48
Latent Markov (All Movers) χ^2 = 110.69, df = 48, p = .00, BIC = 99.55

Finally, the MMLC analyses tell us even more about the properties of party identification in Britain. An MMLC model for the very first BES four-wave panel (1963-64-66-70) fits the data much better than its rivals (see Table 6). Moreover, consonant with the response turnover data presented in Figure 5 above, the percentage of persons in the mover chain for this early panel is substantial – nearly 31%. The implication of this finding is far-reaching; not only is the traditional Michigan model of directionally stable party identification incorrect in the 1990s; it also was incorrect in the 1960s. If a golden age of serenely stable individual-level party identification ever existed in Britain, it is shrouded in the distant past.

TABLE 6
MIXED MARKOV MODEL PARAMETER ESTIMATES FOR
PARTY IDENTIFICATION, 1963-64-66-70 BES PANEL

	Parameter Movers	Stayers
Mixture Proportion (π)	.308	.692
Initial State (δ):		
Conservative	.219	.448
Labour	.356	.378
Other	.426	.174
Response Probabilities (ρ):		
	True	True
Measure:		
Conservative	.973	.943
Labour	.935	.990
Other	.876	.252

Transition Probabilities (τ) for Movers:		Con	Lab	Other
Conservative:	Wave 1 – Wave 2	.545	.227	.228
	Wave 2 – Wave 3	.546	.409	.045
	Wave 3 – Wave 4	.724	.173	.104
Labour:	Wave 1 – Wave 2	.291	.629	.080
	Wave 2 – Wave 3	.112	.724	.164
	Wave 3 – Wave 4	.474	.526	.000
Other:	Wave 1 – Wave 2	.000	.000	1.000
	Wave 2 – Wave 3	.025	.016	.959
	Wave 3 – Wave 4	.217	.074	.709

Rival Models:
MMLC (Movers and Stayers) χ^2 = 82.62, df = 45, p = .00, BIC = 72.04
Classic Latent Class (All Stayers) χ^2 = 158.79, df = 54, p = .00, BIC = 148.03
Latent Markov (All Movers) χ^2 = 114.80, df = 48, p = .00, BIC = 104.16

Conclusion: The Dynamics of Partisanship Reconsidered

In their pathbreaking book, *Political Change in Britain*, Butler and Stokes argued that 'most electors think of themselves as supporters of a given party in a lasting sense, developing what may be called a 'partisan self-image' (Butler and Stokes, 1976: 22). Although Butler and Stokes (e.g. 1976: 23) cautioned readers that not all of those participating in their national panel surveys indicated that they had such 'lasting' partisan attachments, many analysts have failed to appreciate the full extent of the individual-level dynamics in partisanship revealed in these and later panel studies. In national four-wave panel surveys conducted in the 1960s, 1970s and 1990s, no more than 70% of the respondents consistently report identifying with the same party, and upwards of 30% indicate that they have changed their party identification one or more times. It bears emphasis that this reported instability is not simply an artifact of random measurement error. Analyses of these panel data using newly available mixed Markov latent class techniques testify that the instability numbers generated by the panel 'turnover tables' are accurate reflections of reality. The MMLC estimates indicate that substantial minorities of the respondents in all of the multi-wave panel surveys are partisan 'movers'.

The individual instability in party identification is sufficient to permit large-scale changes in aggregate-level party support. In fact, such changes have occurred – parties have suffered (or enjoyed) massive reversals of political fortune over the relatively short-time intervals between successive general elections. The dramatic erosion of Conservative support shortly after the 1992 election and the concomitant rise in Labour support is the most recent realization of what is an ongoing possibility. Both the Gallup and the BEPS data presented above reveal that New Labour gained many new partisans as well as many new voters. Several factors were responsible for these shifts in party identification. Voters' images of the parties and party leaders, as well as their attitudes towards Britain's role in the European Union, and their judgements concerning the delivery of social policies and the health of the economy changed substantially after the 1992 election. Starting shortly after that contest, these changes worked to enhance the size of Labour's cohort of party identifiers and to decrease the size of the Conservative cohort. The flood tide of electoral support that swept Tony Blair and his party to power in the 1997 election thus reflected partisan dynamics that had been at work for much of the preceding five years.

New partisans are, of course, good news for New Labour. But the larger message of our analyses is that these partisans are not necessarily New Labour for good. National survey data gathered over the past three decades consistently indicates that many voters have unstable partisan attachments, and there is no reason to believe that this dynamic has ended. Voters who have changed their party identifications in the past may do so again. Since at least the 1960s, partisanship in the British electorate has been a resource that can be depleted – as well as renewed. Partisan instability is a major source of political change in Britain.

NOTES

1. Question batteries have been included on monthly Gallup surveys since January 1992 using research funds provided by National Science Foundation (US). The fieldwork was conducted

under the direction of Robert Wybrow, Rory Fitzgerald and Sheri Weber. The authors wish to thank these individuals, the Gallup Organization, and the National Science Foundation for their generous assistance with this project. Neither the NSF nor Gallup is responsible for the analyses and interpretations of the data presented in this article.

2. Conservative, Labour and Liberal Democrat party identifications are the percentages mentioning one of these parties in response to the question 'Generally speaking, do you think of yourself as Conservative, Labour, Liberal Democrat, or what?' The SNP and Plaid Cymru also are mentioned in Scotland and Wales, respectively.

3. Party images are summarized as factor scores derived from exploratory factor analyses using the following party image variables: moderate/extreme, united/disunited, good for all classes/good for one class, capable of strong leadership/not capable of strong leadership, keeps promises/breaks promises. The factor analysis of Conservative Party images yielded two factors that collectively explained 65.0% of the item variance, whereas the factor analyses of Labour and Liberal Democratic Party images yielded one factor in both cases. This factor explained 39.5% and 35.7%, respectively, of the item variance in the Labour and Liberal Democratic analyses. Party leader images are additive indices based on perceptions of whether Messrs Major, Blair, and Ashdown were: moderate/extreme, good for all classes/good for one class, capable of strong leadership/not capable of strong leadership, keeps promises/breaks promises. Economic evaluations are summarized using a factor score variable generated by an exploratory factor analysis of questions asking respondents if unemployment, inflation, taxes, interest rates and the general standard of living had increased/decreased since the last general election. An item measuring perceptions of whether the British economy had got stronger or weaker over the last year was also included. A factor analysis of these items explained 42.6% of their variance. Attitudes towards the European Union are measured as a factor score generated by an exploratory factor analysis of responses to questions whether Britain should 'unite fully' with the EU, remain a member of the EU now or leave the EU in the long term, and the future of the pound in the EU. A factor analysis explained 59.5% of the item variance. Social policy evaluations are an additive index based on responses to two questions regarding the performance of the National Health Service and the educational system. Social class is measured as a upper/middle (A, B, C1) versus (C2, D, E) dichotomy; age is measured in years; gender is scored women = 1, men = 0; region is a series of dummy variables with the North, North West and Yorkshire and Humberside serving as the reference category. Additional details concerning the measurement of the variables used in the logit analyses are available from the authors upon request.

4. Formally, $PID_t = \Sigma\beta_{t-i,k}EVAL_{t-i,k}\ \varepsilon_t$, where PIDt is party identification at time t, $EVAL_{t-i,k}$ is a vector of current and past party performance evaluations, and ε_t is $\sim N(0,\sigma^2)$. If party performance evaluations are viewed as an infinite distributed lag where the effects of prior evaluations decline at a geometric rate (λ^j), a Koyck transformation may be employed for estimation purposes, i.e. $PID_t = \alpha(1-\lambda) + \Sigma\beta_{t,k}EVAL_{t,k} + \lambda PID_{t-1} + v_t$, where $v_t = \varepsilon_t - \lambda\varepsilon_{t-1}$. The model may be theoretically motivated as a partial adjustment process. If so, the error process is Gaussian. See, e.g. Gujarati (1988: 519-21). Individual-level analyses using these types of models in the British context include Alt (1984) and Clarke and Stewart (1984).

REFERENCES

Abramson, Paul R. and Charles W. Ostrom (1991) 'Macropartisanship: An Empirical Assessment'. *American Political Science Review* 85: 181–92.

Achen, Christopher H. (1992) 'Social Psychology, Demographic Variables, and Linear Regression: Breaking the Iron Triangle in Voting Research'. *Political Behavior* 14: 195–212.

Alt, James E. (1984) 'Dealignment and the Dynamics of Partisanship in Britain'. in Paul Allen Beck, Russell Dalton and Scott Flanagan (eds) *Electoral Change in Advanced Industrial Societies*, pp.298–339. Princeton: Princeton University Press.

Bishop, George F., *et al.* (1994) 'Question Form and Context Effects in the Measurement of

Partisanship: Experimental Tests of the Artifact Hypothesis'. *American Political Science Review* 88: 945–58.

Box-Steffensmeier, Janet M. and Renée Smith (1996) 'The Dynamics of Aggregate Partisanship'. *American Political Science Review* 90: 567–80.

Budge, Ian, Ivor Crewe and Dennis Farlie (eds) (1976) *Party Identification and Beyond: Representations of Voting and Party Competition.* New York: John Wiley & Sons.

Butler, David and Donald E. Stokes (1976) *Political Change in Britain,* 2nd College Edition. New York: St. Martin's Press.

Campbell, Angus, Philip E. Converse, Warren E. Miller and Donald E. Stokes (1960) *The American Voter.* New York: John Wiley & Sons.

Campbell, Angus, Philip E. Converse, Warren E. Miller and Donald E. Stokes (1966) *Elections and the Political Order.* New York: John Wiley & Sons.

Campbell, Angus, Gerald Gurin and Warren E. Miller (1954) *The Voter Decides.* Evanston: Row, Peterson and Company.

Clarke, Harold D. and Allan L. McCutcheon (1998) 'Mixed Markov Latent Class Models for the Dynamics of Party Identification'. unpublished manuscript, Department of Political Science, University of North Texas.

Clarke, Harold D. and Marianne C. Stewart (1984) 'Dealignment of Degree: Partisan Change in Britain 1974–83'. *Journal of Politics* 46: 689–718.

Clarke, Harold D., Marianne C. Stewart and Paul Whiteley (1997) 'Tory Trends: Party Identification and The Dynamics of Conservative Support Since 1992'. *British Journal of Political Science* 26: 299–318.

Clarke, Harold D., Marianne C. Stewart and Paul F. Whiteley (1998) 'New Models for New Labour: The Political Economy of Labour Party Support, January 1992–April 1997'. *American Political Science Review* 92: 559–75.

Clarke, Harold D. and Motoshi Suzuki (1994) 'Partisan Dealignment and the Dynamics of Independence in the American Electorate, 1953–88'. *British Journal of Political Science* 24: 57–78.

Converse, Philip E. (1976) *The Dynamics of Party Support: Cohort-Analyzing Party Identification.* Beverly Hills: Sage Publications.

Crewe, Ivor, Bo Sarlvik and James E. Alt (1977) 'Partisan Dealignment in Britain, 1964–1974'. *British Journal of Political Science* 7: 129–90.

Enders, Walter (1995) *Applied Econometric Time Series.* New York: John Wiley & Sons.

Fiorina, Morris P. (1981) *Retrospective Voting in American National Elections.* New Haven: Yale University Press.

Franklin, Charles H. (1984) 'Issues, Preferences, Socialization and the Evolution of Party Identification'. *American Journal of Political Science* 28: 459–78.

Franklin, Charles H. (1991) 'Measurement and the Dynamics of Party Identification'. *Political Behavior* 4: 297–310.

Franklin, Charles H. and John E. Jackson (1983) 'The Dynamics of Party Identification'. *American Political Science Review* 77: 957–73.

Green, Donald, and Bradley Palmquist (1990) 'Of Artifacts and Partisan Instability'. *American Journal of Political Science* 34: 872–902.

Green, Donald, Bradley Palmquist and Eric Schickler (1993) 'A Multiple Method Approach to the Measurement of Party Identification'. *Public Opinion Quarterly* 57: 503–35.

Gujarati, Damodar (1988) *Basic Econometrics,* 2nd Edition. New York: McGraw-Hill.

Heath, Anthony *et al.* (eds) (1994) *Labour's Last Chance?* Aldershot: Dartmouth Publishing Company Ltd.

Heath, Anthony, and Sarah-K. MacDonald (1988) 'The Demise of Party Identification Theory?' *Electoral Studies* 7: 95–108.

Heath, Anthony and Roy Pierce (1992) 'It was Party Identification all Along: Question Order Effects on Reports of Party Identification in Britain'. *Electoral Studies* 11: 93–105.

Long, J. Scott (1997) *Regression Models for Categorical and Limited Dependent Variables.* Thousand Oaks, CA.: Sage.

MacKuen, Michael B., Robert S. Erikson and James A. Stimson (1989) 'Macropartisanship'.

American Political Science Review 83: 1125–42.

MacKuen, Michael B. *et al.* (1992) 'Controversy: Question Wording and Macropartisanship'. *American Political Science Review* 86: 475–86.

Miller, Warren E. (1991) 'Party Identification: Back to Basics'. *American Political Science Review* 85: 557–70.

Sarlvik, Bo, and Ivor Crewe (1983) *Decade of Dealignment: The Conservative Victory of 1979 and Electoral Trends in the 1970s.* Cambridge: Cambridge University Press.

Schickler, Eric and Donald Green (1997) 'The Stability of Party Identification in Western Democracies: Results From Eight Panel Surveys'. *Comparative Political Studies* 30: 450–83.

Whiteley, Paul (1997) 'The Conservative Campaign'. *Parliamentary Affairs* 50: 542–54.

'Independents', 'Switchers' and Voting for Third Parties in Britain 1979–92

David W.F. Huang

Voting for 'third' parties in Britain (that is, parties other than Labour and the Conservatives) increased sharply after 1970. Between 1945 and 1970 the share of votes obtained by the two major parties averaged about 90 per cent but this fell to about 75 per cent between 1974 and 1992. In contrast, the combined vote share of other parties (including the Liberal Democratic Party, Scottish National Party, Plaid Cymru, etc.) increased steadily. At the same time, according to most theorists, Britain was undergoing a process of partisan dealignment. Party identification weakened from the end of 1960s and voters became more likely to profess no party affiliation. As a consequence, it was argued, voters also became more volatile, more likely to switch their party choices between two adjacent elections. These developments led scholars to question whether Britain's two-party system was crumbling (see Crewe, 1982, 1983; Garner and Kelly, 1993; Williams, 1984; Clarke and Stewart, 1984; Sarlvik and Crewe, 1983).

The increase in third party support was often assumed to be a consequence of the weakening of party identification and the growth in the proportion of switchers but despite being theoretically plausible, this assumption has not been subjected to rigorous empirical verification. The socio-economic background and political attitudes of third party supporters have, of course, been investigated in the context of dealignment. In some cases, however, the main focus is whether there has been a dealignment or realignment (see Crewe, 1982; MacIver 1996; Curtice, 1996) while in others dealignment is taken as given when exploring short-term influences on third party voting. Party identification is usually controlled for in multivariate models designed to test whether salient issues and policies, party and leadership images, personal and national economic conditions, and other short-term factors have significant effects on third party voting (see Studlar and McAllister, 1987; Lutz, 1991; Eagles and Erfle, 1993; Levy, 1988; Clarke and Zuk, 1989).

This article attempts to examine whether non-party identifiers and vote switchers are more likely than others to vote for third parties, using the

1979–92 British Election Study (BES) cross-sectional survey data. The 1979–92 BES data are used, partly because the most recent 1997 BES data were not available at the time of writing. There is also a theoretical justification for restricting my analyses to this period, however. Pinard argued three decades ago that third parties were most likely to rise and prosper when one party consistently dominated in a two-party system (Pinard, 1967; Eagles and Erfle, 1993) and the Conservative Party was clearly dominant in Britain from 1979 to 1992.[1] Given that on this hypothesis conditions were very favourable for third parties, an absence of evidence to support the contention that non-identifiers and switchers are more likely to vote for third parties, would seriously undermine the argument that there is a link between the dealignment thesis and third party voting.

In the next section I first define major terms before presenting crosstabulations showing the relationship between party identification and vote switching on the one hand and third party voting on the other. Subsequently, multivariate logistic regressions are used to control for other influences on third party voting and the major findings and their implications discussed.

Definitions of Terms and Initial Results

BES survey respondents who said that they had no party identification are called 'independents', the remainder being 'party identifiers'. 'Switchers' are defined as voters who voted for different parties in two consecutive elections or who voted in one election but not in the other.[2] Finally, 'third party' voters (or supporters) are defined as those whose party choice was anything other than Conservative or Labour. This includes supporters of minor parties other than the Liberal Democrats (the 'major minor' party) but all minor parties share similar features. They are not in the running to form a government, and the first-past-the-post electoral system makes it difficult for third party candidates to win seats. Therefore, third party supporters are similar as a group in that they may base their votes on motivations other than expecting their own party to govern or even to win the seat.

Table 1 shows the percentages of party identifiers and independents voting for third parties over four elections. Not unexpectedly, third party identifiers are the most likely to vote for third parties (70 per cent on average) and major party identifiers tend to stick to their party in elections. Over the four elections examined, an average of 82 per cent of Conservative identifiers voted for the Conservative Party and 75 per cent of Labour identifiers voted Labour compared with only 5 per cent and 9 per cent voting for third parties. Independents were more likely than Conservative and Labour identifiers to vote for third parties, but the most popular party choice of independents is not third parties. On average, 32 per cent of independents voted for the Conservatives, 14 per cent for Labour, and 21 per cent for third parties. On this evidence, independents do not seem to be a powerful voting bloc for third parties.

Table 2 shows the votes of switchers over the same four elections. With the exception of 1979, when the Conservatives were the main beneficiaries, switchers were clearly more likely to move to third parties than to either of the major parties. Switchers, then, form a pool from which third parties can draw support. The figures in Table 3 emphasize the dependence of third parties on switchers. The two major parties are better than third parties at retaining supporters from the previous election, and switchers rarely constitute more than a quarter of their vote. In contrast more than half of third party voters in these elections had switched their votes from the previous election.

TABLE 1
PARTY IDENTIFICATION AND VOTE FOR THIRD PARTIES 1979–92 (%)

Identification	1979	1983	1987	1992
Conservative	3	4	6	6
Labour	7	10	9	8
Third party	62	72	72	73
Independent	11	26	24	24

Source: BES cross-section surveys 1979–92.
Note: Ns for Conservative identifiers across the four elections are 707, 1406, 1411 and 1357; for Labour identifiers 673, 1220, 1137 and 1115; for Third party identifiers 236, 728, 665 and 588 and for Independents 172, 401, 400 and 319.

TABLE 2
PARTY CHOICE OF SWITCHERS, 1979–92

	1979	1983	1987	1992
Switch to:	%	%	%	%
Con	38	23	24	25
Lab	19	13	21	23
Third	20	37	34	32
Non-voted	24	27	21	20
(N)	(606)	(1471)	(1235)	(1054)

Source: BES cross-section surveys 1979–92.

TABLE 3
SWITCHERS AS A PROPORTION OF PARTY VOTES, 1979–92 (%)

	1979	1983	1987	1992
Con	32	24	21	21
Lab	19	20	26	24
Third	51	67	54	50

Source: BES cross-section surveys 1979–92.
Note: Ns for Conservative voters across the four elections are 718, 1419, 1397 and 1233; for Labour they are 580, 934, 977 and 1024 and for Third parties 235, 819, 767 and 673.

The results of bivariate logistic regression analyses with third party voting as the dependent variable (not shown here) confirm the crosstabulation results. The coefficients for 'being independent' do not achieve significance for 1979, 1987 and 1992. In 1983, however, the coefficient (0.295) is statistically significant. On the other hand, the effect of switchers on third party voting is both strong and significant in all four general elections, and the effect of independents in 1983 becomes non-significant when switchers are added to the model.[3] In order to verify these results, however, we have to take account of other variables likely to impact on third party voting and in the next section a multivariate model is developed to do this.

Building a Multivariate Logit Model of Third Party Voting

Many potential influences on third party voting have been proposed. One major theme relates to 'protest' voting. Rosenstone *et al.* (1984) point out that the rise of third party depends on voters' dissatisfaction with the failures of the major parties while Key argues that third party candidates provide a safety valve for voters to express discontent (Key, 1948: 235–46). Chressanthis and Shaffer (1993) also remark that third parties often thrive when two major parties do not address salient issues, and Pinard (1975) makes it clear that in one-party dominant regions people vote for third parties in order to protest against the governing party. In Britain, a third party vote is also usually seen as protest against the two major parties (Sarlvik and Crewe, 1983: 59; Crewe, 1982: 299, 303, 304).

Unfortunately the BES surveys have not directly asked respondents about dissatisfaction with government performance and we have to rely, therefore, on some proxy indicators. First, for 1992 only, we use as proxies respondents' perceptions of changes in national and personal living standards since the previous general election (NGLIVEN, NGLIVEP) and, for 1979 to 1987, respondents' evaluations of the government's management of inflation and unemployment (NGEMP, NGINF). Second, we use the extent of negative feeling towards the two major parties as an indicator of voters' protest mood (NGPTYC, NGPTYL). The expectation is that those who dislike the two major parties will vote for third parties. Third, we use party image questions (are parties extreme or moderate, united or divided, capable of strong government and do they look after one class or all classes?) to construct an additive index to measure the party images of the Conservatives and Labour (PTYIMGC, PTYIMGL). We would expect voting for third parties to be greater among those with negative images of the major parties.

In addition to negative or protest motivations, people may be attracted to third parties by their positive qualities, such as leadership image and policy positions. Except for 1979, there are questions in the BES surveys exploring voters' perceptions of party leaders – are they extreme or moderate, caring or uncaring, capable of being strong leaders or not; do they look after one class or all classes? Answers to these questions are used to construct an additive index of the image of third party leaders. In the 1979 BES survey, respondents were asked to give party leaders a mark out of 10 and we use this thermometer to measure leadership image in 1979.

Whether issue proximity affects third party voting is still in dispute. Earlier studies in Britain showed that voters did not recognize a clear set of policies or ideology offered by the Liberal Party or the Social Democratic Party (Sarlvik and Crewe, 1983; Crewe, 1982). However, a recent study suggested that the Liberal Democratic Party had formulated a distinctive set of policies that was recognized by its supporters (MacIver, 1996). BES data allow us to calculate the distance between a respondent's position on a series of policy issues (such as giving priority to inflation or unemployment, preferring tax cuts to increased services and favouring nationalization or privatization) and their perceptions of the parties' positions on the same policies. We computed the absolute value of each policy for each voter and each party and then created a series of dummy variables (SPACE) scoring 1 to represent voters whose policy positions are closest to third parties. According to classic spatial voting theory pioneered by Downs (1957) people will vote for a party whose policy positions are closest to their own. There are many problems associated with this single-dimensional spatial model but, for simplicity, we nonetheless use Downs' model to predict third party voting.[4]

Tactical considerations may also influence third party voting. Voters may not want to waste their votes on third parties that apparently have no chance of winning the seat or forming the government. Previous studies using BES data have found that only about 6 per cent of the electorate are motivated by tactical considerations (Heath *et al.*, 1991). But the proportion of third party identifiers who voted for other parties is much higher than that of major-party identifiers. In other words, when tactical voting occurs, it seems likely to work against third parties. We can use the BES data to test the hypothesis that tactical calculations affect third party voting.

In the United States, it is found that third party voting is an expression of distrust of government (Peterson and Wrighton, 1998). This variable (TRUST) is available for 1979 and 1987 and together with other socio-demographic variables – religious attachment, age, education, income, and class – is also included in the model. Although these socio-demographic variables are categorical variables, they are treated as ordinary variables in order to assess the impact of each variable (rather than each category) on third party voting.

We have, then, a multivariate logistic regression model of the following general form:

THIRDV= a + b1(INDP) + b2(SW) + b3(NGGVT) + b4(NGPTY) +
b5(LEADER) + b6(PTYIMG) + B7(SPACE) + b8(TACT) +
b9(TRUST) + b10(AGE) + b11(INC) + b12(CLASS) +
b13(RELIGION)+ e

Further details of the variables, including the coding scheme are given in the Appendix and the results of the analyses are reported in the following section.

The Results of Multivariate Logistic Regressions

The results of this complete version of the logistic regression model are shown in Table 4. In all four equations the coefficients for 'INDP' are not significant, confirming that independent voters are no more likely than party identifiers to vote for third parties. In contrast, switchers are more likely than non-switchers to vote for third parties, the relevant coefficients in all four equations being both large and significant, even when other variables are controlled. This suggests that an increase in the pool of switchers is beneficial to third parties.

In general, most of the controlled variables are both significant and in the expected direction. For example, people who dislike Labour and the Conservatives are more likely to vote for third parties as are those who have negative opinions about the two major parties' images. These findings are consistent with previous studies suggesting that third party voting is largely motivated by negative protest against two major parties. However, the impact of voters' evaluations of government's economic performances is not clear. While voters who are dissatisfied with government's management of unemployment are likely to vote for third parties, voters' evaluations about personal and national economic conditions as well as about government's management of inflation are not significant in explaining third party voting.

Table 4 also shows that the image of third party leaders is positively related to third party voting. The coefficients for 'LEADER' are all positive and significant, meaning that voters who hold a positive opinion about third party leaders are more likely to vote for third parties. Moreover, voters are likely to vote for third parties when these parties' policy positions are closest to their own positions although there are some variations across issues. For example, in three general elections from 1983 to 1992, voting for third parties was significantly associated with being closest to the party on unemployment and inflation (SPACE1). A similar effect is found for the tax and service issue (SPACE2) except in 1983, for nationalization and privatization (SPACE3) in 1983 and 1987, for the economic growth versus redistribution issue (SPACE4) in 1987 and 1992, and the nuclear weapons issue (SPACE5) in 1983. The inconsistency of the effect of issue proximity on third party voting may reflect variations in issue salience across elections. For example, in 1983 and 1987 the controversy over nuclear weapons and privatization attracted media attention. Since these widely reported issues became salient and relevant to voters' decisions, it is not surprising that issue proximity of these two issues affected third party voting in 1983 and 1987 respectively.

TABLE 4

MULTIVARIATE LOGISTIC REGRESSIONS OF THIRD PARTY VOTING (1)

	1979	1983	1987	1992
Variable	B	B	B	B
INDP	0.587	0.272	-0.070	0.008
SW	1.458***	2.420***	1.753***	0.885***
NGLIVEN	–	–	–	0.021
NGLIVEP	–	–	–	0.103
NGEMP	-0.545**	-0.347**	-0.609***	–
NGINF	0.043	-0.005	0.019	–
NGPTYC	-1.210**	-1.185***	-0.808***	-0.799***
NGPTYL	-0.990**	-1.122***	-0.959***	-0.933***
LEADERA	–	–	-	0.288***
LEADERO	–	–	0.170***	–
LEADERJ	–	0.119**	–	–
LEADERS	0.744***	0.274***	0.303***	–
PTYIMGC	-0.056	-0.168***	-0.232***	-0.186***
PTYIMGL	-0.220**	-0.242***	-0.244***	- 0.018
SPACE1	–	0.475**	0.381**	0.473**
SPACE2	1.402***	0.227	0.426***	0.450**
SPACE3	0.176	0.964***	0.728***	0.226
SPACE4	–	–	0.571***	0.398**
SPACE5	–	0.864**	–	–
TACT	-3.222***	-0.179	0.3000	1.3434***
AGE	0.147	0.038	0.101**	0.027
CLASS	0.074	-0.090**	-0.291***	-0.058
EDUC	0.440**	-0.031	0.071	0.146
INC	0.002	–	-0.077	-0.025
RELIGION	-0.056	0.020	-0.037	0.060
Constant	-4.339	2.222	2.418	1.186
-2 Log Likelihood	286.61	1229.27	1279.64	926.67
Model Chi-Square	245.58***	1115.18***	952.97***	320.37***
Overall Correct Prediction	91.5 %	87.2 %	85.7 %	83.2 %
Df	17	19	20	19
N	657	1906	1898	1175

Source: BES, 1979–92

Note: ***p<0.001; **p<0.05, *p<0.10

The impact of tactical considerations on third party voting is also not consistent. In 1979 tactical voters were likely to vote *against* third parties. However, in 1992, tactical voters were likely to vote *for* third parties. In both 1983 and 1987 general elections, tactical voting was not significant in explaining third party voting. Why were the effects of tactical voting reversed between 1979 and 1992? One explanation is that the questions in the two relevant BES surveys are not exactly the same. It may also be, however, that as the Conservative party had been in power for more than 12 years, people might have moved from voting tactically against third parties in 1979 to voting tactically against the Conservative incumbent in 1992. The phenomenon of 'anti-government tactical voting' may be responsible for the beneficial effect of tactical voting on third parties in 1992.

The effects of socio-demographic variables on third party voting are very weak. With the exceptions of age, education and class effects in a few general elections, the impact of these variables is virtually non-existent which confirms the view that third party supporters do not come from a particular socio-economic backgrounds (Butler and Stokes, 1969; Sarlvik and Crewe, 1983; Curtice, 1983). In addition, the effect of trust on third party voting is not significant. However, because the variable 'TRUST' was measured only in the 1979 and 1987 BES data the coefficients are not reported in the tables.

In general, the statistical reliability of the four logistic regressions in Table 4 is adequate. Not only do all the values of model chi-square reach statistical significance, but the percentages of overall correct prediction are very high, ranging from 83 per cent to 92 per cent. It seems that the 'goodness of fit' in the four models is reasonably good. We can be fairly confident that the findings of these four logistic regression models are robust. In sum, switchers are more likely than non-switchers to vote for third parties, but independent voters are no more likely than party identifiers to do so. If, however, independents are not more likely than party identifiers to vote for third parties in Britain then we might ask why previous studies have regarded independents as the biggest hope for third parties (Campbell, 1979: 268; Abramson *et al.*, 1983: 237).

To investigate this question further, we substitute for INDP a categorical variable (PTY4), with separate codes for Conservative, Labour and third party identifiers. The remaining controlled variables are as in Table 4. Following the SPSS categorical variable procedure, we use the first category (i.e. Conservative identifiers) as a reference group and observe the differences between them and the other categories (PTY4(1) = Labour; PTY4(2) = Third Party; PTY4(3) = Independents).

As Table 5 shows, except in 1992, the coefficients of 'PTY4(1)' are not significant. This means that except in 1992, Labour identifiers were not more likely than the Conservative identifiers to vote for third parties. In

1992 Labour identifiers may have wished to bring down the Conservative government after its 12-year dominance in British politics. Table 5 also shows, however, that third party identifiers and independents are more likely than the Conservative identifiers to vote for third parties – the coefficients of PTY4(2) and PTY4(3) are fairly large and significant in all four equations. Overall, including PTY4 in the equations improves the correct prediction for the model by between two and three per cent. Therefore, we know from Table 5 that party identification is significant in explaining third party voting. Moreover, from Table 5, we also find that independents are more likely than Conservative identifiers to vote for third parties. In a similar analysis, with Labour identifiers as the reference group, it was found that independents are also more likely than Labour identifiers to vote for third parties.[5]

TABLE 5
MULTIVARIATE LOGISTIC REGRESSIONS OF THIRD PARTY VOTING (2)

Variable	1979 B	1983 B	1987 B	1992 B
PTY4(1)	0.670	0.088	0.442	1.187***
PTY4(2)	4.307***	3.996***	2.911***	4.447***
PTY4(3)	1.400*	1.715***	1.159***	1.972***
SW	1.965***	2.514***	1.808***	0.910***
NGLIVEN	–	–	–	-0.061
NGLIVEP	–	–	–	0.124
NGEMP	-0.707**	-0.491***	-0.507***	–
NGINF	0.113	0.032	0.031	–
NGPTYC	0.070	-0.364**	-0.510***	-0.333**
NGPTYL	0.341	-0.062	-0.660***	0.654***
LEADERA	–	–	–	0.148**
LEADERO	–	–	0.187***	–
LEADERJ	–	0.137**	0.187***	–
LEADERS	0.662***	0.231**	0.200***	–
PTYIMGC	-0.203*	-0.159**	-0.209***	-0.100*
PTYIMGL	-0.249*	-0.232***	-0.216***	0.056
SPACE1	–	0.350*	0.403**	0.366*
SPACE2	0.737*	0.121	0.196	0.164
SPACE3	0.108	0.733***	0.500**	-0.070
SPACE4	–	–	0.400**	0.161
SPACE5	–	0.702***	–	–
TACT	-3.590**	-0.395	0.273	1.578***
AGE	0.274	0.098*	0.123**	0.068
CLASS	0.129	-0.068	-0.269**	0.043
EDUC	0.485**	0.119	-0.019	0.183
INC	0.093	–	-0.033	0.180
RELIGION	-0.085	-0.061	0.033	0.056
Constant	-9.469	-2.415	1.075	-1.064
-2 Log Likelihood	221.757	933.257	1053.854	645.358
Model Chi-Square	310.438***	1411.197***	1178.756***	601.675***
Overall Correct Prediction	93.9 %	90.4 %	87.8 %	89.9 %
Df	19	21	22	21
N	657	1906	1898	1175

Source: BES, 1979–92
Note: ***p<0.001¡ **p<0.05, *p<0.10

TABLE 6
MULTIVARIATE LOGISTIC REGRESSIONS OF THIRD PARTY VOTING (3)

Variable	1979 B	1983 B	1987 B	1992 B
PTY4(1)	0.670	0.133	0.456	1.182**
PTY4(2)	3.971***	3.978***	2.710***	3.743***
PTY4(3)	-0.259	0.351	0.048	0.131
SW	1.965***	2.539***	1.787***	0.910***
NGLIVEN	–	–	–	-0.061
NGLIVEP	–	–	–	0.124
NGEMP	-0.707**	-0.508***	-0.499***	–
NGINF	0.113	0.045	0.027	–
NGPTYC	0.070	-0.352**	-0.492***	-0.333**
NGPTYL	0.342	-0.075	-0.663***	-0.654***
LEADERA	–	–	–	0.148**
LEADERO	–	–	0.186***	–
LEADERJ	–	0.135**	–	–
LEADERS	0.666***	0.230**	0.201***	–
PTYIMGC	-0.203*	-0.156**	-0.214***	-0.100*
PTYIMGL	-0.249*	-0.229***	-0.218***	0.056
SPACE1	–	0.347*	0.419**	0.366*
SPACE2	0.737*	0.124	0.194	0.164
SPACE3	0.108	0.761***	0.478**	-0.070
SPACE4	–	–	0.390**	0.161
SPACE5	–	0.722***	–	–
TACT	-3.590***	-0.419	0.253	1.578***
AGE	0.274	0.103*	0.115**	0.068
CLASS	0.129	-0.070	-0.259**	0.043
EDUC	0.485**	0.118	-0.009	0.183
INC	0.093	–	-0.034	0.108
RELIGION	-0.085	-0.063	-0.031	0.056
Constant	-7.875	-2.465	1.033	-1.064
-2 Log Likelihood	221.757	925.216	1059.443	645.358
Model Chi-Square	310.438**	1410.472***	1181.054***	601.675***
Overall Correct Prediction	93.9 %	90.6 %	87.6 %	89.9 %
Df	19	21	22	21
N	657	1906	1898	1175

Source: BES, 1979–92
Note: ***p<0.001¡ **p<0.05, *p<0.10

Finally, in Table 6 we explore whether independents are more likely than third party identifiers to vote for third parties. In this case, Conservative identifiers are again the reference group but the SPSS 'difference procedure' has been used for comparison. With this procedure the effect of each category in PTY4 is compared with that of the previous category. We find that PTY4(3) is insignificant in all equations, meaning that independents are no more likely than third party identifiers to vote for third parties. One policy implication that follows from this finding is that third party leaders should cultivate their own identifiers rather than trying to attract independent voters.

The foregoing analysis suggests two main conclusions. First, independent voters are more likely than identifiers with the two major parties to vote for third parties but they are no more likely to do so than third party identifiers. Second, volatile voters are more likely than non-volatile voters to vote for third parties. These two conclusions hold true even when we control for other influences of third party voting. Indeed, the interpretations of controlled variables in Tables 5 and 6 would be virtually the same as for those in Table 4. As with Table 4, the goodness of fit for the models in Table 5 and Table 6 is very strong with the percentages of correct predictions ranging from 87 per cent to 94 per cent.

A few qualifications to these conclusions are necessary. First, the BES data used for the analyses are not time-series panel data. We cannot, therefore, make any inferences from our data about changes in individual voters' political attitudes or voting orientations. Although we expect that the longer the Conservative dominated the government, the more likely voters became to opt for third parties, the cross-sectional BES data simply cannot verify this hypothesis. What we have done is to verify whether or not independents and switchers in each of four elections were likely to vote for third parties. We may compare the sign and significance level of coefficients across different equations and give an educated guess about their trends but we cannot confirm these trends. Second, the main purpose of our multivariate logistic regressions is to control for other influences of third party voting while observing the effects of independent and switchers. For this purpose, our models are adequate as they are properly specified and the results more often than not confirm our theoretical expectations. Judging from the goodness of fit of the models, we can be confident about the conclusions.

Conclusion

The results of this investigation into third party voting suggest that we need to revise the party dealignment thesis. It is certainly true that the strength of party identification has weakened and that the number of switchers has increased. However, the weakening of party identification did not automatically translate into support for third parties. In fact, independents are no more likely than third party identifiers to vote for third parties. For this reason, it is doubtful that independents are the biggest hope for third parties. On the other hand, switchers appear to be more likely to vote for third parties. Based on evidence presented in the previous section, we believe that switchers provide third parties with a larger pool of potential supporters. It is in producing more volatile voters rather than non-party identifiers that dealignment has proved beneficial to third parties.

ACKNOWLEDGEMENTS

An earlier version of this article was presented at the 1998 EPOP conference at Manchester Business School, UK. The author wishes to thank David Denver, Tony Tam, Clive Payne and Yon-Tai Hung for helpful comments on the earlier version and acknowledges the assistance of the Data Archive, University of Essex, in providing the 1979–92 BES data and the financial support given by the National Science Council of Taiwan (grant NSC 87-h-001-005).

NOTES

1. Pinard's hypothesis is partially confirmed by Eagles and Erfle who find that support for third parties tends to be high in one-party dominant constituencies (see Eagles and Erfle, 1993).
2. Vote in the previous election is based on recall at the time of the current election.
3. In the 1983 equation the coefficient for Independents reduced to 0.141 (which is not significant) when switchers were added. The (statistically significant) coefficient for switchers is 1.476.
4. For example, a single-dimensional spatial model may suffer 'confounding' effects when voting is determined by multi-dimensional issues and people may use issue preferences as a 'projection' of their party preferences (see Conover and Feldman, 1982; Hinich and Munger, 1994).
5. When Labour identifiers are used as the reference group the coefficients for PTY4(3) (Independents) are as follows: 1979 = 0.6089 (not significant); 1983 = 1.6108; 1987 = 0.7232; 1992 = 1.1845.

REFERENCES

Abramson, P.R. and J.H. Aldrich and D.W. Rohde (1983), *Changes and Continuity in the 1980 Elections*, Washington D.C.: CQ Press.
Butler, D. and D. Stokes (1969), *Political Change in Britain*, London: Macmillan.
Campbell, B.A. (1979), *The American Electorate*, New York: Holt, Rinehart & Winston.
Chressanthis, G. and S. Shaffer (1993), 'Major-Party Failure and Third Party Voting in Presidential Elections, 1976–1988', *Social Science Quarterly* 74: 64–273.
Clarke, H.D. and M.C. Stewart (1984), 'Dealignment of Degree: Partisan Change in Britain, 1974–1983', *Journal of Politics* 46: 689–718.
Clarke, H.D. and G. Zuk (1989), 'The Dynamics of Third Party Support: The British Liberals, 1951–79', *American Journal of Political Science* 33: 1, pp.196–221.
Conover, P. and S. Feldman (1982), 'Projection and the Perception of Candidate', *Western Political Quarterly* 35: 228–44.
Crewe, I. (1982), 'Is Britain's Two-party System Really About to Crumble? The Social Democratic–Liberal Alliance and the Prospects for Realignment'. *Electoral Studies* 1: 275–313.
Crewe, I. (1983), 'The Electorate: Partisan Dealignment Ten Years On', *West European Politics* 6: 183–215.
Curtice J. (1983), 'Liberal Voters and the Alliance: Realignment or Protest?' in V. Bogdanor (ed.), *Liberal Party Politics*, pp. 99–122. Oxford: Oxford University. Press.
Curtice, J. (1996), 'Who Votes for the Centre Now?' in D. MacIver (ed.), *The Liberal Democrats*, pp.191–204. Hemel Hempstead: Harvester Wheatsheaf
Downs, A. (1957), *An Economic Theory of Democracy*, New York: Harper and Row.
Eagles, M. and S. Erfle (1993), 'Variations in Third/Minor Party Support in English Constituencies', *European Journal of Political Research* 23: 1, pp.91–116.

Garner, R. and R. Kelly (1993), *British Political Parties Today*. Manchester: Manchester University Press.

Heath, A., R. Jowell, J. Curtice, G. Evans, J. Field, and S. Witherspoon (1991), *Understanding Political Change: The British Voter 1964–87*. Oxford: Pergamon.

Hinich, M.J. and M.C. Munger (1994), *Ideology and Theory Political Choice*, Ann Arbor, MI.: University of Michigan Press.

Key, V.O. (1948), *Politics, Parties, and Pressure Groups* 2nd edition. New York: Thomas Crowell Company

Levy, E. (1988), 'Third Party Decline in the UK: The SNP and SDP in Comparative Perspective', *West European Politics* 11: 57–74.

Lutz, J. (1991), 'Marginality, Major Third Parties and Turnout in England in the 1970s and 1980s: A Re-Analysis and Extension', *Political Studies* 39: 721–26.

MacIver, D. (ed.) (1996), *The Liberal Democrats*, Hemel Hempstead: Harvester Wheatsheaf.

Peterson, G. and J.M. Wrighton (1998), 'Expressions of Distrust: Third Party Voting and Cynicism in Government', *Political Behavior* 20 (1): 17–34, p.22, Table 2.

Pinard, M. (1975), *The Rise of a Third Party*, Montreal: McGill-Queen's University Press.

Rosenstone, S.J., R.L. Behr and E.H. Lazarus (1984), *Third Parties in America*, Princeton: Princeton University Press.

Sarlvik, B. and I. Crewe (1983), *Decade of Dealignment*, Cambridge: Cambridge University Press.

Studlar, D.T. and I. McAllister (1987), 'Protest and Survive? Alliance Support in the 1983 British General Election', *Political Studies* 35: 39–60.

Williams, P. (1984), 'Party Realignment in the United States and Britain', *British Journal of Political Science* 15: 97–115.

APPENDIX
Variables and Coding

THIRDV voted for the third party: 0 = not vote for third party ; 1 = voted for third party.

INDP non-party identifiers: 0 = party identifier; 1 = not party identifier.

SW party switchers: 0 = non-switcher; 1 = switcher.

NGLIVEN assessment of national living standard since last general election: 0 = fallen a lot; 2 = fallen a little; 3 = stayed the same; 4 = increased a little; 5 = increased a lot.

NGLIVEP assessment of personal living standard since last general election: 1 = fallen a lot; 2 = fallen a little; 3 = stayed the same; 4 = increased a little; 5 = increased a lot.

NGEMP assessment of how well government handled unemployment: 0 = not at all well; 2 = not very well; 3 = fairly well; 4 = very well.

NGINF assessment of how well government handled inflation 1 = not at all well; 2 = not very well; 3 = fairly well; 4 = very well.

NGPTYC feeling against the Conservatives: 1 = strong against; 2 = against; 3 = neither; 4 = in favour; 5 = strongly favour. (**1979**) 1 = strongly against; 2 = not very strongly against; 3 = not applicable.

NGPTYL feeling against Labour: 1 = strong against; 2 = against; 3 = neither; 4 = in favour; 5 = strongly favour. (**1979**) 1 = strongly against; 2 = not very strongly against; 3 = not applicable.

LEADERA leader image Ashdown (ld1+ld2+ld3+ld4).
LEADERO leader image Owen (ld1+ld2+ld3+ld4).
LEADERS leader image Steel (ld1+ld2+ld3+ld4).
LEADERJ leader image Jenkins (ld1+ld2+ld3+ld4).
-4 = worst image; 0 = neither or dk; 4 = best image.
ld1 = extreme~moderate; ld2 = look after one or all classes; ld3 = capable of being strong leader; ld4 = caring–uncaring.

PTYIMGC Conservative Party image (img1+img2+img3+img4).

PTYIMGL Labour Party image (img1+img2+img3+img4):
-4 = worst image; 0 = neither or dk; 4 = best image; img1=extreme~
moderate; img2=united or divided; img3=good for one or all classes;
img4=capable of strong government. **(1979)** (0–10 thermometer): 0 = not
favour; 10 = strongly favour.

SPACE1 distance closest to the third parties (employment–inflation).

SPACE2 distance closest to the third parties (taxation–services).

SPACE3 distance closest to the third parties (nationalization–privatization).

SPACE4 issue distance closest to the their parties (redistribution of wealth).

SPACE5 distance closest to the third parties 83 (nuclear weapons, keep or get rid): 0
= closer to one of the major parties; 1 = closest to the third parties.

TACT tactical voters: 0 = not tactical voter; 1 = tactical voter.

AGE age groups: 1 = 17–25; 2 = 26–35; 3 = 36–45; 4 = 46–55; 5 = 56–65; 6 = 66
and over (Respondent's age last birthday).

CLASS class groups: 1 = higher managerial; 2 = lower managerial; 3 = skilled non-
manual; 4 = lower non-manual; 5 = skilled manual 6 = unskilled or semi-
skilled manual; 7 = unemployed/NA.

EDUC education groups (age when completed full-time education): 1 = 13 or less;
2 = 14–16; 3 = 17–18; 4 = 19–21; 5 = 22 and over.

INC income groups: 1 = less then £6000; 2 = £6000–£11999; 3 =
£12000–£17999; 4 = £18000–£24000; 5 = £25000 and over. **(1979)** 1 = less
than £18 per week; 2 = £19–£28; 3 = £29–£38; 4 = £39–£58; 5 = £59–£96;
6 = £97 and more per week.

RELIGION religious attachment: 0 = never attend church; 1 = attend one or less than
once a year; 2 = attend several times a year; 3 = attend once or more a month;
4 = attend once or more a week.

Improving the Measurement of
Party Identification in Britain

John Bartle

The idea that many voters have an enduring attachment to a political party is of central importance to the study of voting behaviour. In the 1950s scholars at the University of Michigan devised the concept of party identification in order to account for the overwhelming stability of voting behaviour (Campbell *et al.*, 1960). In this early work party identification was held to represent a generalized psychological attachment between voter and party which could be used to predict voting behaviour and specific opinions (e.g. policy preferences, evaluations of the economy and party leaders). So influential were these early studies that the theory of party identification was applied in many other countries.

Yet ever since the concept was first applied to the British electorate (Butler and Stokes, 1974), there has been unease about its close relationship with current party preference (Budge *et al.*, 1976). Far higher proportions of identifiers vote for their party in Britain than do so in the United States. The very closeness of this relationship has led some analysts to conclude that party identification cannot be looked upon as a genuinely causal factor operating on the vote (Brynin and Sanders, 1997). Other analysts have argued that the apparent closeness of the relationship between party identification and vote is the result of a methodological artefact (Heath and Pierce, 1992). In particular it has been suggested that the close relationship is due to the fact that 'reported vote' appears *before* the party identification item on the British Election Study (BES) survey questionnaire. Respondents who have previously reported that in the *specific* election concerned they voted for party X may bring their *general* party identification 'into line' with their vote even if they really identify with another party. When the question order is reversed, so that the question about general party identification item appears before specific vote, there should be less of a tendency to distort reported party identification.[1]

The argument of this article is that the current measure of party identification is seriously flawed and should be abandoned for the purpose of explaining vote choices. In the next section I put forward a formal definition of party identification in order to provide a benchmark against which survey items can be compared. This is followed by an examination of the traditional measure of party identification and an outline of the evidence that suggests that it does not measure *enduring* identities. I then propose a more theoretically defensible measure of party identification and present empirical evidence that suggests that the actual number of non-identifiers in the electorate may be very much higher than is suggested by the traditional BES item. It appears that the effect of the BES survey question has been to artificially inflate the relationship between party identification and vote and it has thus provided ammunition for those who suggest that party identification is tautological. In the final sections I indicate what additional evidence is required in the light of this preliminary analysis and discuss some of the implications of my results for voting research.

A Formal Definition of Party Identification

Party identification is a term that has been thoroughly muddied by diverse definitions and uses (Catt, 1996: 79). Before exploring the ways in which party identification has traditionally been measured in Britain, it is vitally important to define the concept with some degree of clarity. This is no easy task, for as Miller (1976: 22) has conceded, 'It may be that the time has passed when a single "Michigan view"...can be specified'. In order to remove some of the idiosyncratic differences between individual scholars therefore, I will take the work of Miller (working either singly or in collaboration with colleagues such as Shanks) as representing the 'definitive' account of the Michigan approach.[2]

Campbell *et al.* (1960: 121) defined party identification as '...the individual's affective orientation to an important group object in his environment'. Somewhat less formally, party identification represents a general psychological attachment to a political party. The Michigan approach is therefore based on the assumption that 'our individual sense of personal identity is derived from groups to which we belong' (Miller, 1976: 22). This generalized sense of belonging leads to a long-term tendency to describe oneself using a party label, such as 'I am a Conservative' or 'I am Labour'. This sense of belonging may in turn be associated with negative feelings towards another party, but need not be (Miller and Shanks, 1996: 121 *cf.* Crewe, 1976). All that is required to be a party identifier is to think of oneself as 'being Conservative', 'being Labour' or whatever. The two central elements of party identification are, therefore:

• A self-identity; and
• An extended time horizon.

The possession of this enduring self-identity and acceptance of a party label can have several consequences. Party identifiers are likely to vote in accordance with their 'long-term' allegiances, unless 'short-term' forces (such as policies or party performance) propel them to support another party. They are likely to adopt those positions and support those policies that are advocated by the leaders of their party. They are likely to evaluate politicians from their party more favourably than those from another, simply because they have the party label as a guide. Moreover, party identifiers are also likely to give information a partisan bias, discounting information that is critical of their party while accepting information that is critical of other parties. A party identifier can, therefore, view the world almost entirely in terms of convenient party stereotypes.

Given the basic stability of party identification revealed by American surveys, it made sense to conclude that party identification was a cause – rather than a consequence – of more transient preferences, such as evaluations of economic performance and leadership traits.[3] This in turn implied that in order to estimate the effect of these less stable variables on vote, one should 'control for' party identification in order to allow for the indirect effect of party identification on transient preferences. As many analysts have discovered, once controls for party identification are added many apparently strong statistical relationships between other variables and vote are greatly diminished.

Given that party identification has all these possible consequences it is often tempting to define party identification in terms of those consequences and select operational measures accordingly. Yet as Campbell *et al.* (1960: 131) and Miller and Shanks (1996: 124) have emphasized, party identification is one among many causes of political preferences. Thus a measure of party identification in terms of past vote would capture factors other than party identification (for example, short-term forces at the previous election). Campbell *et al.* (1960: 122) argue that a definition of party identification in terms of its consequences would:

blur the distinction between the psychological state and behavioural consequences. We have not measured party attachments in terms of the vote or the evaluations of partisan issues because we are interested in exploring the influence of party identification on voting behaviour and its immediate determinants. When an independent measure of party identification is used it is clear that even strong party adherents at times may think and act in contradiction to their party allegiance. We could never establish the conditions under which this will occur if lasting partisan orientations are measured in terms of the behaviour they are thought to affect.[4]

Having rejected the idea of measuring party identification in terms of its consequences there are, of course, still a whole host of potentially valid measures of party identification available to analysts. In the next section I will examine the traditional BES measure of party identification and suggest several ways in which it may be defective.

The Traditional BES Measure of Party Identification

The BES surveys use the following question to elicit party identification:

> *Generally speaking, do you think of yourself as Conservative, Labour, Liberal Democrat or what?*[5]

At first glance, this item appears well suited to its task of measuring party identification. The 'self-identity' component of party identification is reflected by the phrase 'think of yourself as'; while the 'extended time horizon' component is captured by the 'Generally speaking' clause. However, the item has several potential defects:

* *Lack of a clear temporal dimension.* Party identification is a relatively subtle theoretical construct. It would perhaps be surprising if any item could convey its meaning to respondents in a little over a line and a half, particularly when there is no practice of registering as a party supporter in Britain, as happens in America. The traditional BES measure does not explain that it is perfectly possible to think of oneself as X and yet vote for Y in certain circumstances. It does not raise considerations of long-term *identities*. Respondents may interpret the question as referring to their voting history – the way that they *generally* vote. Given the general consistency of voting behaviour, past vote and identity may be the same for most voters. However, if the voter is young and has voted in only one election, then such a response may be thoroughly misleading since short-term forces (such as economic evaluations) may have propelled them to vote for a party other than the one with which they really identify. More worrying still, respondents could interpret the item as referring to how they have voted in the most recent general election. The possibility of rationalization is strengthened by the fact that the question about party identification usually appears *after* the one asking about voting behaviour in the BES questionnaire.[6] This ordering might produce a desire to appear consistent and lead the respondent to bring their reported identity into line with their vote (Heath and Pierce, 1992). Moreover, the term 'generally speaking' may be interpreted as meaning 'over most issues'. If any of these processes are at work we would expect to find that party identification and vote would move in tandem in panel studies.

• *Failure to highlight non-identification.* Another problem with this question is that the response categories appear relatively restricted. In particular, the 'or what?' clause at the end may be interpreted as meaning 'or what other *party*'. Yet, as party identification theorists have emphasized, it is perfectly possible not to identify with *any* party (Campbell *et al*, 1960: 123). In the traditional BES question respondents have to assert positively that they do not belong to any political party. This item may therefore count as identifiers a large proportion of the electors who do not actually think of themselves as 'Conservative', 'Labour' or 'Liberal Democrat', but who feel constrained by the question to report a party identity (Johnston, 1992). Moreover, it seems plausible to suggest that such respondents will report an identification with the party that they currently prefer – thus inflating the strength of relationship between party identification and vote.[7] If this process is at work then party identification and vote are again likely to move in tandem; although in reality the voter may be a consistent non-identifier.

There is good evidence from the United States that party identification as measured by the traditional Michigan item is more stable than other attitudes. Converse (1964) presented evidence which demonstrated that while many attitudes appeared to vary almost at random, American voters' basic sense of being 'Republican', 'Independent' or 'Democrat' is highly stable and resistant to election-specific forces. In America, voters who switched parties tended to retain their prior party identification. For example, in the 1950s many identifiers with the Democrats voted for Eisenhower, the Republican presidential candidate, while retaining their previous identification. It made a great deal of sense, therefore, to assume that, on the whole, the causal direction ran from (stable) party identification to (less stable) attitudes. More recently debate has raged about the stability of the traditional measure of party identification in the United States,[8] but – on the whole – political scientists are still prepared to endorse the assumption that party identification is a cause of other politically-relevant opinions (such as evaluations of the economy and party leaders) rather than *vice versa*.

In Britain by contrast, the concept of party identification – as measured by the traditional Michigan item – has been less successful. Butler and Stokes (1974: 42) noted a disturbing tendency for party identification and vote to 'travel together': previously Labour identifiers switching their vote to the Conservatives would also change their reported identification. Not surprisingly in these circumstances, Butler and Stokes often treated party identification as the dependent variable to be explained, rather than as a cause of other preferences (Miller *et al.*, 1986: 34). More recently there has been a large number of articles suggesting that party identification in Britain is far from stable[9] or that it is too close to current political preference to be genuinely explanatory.[10] Analysts exploring the effects of other variables (for example, leadership traits) are constantly frustrated in their research since many significant statistical relationships vanish once controls for party identification are added. Meanwhile, aggregate studies have suggested that party identification, as conventionally measured in the BES, tracks vote intention very closely in the polls, suggesting that it is only 'mildly exogenous' – part cause and part consequence – of vote (Clarke et al., 1997).

Some analysts appear to suggest that the main conclusion to be drawn from these studies is that party identification theory is deeply flawed. What they have clearly demonstrated, however, is that the current *measure* of party identification is far from satisfactory. They have not demonstrated the weakness of party identification *theory* because there are strong grounds for believing that the current *measure* is seriously inadequate for the reasons set out above. In the next section I will outline what I believe to be a more defensible measure of party identification and following that I will present results from an experiment carried out by the Gallup Organisation that reinforce these arguments.

An Alternative Measure of Party Identification

I suggested above that there are whole hosts of potentially valid measures of party identification and that the traditional BES measure is clearly seriously inadequate. It is vitally important that the measure of party identification be revised. The survey item I propose is:

> *Many people think of themselves as being Conservative, Labour, Liberal Democrat (or Nationalist), even if they don't always support that party. How about you? Generally speaking do you think of yourself as Conservative, Labour, Liberal Democrat, Nationalist, or don't you think of yourself as any of these?*[11]

My general approach is to provide a longer preamble to the basic question in order to clarify the meaning of party identification for the respondent. For example, the opening statement makes clear that it is perfectly possible to think of oneself as X and yet temporarily express support for party Y. When read in conjunction with the rest of the item it clearly establishes an extended temporal dimension. The use of the word 'support' rather than 'vote' underlines the fact that a party identifier might vote for another party, at a local election for example, or express disapproval of their party from time to time. The second sentence ('How about you?') may initially appear superfluous, but it is designed to get the respondent to stop and think about the difference between current support and enduring identity before answering the party identification question itself. The latter is contained in the third sentence and is made up of the traditional BES item, with the clause *'or don't you think of yourself as any of these?'* added. The purpose of this clause is again to underline the nature of an identity ('think of yourself as') and to re-emphasize that it is perfectly possible not to identify with *any* party.

There is probably no uniquely correct way of measuring party identification, but it appears to me that this item is more likely to tap the theoretical construct of party identification than the traditional BES item; in other words, it has greater 'face validity'.[12] To be sure, it could be argued that the item is too long, that respondents will have forgotten the first sentence by the time they respond and that they will still give an unreflective 'top of the head' response (Zaller, 1992). Ultimately the real test is an empirical one. In the next section, therefore, I describe the results of preliminary research carried out by the Gallup Organisation which suggest that the BES item may have systematically overstated the level of identification with the major parties ever since the first survey in 1963.

Report of Preliminary Gallup Results

During the period 5–11 March 1998, the Gallup Organisation conducted a mini-experiment to test the effect of the new and traditional questions on reports of party identification. The sample (containing around 2,000 respondents) was split into two groups. The social composition and voting intentions of these groups were virtually identical. However, the two groups were asked different party identification questions. Since the interviews took place at the same time, other contextual effects are controlled (such as the tendency for partisanship to decrease as memories of an election recede).

Group A was asked the 'traditional' BES item and the results are set out in Table 1. Labour's lead over the Conservatives in terms of voting intention was 26 points (53 to 27 per cent). Their lead in terms of long-term party identification was only slightly smaller at 19 points (44 to 25 per cent). Only 10 per cent of the sample did not identify with a party by positively asserting that they did not think of themselves as being 'any party'. Moreover, although party identification theory suggests that a sense of identification should develop with experience, the level of non-identification in this case actually increased in the oldest age cohort (see Figure 1).

Table 2 shows that, among Group A respondents, 85 per cent of Labour identifiers intended to vote for their party, while 77 per cent of

Conservatives and 60 per cent of Liberal Democrats intended to vote for their respective parties. Not surprisingly, given that Labour was riding high in the polls, virtually all its identifiers expressed an intention to vote for their party. The Conservatives, however, were clearly still suffering from the effects of their recent period in office; while the Liberal Democrats, who are presumably faced with tactical voting considerations, were the least likely to intend to vote for their party.

The political implications of the data in Table 1 are – to put it mildly – somewhat implausible. If the results based on the traditional BES question are to be believed then the Conservatives face a considerable electoral obstacle. Winning over the small proportion of non-identifiers (just 10 per cent of respondents according to the BES measure) is not enough. They *also* have to 'convert' voters who currently appear to have long-term Labour and Liberal Democrat identities. If the Michigan model is correct and party identification responds only slowly to political experience, then – short of some unforeseen catastrophe for the Labour government – the Conservatives appear to have little or no chance of winning the next election.

TABLE 1
PARTY IDENTIFICATION AND VOTE INTENTIONS

	Group A (Traditional BES)		Group B (New Item)	
	% Party ID	% Vote	% Party ID	% Vote
Conservative	25	27	26	29
Labour	44	53	32	53
Lib. Dem.	14	15	10	14
None	10	5	28	4

Source: Gallup Organisation, Fieldwork 5–11 March 1998.

TABLE 2
THE RELATIONSHIP BETWEEN PARTY IDENTIFICATION AND VOTE INTENTION

	Group A Voting Intention (%)				Group B Voting Intention (%)			
	Con.	Lab.	Lib.	Other/DK	Con.	Lab.	Lib.	Other/DK
Conservative	77	11	5	7	72	12	6	10
Labour	2	85	5	8	1	88	4	7
Lib. Dem.	10	18	60	12	8	24	55	13

Source: Gallup Organisation, Fieldwork 5–11 March 1998.)

FIGURE 1
PROPORTION NON-IDENTIFIERS BY AGE GROUP (TRADITIONAL MICHIGAN ITEM)

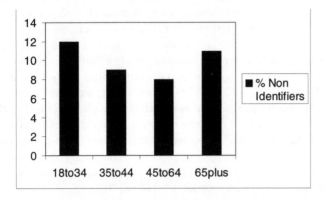

FIGURE 2
PROPORTION NON IDENTIFIERS BY AGE GROUP (NEW ITEM)

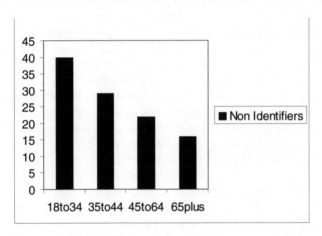

The implausibility of these findings is underlined by the data in Table 1 which sets out the results for respondents in Group B, who were asked the new party identification question. Although Labour's lead over the Conservatives in terms of vote intention was again very healthy at 24 points (53 per cent to 29 per cent), its lead in terms of party identification was whittled down to a mere 6 points (32 per cent to 26 per cent). Equally striking is the fact that 28 per cent of this sample did not appear to identify with *any* political party. It appears that when longer-term and non-partisan considerations are raised more clearly many more voters decline a party identity.

In the case of Group B the level of non-identification varies inversely and monotonically with age (see Figure 2). Fully 40 per cent of voters aged 18–34 were without a party identification, compared with 29 per cent among those 35–44, 22 per cent among those 45–64 and only 16 per cent among those aged above 65. These data are fully in line with party identification theory which suggest that one's sense of being 'Conservative' or being 'Labour' is something that develops over time and with political experience (Butler and Stokes, 1974). They imply that the support of younger voters may be particularly soft and 'up for grabs'. Whether this reflects a life-cycle or cohort effect is not clear from these data, but these results suggest that this would be an interesting research question in itself. If the high proportion of non-identifiers among the youngest cohort is a consequence of a life cycle effect then we would expect levels of non-identification for any given cohort to fall as they gain in political experience. If however this is a cohort effect, this group will continue to think of themselves as non-identifiers and there is the potential for increased electoral volatility. In either case, the new item identifies an area for research that was obscured by the traditional measure.[13]

Table 2 demonstrates that, in the case of Group B respondents, 88 per cent of Labour identifiers intended to vote for their parties (up 3 points compared with Group A respondents) while 72 per cent of Conservatives (down 5 points) and 55 per cent of Liberal Democrats (down 5 points) intended to vote for their respective parties. While the relationship between party identification and vote is apparently not very different from that found for Group A it must be noted that, according to the revised measure, there are nearly three times as many *non-identifiers* in total. The relationship between party identification and vote is thus diminished among Group B respondents, presumably because many of those currently expressing an intention to vote Labour declined a Labour identity when given the opportunity to do so. This is demonstrated in Table 3, which shows the partisan origins of party support according to both measures. According to the traditional BES measure, Labour obtained 79 per cent of its support from its own identifiers and just 6 per cent from those who asserted that they did not identify with any party. The new measure tells a very different story. In this case only 60 per cent of Labour support came from its identifiers and 27 per cent from those without any identity. Similarly, the Liberal Democrats obtained 54 per cent of their support from their identifiers according to the BES measure and just 44 per cent according to the new measure. Moreover, while the Liberal Democrats received just 11 per cent of their support from non-identifiers according to the BES measure, they received 31 per cent from non-identifiers according to the new measure. In both cases however, the Conservatives received three-quarters of their support from Conservative identifiers. It appears that, in March 1998, few other than Conservative identifiers had much affection for the Conservative Party under Mr Hague.

These results are substantively important. They represent 'good news' for William Hague since they suggest that Labour's long-term advantage is greatly exaggerated by both the traditional measure of party identification *and* voting intentions. They also appear to confirm Tony Blair's belief that support for 'New Labour' is conditional. They suggest that much of the support for Labour in March 1998 was relatively superficial and a reflection of the pro-Labour (or anti-Conservative) mood in the country. People were prepared to indicate short-term support for Labour, but far fewer were prepared to express a long-term identity. Short-term forces may well keep Labour high in the polls and inflate the levels of identification as measured by the Michigan item. However, if New Labour performs badly the new measure suggests that support for it will fall as non-identifiers switch to another party. Although one should always be careful of placing too much reliance upon intuition, it must also be said that the new item 'feels right'. In theory, party identification should build relatively slowly over time. Labour has been ahead in the polls for something approaching six years. It makes some sense to say that Labour has a lead over the Conservatives in terms of long-term allegiances, but it is stretching credulity to maintain that Labour's long-term lead is in the area of 19 points.[14]

TABLE 3
THE PARTISAN SOURCE OF PARTY SUPPORT

	% Conservative		% Labour		% Liberal Democrat	
	BES	New	BES	New	BES	New
Conservative	81	74	6	7	10	12
Labour	4	2	79	60	17	10
Lib. Democrat	5	3	5	5	54	44
Non-Identifier	6	19	6	27	11	31

Source: Gallup Organisation, Fieldwork 5–11 March 1998.

Future Research

These results are suggestive, but much work on the new measure remains to be done. It would be useful to carry out further experiments to find out which of the two innovations (the preamble *or* the addition of the non-identity clause) is responsible for inflating the number of non-identifiers. For example, if we were to find that the addition of the preamble, without the non-identification clause, produced little difference, then we could improve the traditional BES item merely by replacing 'or what?' with the clause 'or don't you think of yourself as any of these?'. However, it may well be that the two innovations work in tandem and that it is necessary to incorporate both non-identification and long-term considerations. It is also vitally important to compare the stability of responses to the new item with the traditional Michigan question using a panel study design. Responses to the new question should be more stable over time. If the new question is tapping an enduring psychological attachment, then fewer voters should change their party identification when changing their vote. We might find that the proportion of the electorate retaining their identification while switching vote reaches American levels. Moreover, if time series data on the new question were collected I would expect that aggregate levels of identification would be far more stable than either vote intention or the traditional BES measure. It may be that aggregate studies which have emphasized dynamic change in party identification have, to a large extent, merely demonstrated that the traditional measure is hopelessly polluted by short-term forces, such as economic and leader evaluations. If party identification had been measured properly it may have been found that party identification is 'a remarkably stable predisposition' (Miller and Shanks, 1996: 119) but that there are fewer 'party' votes in total. The collection of data on a more clearly exogenous variable would have considerable benefits for studies of both individual vote decisions and aggregate opinion trends. Studies of individual voting behaviour would have less need to estimate the reciprocal links between party identification and issue positions or retrospective evaluations (Fleury and Lewis-Beck, 1993; cf. Converse and Pierce, 1993). Studies of aggregate opinion poll trends would also be able to impose assumptions about the causal ordering among explanatory variables without having to rely on dubious statistical tests for causality (Clarke et al., 1997).

Summary and Discussion

My argument can be summarized by four inter-related propositions. First, party identification is potentially an enormously important explanatory variable because it appears well able to account for the impressive continuity of political preferences found by survey research. Second, it is virtually certain that the traditional measure of party identification is seriously inadequate or even quasi-tautological. Third, any individual level model relying on the traditional measure of party identification will produce biased estimates of the effect of party identification, and any model of the dynamics of party identification may give an inflated estimate of the effect of other variables (such as performance evaluations) on party identification (Green and Palmquist, 1992 and 1994). Fourth, given the enormous theoretical payoffs from party identification theory, it is vitally important that we consider alternative measures of party identification.[15] The item outlined here is one potential approach. To repeat, there is probably no perfect way of measuring party identification but there can be little doubt that the traditional measure is deeply flawed.

There are some analysts who will take the view that it is important to preserve long-established time series data in surveys such as the BES. It could be argued that, even if the current measure is biased, as long as the bias is consistent over time, trends in aggregate party identification levels revealed by the traditional Michigan item from repeated cross-sectional studies are informative. Yet the role of surveys such as the BES surely cannot be restricted to documenting change over long periods of time. The goal of political scientists is surely both to explain why any given individual votes as they do and why one party receives a greater share of the aggregate vote (Achen, 1982). If these are common goals, then we must give priority to ensuring that our measures of concepts such as party identification are valid.

It might also be objected that the proposed item is radically different from the American National Election Study measure of party identification, which would make cross-national US/UK comparisons problematic. It should be noted, however, that there are strong reasons for believing that British respondents require an explanation of party identification. In the United States many voters can register as Democrats or Republicans and therefore must give some consideration to their basic partisan predisposition. There are also far more elections in the United States and consequently a greater need to judge candidates according to party labels (Harrop and Miller, 1987: 139). My approach is based on the assumption that British voters are just as familiar with the idea of party identification as American voters, but that long-term and non-partisan considerations need to be flagged for the British voter.[16] It is also worth noting that the levels of non-partisanship revealed by the experimental group in the Gallup survey are similar to the proportion of the American electorate that considers themselves to be 'Independent' (Keith et al., 1992: 14).

In general, there can be no assumption that the same questionnaire item can be used in all contexts. Indeed this is the chief problem with the Michigan measure – it was directly imported from one party system to another with insufficient thought as to substantive differences between those two countries. Butler and Stokes (1974: 44, n.1) considered and rejected the addition of an 'Independent' choice category in the BES measure. They rejected it because of poll evidence that few British voters appeared to understand the term. Yet the substantive meaning of being an 'Independent' is simply that the voter does not have a long-term party identification, so it seems perfectly reasonable to ask if respondents do not think of themselves as identifying with a party.

The new item raises many questions, but for the moment it is instructive to focus on one. In the United States, 'partisan dealignment' took the form of an increasing number of voters thinking of themselves as 'Independent' (Keith *et al.*, 1992), while in Britain dealignment took the form of a decline in strength of party identification (Crewe *et al.* 1977: 144–5). It may well be that, had the non-identification option been clearly signalled in the 1970s, the processes of dealignment in Britain may have taken the same form as in the United States, an increase in non-identification.

A great deal of electoral research has relied on an inherently flawed measure of party identification. Too many researchers have taken negative findings about party identification as an indication that party identification does not exist, is tautological or vapid. It is understandable that analysts are anxious to resolve big questions such as why people vote the way they do. However, in the social sciences there is often considerable slippage between the theoretical construct and operational measure, so that progress is continually hindered by measurement problems (Miller and Shanks, 1996: 127). Given the practical advantages to both social-psychological and rational choice theories that an improved measure of party identification would bring, it is well worth devoting time and resources to an attempt to make such an improvement.

ACKNOWLEDGEMENTS

I would like to thank Andrew Wroe of the University of Essex for detailed comments on an earlier version of this article and also Jon Burton, Ivor Crewe, David Denver, Anthony King, Jack Kneeshaw, Anthony Lyons, Warren E. Miller and Michael J. Smith for many stimulating discussions on the subject of party identification. In addition I record my gratitude to the Gallup Organisation.

NOTES

1. The results of experiments on question order are not conclusive, but there can be little doubt that differences in question order do have some effect on responses.
2. Sources therefore include Campbell *et al.* (1960), Miller (1976), Miller (1991) and Miller and Shanks (1996). Taken as a whole these works tell a remarkably consistent story about party identification.
3. Converse and Pierce (1992: 240) argue that, '*for most voters, most of the time*, the predominant causal flow is from partisan attachment to other specific political sentiments, including vote choices, rather than vice-versa'. It is left unclear what issues, and in what circumstances, might affect party identification. See also Campbell *et al.* (1960: 135–6).
4. The validity of the measure can still be assessed, however, by establishing whether it has certain predicted relationships with other variables.
5. Until 1970 the item read, 'Generally speaking, do you *usually* think of yourself as Conservative, Labour, Liberal Democrat or what?' In correspondence Warren E. Miller has indicated that he thinks the inclusion of the word 'usually' may help to clarify the question for British respondents. If he is right there has already been a break in the continuity offered by the traditional BES measure.

6. In 1992 the BES conducted an experiment in which half the respondents were asked about vote before party identification and the other half were asked about party identification before vote. The results were not encouraging to the question order hypothesis, as there was little difference between the groups.

7. Butler and Stokes (1974: 44, n.1) considered adding an 'Independent' option in their study, but rejected the idea after gathering evidence that the term was not understood by the British electorate.

8. On individual level data see Jackson (1975), Fiorina (1981) and Green and Palmquist (1990, 1994). On aggregate data see MacKuen et al. (1992) and Abramson and Ostrom (1992).

9. Johnston and Pattie (1996) point out that the strength of party identification varies over relatively short periods. However, a recalculation of their figures suggests that relatively few voters switch between parties.

10. Brynin and Sanders (1995: 74). These authors conclude that it is wisest to 'seek to specify and estimate separate models of vote choice and party identification which by definition exclude the other from the right-hand side of the specified equation'.

11. I do not claim any great originality for this question. A similar item was contained on the 1992 BES self-completion supplement. The wording of this item is: 'Many people lean towards a particular party for a long time, although they may occasionally vote for a different party. How about you? Do you in general lean towards a particular party? If so, which?' This item appears to be rather better than the traditional item. Those who do not lean towards a party can be classified as non-leaners. Moreover, the item does not refer to any political party and so might carry fewer partisan cues. It is unclear whether the use of the term 'lean towards' is the same as 'thinking of oneself as', but it would certainly be interesting to compare this item with both the traditional and new items.

12. It could be argued that we should use the word 'belonging' instead of 'think of yourself as', but this would raise additional problems. A clause would have to be added to the item to stress that it is perfectly possible to 'belong' without being a formal member. Indeed, the word 'belong' may be too strong – forcing many people who 'think of themselves as' being Conservative or as being Labour to reject an identity. However, such an item might still serve a useful purpose by providing a minimum estimate of levels of party identification.

13. An examination of the BES data on party identification by age group for 1983, 1987, 1992 and 1997 suggests that the traditional Michigan item does produce the negative relationship between age and non-identification uncovered by the new item in three out of four recent elections (1992 being the exception). If the figures for non-identification are multiplied by a constant (equal to the number of non-identifiers in Group B, divided by those in Group A) the relationship between age and non-identification is just as strong. I would like to thank Jack Kneeshaw of the University of Essex for drawing this to my attention.

14. I am grateful to Anthony King for this observation.

15. It is certainly worth noting that rational choice theorists have demonstrated an interest in the habitual element of the vote. See Downs (1957: 85), Fiorina (1981) and Grofman (1995).

16. Harrop and Miller (1987: 139) make a similar point, 'The difficulty of measuring partisanship outside the United States does not mean the concept should be abandoned. European electors are unfamiliar with the *term* party identification, but not with the *concept* or the *spirit*' (emphasis added).

REFERENCES

Abramson, Paul R. and Charles W. Ostrom (1992) 'Response to Mackuen et al.', *American Political Science Review* 88: 481–6.

Achen, Christopher H. (1982) *Interpreting and Using Regression,* Sage University Paper Series on Quantitative Applications in the Social Sciences 007-029. Beverley Hills: Sage Publications.

Achen, Christopher H. (1992) 'Social Psychology, Demographic Variables and Linear Regression: Breaking the Iron Triangle in Voting Research', *Political Behaviour* 14: 195–211.

Brynin, Malcolm and David Sanders (1997) 'Party Identification, Political Preferences and Material Conditions: Evidence from the British Household Panel Survey, 1991–2', *Party Politics* 3: 53–77.

Budge, Ian, Ivor Crewe and Denis Farlie (1976) 'Editors Introduction' in Ian Budge, Ivor Crewe and Denis Farlie (eds) *Party Identification and Beyond*. pp.3–20. London: John Wiley.

Butler, David and Donald Stokes (1974) *Political Change in Britain: The Evolution of Electoral Choice, 2nd Edition*. London: Macmillan.

Campbell, Angus, Philip Converse, Warren E. Miller and Donald Stokes (1966) *Elections and the Political Order*. London: John Wiley.

Catt, Helena (1996) *Voting Behaviour: A Radical Critique*. London: Leicester University Press.

Clarke, Harold D., Marianne C. Stewart and Paul Whiteley (1997) 'Tory Trends: Party Identification and the Dynamics of Conservative Support Since 1992', *British Journal of Political Science* 27: 299–331.

Converse, Philip E. (1964) 'The Nature of Belief Systems in Mass Publics' in D. Apter (ed.), *Ideology and Discontent*. pp.206–61. New York: Free Press.

Converse, Philip E. and Roy Pierce (1992) 'Partisanship and the Party System', *Political Behaviour* 14: 239–59.

Converse, Philip E. and Roy Pierce (1993) 'Comment on Fleury and Lewis-Beck: Anchoring the French Voter: Ideology Versus Party', *Journal of Politics* 55: 1110–7.

Crewe, Ivor (1976) 'Party Identification Theory and Political Change in Britain' in Budge, Ian, Ivor Crewe and Denis Farlie (eds), *Party Identification and Beyond*. pp.33–61. London: John Wiley.

Crewe, Ivor; Bo Sarlvik and James Alt (1977) 'Partisan Dealignment in Britain 1964–74', *British Journal of Political Science* 7: 129–90.

Downs, Anthony (1957) *An Economic Theory of Democracy*. New York: Harper Row.

Fiorina, Morris P. (1981) *Retrospective Voting in American National Elections*. New Haven: Yale University Press.

Fleury, Christopher J. and Michael S. Lewis-Beck (1993) 'Anchoring the French Voter: Ideology Versus Party', *Journal of Politics* 55: 1100–9.

Green, Donald Philip and Bradley Palmquist (1990) 'Of Artifacts and Partisan Instability', *American Journal of Political Science* 34: 872–902.

Green, Donald Philip and Bradley Palmquist (1994) 'How Stable is Party Identification?', *Political Behaviour* 16: 437–66.

Grofman, Bernard (ed.) (1995) *Information, Participation & Choice: An Economic Theory of Democracy in Perspective*. Ann Arbor: University of Michigan Press.

Harrop, Martin and William L. Miller (1987) *Elections and Voters: A Comparative Introduction*. Basingstoke: Macmillan.

Heath, Anthony and Roy Pierce (1992) 'It Was Party Identification All Along; Question Order Effects on Reports of Party Identification in Britain', *Electoral Studies* 14: 93–105.

Jackson, John A. (1975) 'Issues, Party Choices and Presidential Votes', *American Journal of Political Science* 19: 161–85.

Johnston, Richard (1992) 'Party Identification Measures in the Anglo-American Democracies: A National Survey Experiment', *American Journal of Political Science* 36: 542–59.

Johnston, R.J. and Charles Pattie (1996) 'The Strength of Party Identification Among the British Electorate: An Exploration', *Electoral Studies* 15: 295–309.

Keith, Bruce E., David B. Magleby; Candice J. Nelson, Elizabeth Orr, Mark C. Westyle and Raymond E. Wolfinger (1992) *The Myth of the Independent Voter*. Berkeley: University of California Press.

Mackuen, Michael, Robert S. Erikson and James A. Stimson (1992) 'Question Wording and Macropartisanship', *American Political Science Review* 86: 475–81.

Miller, Warren E. (1976) 'The Cross-National Use of Party Identification as a Stimulus to Political Inquiry' in Ian Budge, Ivor Crewe and Denis Farlie (eds), *Party Identification and Beyond*. pp.21–31. London: John Wiley.

Miller, Warren E. (1991), 'Party Identification, Realignment and Party Voting: Back To Basics', *American Political Science Review* 82: 557–67.

Miller, Warren E. and J. Merrill Shanks (1996) *The New American Voter.* Cambridge, MA: Harvard University Press.

Miller, William, S. Tagg and K. Britto (1986) 'Partisanship and Party Preferences in Government and Opposition: The Mid-term Perspective', *Electoral Studies* 5: 31–46.

Zaller, John R. (1992) *The Nature and Origins of Mass Opinion.* Cambridge: Cambridge University Press.

Settled Will or Divided Society? Voting in the 1997 Scottish and Welsh Devolution Referendums

Charles Pattie, David Denver, James Mitchell and Hugh Bochel

At least partly because they appear to undermine the doctrine of parliamentary sovereignty, referendums have been rare events in the United Kingdom. The only UK-wide referendum was in 1975 (on membership of the European Community) and before 1997 there had been only three other significant sub-national referendums – in Northern Ireland (1973) and in Scotland and Wales on proposals for devolution (1979).[1] The election of a Labour government in 1997 has resulted in a revival of interest in the device, however, and during the first 12 months of the new parliament there were four significant referendums – on a devolved parliament for Scotland, a representative assembly for Wales, the peace proposals and a parliament for Northern Ireland, and the government of London. Further referendums have been mooted on electoral reform, membership of the European single currency, and devolution to the English regions.

The results of the referendums held so far are reported in Table 1. In each case the government's proposals were endorsed – although the endorsement was rather more ringing in some cases than in others.

TABLE 1
UK REFERENDUMS 1997–98

	% voting Yes	% turnout
Scotland (11 September 1997)		
Q1. Support a Scottish parliament?	74.3	60.4
Q2. Give parliament tax-varying powers?	63.5	–
Wales (18 September 1997)		
Support a Welsh assembly?	50.3	50.1
London (7 May 1998)		
Support a directly elected executive mayor?	72.0	34.1
Northern Ireland (22 May 1998)		
Support the Good Friday Agreement?	71.0	81.0

The new wave of referendums is something of a novel experience for Britain's voters. Prior to 1997, (older) voters in Scotland, Wales and Northern Ireland could have taken part in only two referendums, and those in England in only one. The current electorate has had, therefore, very little experience of this form of direct democracy, especially compared with their accumulated, and increasingly sophisticated, practical knowledge of how to act in parliamentary elections. The contrasts between election and referendum voting are clear. Elections recur at regular intervals, are organized around and by long-established political parties, each of which has at least some loyal supporters, and are 'about' the same things – passing judgement on the old government, electing the new, and so on. Most electors will have voted in previous elections, and almost all will know people who have done so. Party competition is well-entrenched and ongoing, making for fairly clearly defined and stable alternatives. Referendums, by contrast, are one-off events. They are about a single issue where elections are multi-issue. In some cases, as with the 1975 EEC referendum, the issues at stake are ones on which the parties themselves are divided or have no clear view, and so party loyalty is not a good guide for voters (see Butler and Kitzinger, 1976). In other cases, as with the 1997 Scottish and Welsh referendums, party positions are clear (although some internal dissension was still in evidence). Furthermore, there are rarely long-established and high profile pre-existing political organizations which have campaigned on the issue over a long period: voters may have to make up their minds on the basis of arguments put forward by short-lived, *ad hoc* organizations which themselves have few campaigning resources to draw upon. Additionally, most British voters rely on television as their major source of political information but, whereas the rules governing television coverage during election campaigns are relatively clear and scrupulously observed (particularly with regard to the parties' own broadcasts), there are no equivalent rules for coverage in referendums.[2] In recent referendums, broadcasters have dealt with the problem by denying campaign groups and parties the opportunity to make their own 'referendum political broadcasts'.

There is, therefore, a great deal of uncertainty surrounding referendum voting in Britain. Campaigners and voters alike have had to operate in a new world, with few of the familiar landmarks that are available during conventional elections. How do voters negotiate their way through this uncertain environment? How do they decide which way to vote? Data deriving from surveys of the Scottish and Welsh electorates undertaken at the time of their respective referendums give us an opportunity to examine these questions.[3]

The Context of the Referendums

Scotland and Wales both have long traditions of political distinctiveness within the United Kingdom (see Kellas, 1973; Miller; 1981, Field, 1997). Both countries have been strongholds of radical politics – Liberal in the nineteenth century, Labour in the twentieth. Furthermore, distinctive national identities have been preserved in both countries which have formed the basis for periodic nationalist and home rule movements (see Mitchell, 1996; Jones, 1997) and since the late 1960s both countries have seen the emergence of nationalist parties as significant electoral forces. The introduction of devolution legislation by the minority Labour government of the late 1970s was largely a response to the electoral success – and hence electoral threat – of the SNP and Plaid Cymru.

While there are these similarities between Scotland and Wales, there are also important differences. Welsh nationalism is closely associated with the survival of the Welsh language and culture even although only around 20% of the Welsh population are Welsh speakers. Furthermore, Wales contains a large minority of residents born outside Wales (23% in 1991, of whom the great majority were born in England). The combination of the language divide and the relatively large non-Welsh population has created a fractured sense of Welsh national identity. As the second column of Table 2 shows, only 17% of Welsh residents in 1997 felt solely Welsh, and a further 25% felt more Welsh than British. More detailed figures for Wales (columns 3 to 5) show that Welsh identity is strongest among Welsh-born Welsh speakers – 29% of these respondents felt 'solely Welsh' and 68% felt either Welsh or more Welsh than British. Among those born in Wales but unable to speak the language, the sense of Welshness was somewhat weaker – just under 50% felt at least more Welsh than British. Not surprisingly, Welsh identity was weak among those not born in Wales with only 7% feeling more Welsh than British. Denis Balsom (1985) has suggested that in terms of language and national identity Wales is geographically divided into three distinct areas. In 'Welsh Wales', the southern industrial strip, people mainly speak English but think of themselves as Welsh; in 'British Wales', comprising the areas which border England and the extreme South West, English is spoken and Welsh identity weak; in north and west Wales (*Y Fro Gymraeg* – 'the Welsh parish') both the Welsh language and Welsh identity are strong.

In contrast, there is a stronger and more unified sense of national identity in Scotland. A larger proportion of the Scottish population is native to the country (89% Scottish-born in 1991) and there is no significant cultural–linguistic division. A very small minority, predominantly in the far North West speaks Gaelic. Unlike the Welsh, the Scots can look to a shared history of independent statehood prior to the 1707 Act of Union, and

Scotland retains its own legal, education and banking systems, as well as its own Presbyterian established church (see Kellas, 1980; Brown et al, 1996). These institutions underpin a civil society that is sufficiently different from England in key respects to maintain a shared sense of Scottishness, albeit leavened to a considerable extent by a common British history. Most of those resident in Scotland feel a dual sense of nationality. In contrast to Wales, however, the majority (63% in 1997) feel more Scottish than British, and a significant minority (28%) of all Scottish residents feel exclusively Scottish.

TABLE 2
NATIONAL IDENTITY IN SCOTLAND AND WALES (%)

	Scotland	Wales	Welsh-born W. speak	W. speak	Not W. born
Scots/Welsh not Brit.	28	17	29	20	1
More Scots/Welsh than Brit.	35	25	39	28	6
Equally Scots/Welsh and Brit.	29	33	31	42	20
More Brit. than Scots/Welsh	3	10	1	5	23
Brit. not Scots/Welsh	3	12	0	4	38
Other/none	2	4	+	1	13
(N)	(2307)	(686)	(157)	(300)	(174)

Note: + = less than 0.5%. 'W. speak' = Welsh speaker.

Sources: In this and all subsequent tables data are from the Scottish Referendum survey undertaken by the authors and the CREST Welsh Referendum survey.

Not surprisingly, then, pro-home rule sentiment has been stronger in Scotland than in Wales (see Mitchell, 1996). Plaid Cymru, has never escaped its association with the Welsh language, and has never made electoral inroads outside its heartland in north west Wales (see Balsom et al., 1983; Borland et al., 1992; Fisher, 1997; McAllister, 1998a). It has been notably unsuccessful in the mainly English-speaking communities of the South Wales valleys. On the other hand, since its breakthrough in the late 1960s the SNP has won seats in different parts of Scotland, in both urban and rural areas, and has achieved significant support throughout the country. Furthermore, when devolution proposals were last put to Scottish and Welsh voters in 1979, the Welsh electorate decisively rejected an elected assembly – only 20% of those voting supported devolution, less than 12% of the eligible electorate. A majority of Scottish voters (51.9%) favoured an assembly although this fell well short of 40% of the electorate, which was the qualified majority condition imposed by the relevant legislation (see Bogdanor, 1980; Bochel et al., 1981).

The 1979 referendums gave a mixed message. In Wales, devolution was clearly rejected whereas the Scottish result was much more equivocal and the issue remained unresolved. The consequences of the referendum votes for the devolution cause were severe, however. The major UK parties had all experienced divisions in both Scotland and Wales over the issue (with, for instance, prominent Scottish Conservatives campaigning for an assembly, and a high-profile 'Labour Vote No' campaign). More importantly, the minority Labour government's failure to carry the devolution votes contributed directly to its downfall, as Nationalist MPs withdrew their support in a parliamentary vote of confidence. In the subsequent 1979 General Election, Labour and the Nationalists saw their support and their parliamentary representation decline, and the Conservatives were elected to government with a large majority.

Under the strongly Unionist leadership of Mrs Thatcher, the new Conservative administration abandoned its (partly strategic) qualified support for devolution and the issue was kept off the Westminster agenda for the next 18 years. Although the Conservatives lost ground in both Scotland and Wales in almost all elections after 1979, their majorities in Parliament were sufficiently large to insulate them from any demands for home rule. Indeed, Mrs Thatcher's successor as party leader, John Major, attributed the (very small) improvement in the Conservatives' performance in Scotland at the 1992 general election to his last-minute appeals to preserve the Union against the threat posed by Labour's devolution plans. Ironically, however, Conservative opposition to home rule was itself a factor in reviving the argument for devolution after the 1979 referendum defeat. Throughout the 1980s and early 1990s, Scottish and Welsh voters were governed by a party, the Conservatives, which they increasingly rejected at the polls.

In Scotland in particular, the government came to be seen (rightly or wrongly) as anti-Scottish. Many former opponents of devolution in the Scottish Labour Party, contrasting their success with Labour's failure in the South, began to change their minds. By the late 1980s, a pro-constitutional change consensus was developing among the opposition parties in Scotland. An important manifestation of this was the establishment of the Scottish Constitutional Convention in 1988. The Convention brought together Labour and Liberal Democrat politicians, trades unionists and some Scottish churchmen. The SNP, however, after some initial indecision, remained aloof, fearing that the Convention would lead to a dilution of its demands for full Scottish independence. The nationalists' boycott notwithstanding, the Convention became an important forum within which proponents of devolution could reach agreement on the broad principles of a scheme.

In Wales, too, support for devolution grew among political elites in the opposition parties. Nonetheless, compared with Scotland, a large number of Welsh Labour activists and MPs remained sceptical, and even opposed. Wales remained the Achilles' heel of Labour's devolution plans.

During the 1992 Parliament, the devolution debate moved on. Labour's new leader, John Smith, had helped pilot earlier devolution proposals through the Commons in the late 1970s, and was now a strong advocate of devolution to Scotland and Wales, as part of a wider commitment to constitutional change. A commitment to devolution was, he claimed, 'the settled will' of the Scottish people. Reflecting the rather different situation in each country Labour's proposals for Scotland and Wales differed. While Scotland was to be offered a parliament with legislative responsibilities and (although this was more controversial) some limited but symbolically important powers over taxation, Wales was to receive a weaker assembly that could discuss, but not pass, primary legislation.

Tony Blair succeeded Smith as Labour leader on latter's death and was more cautious in his approach to home rule than his predecessor. Devolution remained official Labour Party policy, but it was decided that any future Labour government would seek endorsement of its proposals in Scottish and Welsh referendums. In Scotland, two questions would be put to voters: whether a Scottish parliament should be established and whether that parliament should be given tax-varying powers. In Wales, only one was needed – whether an assembly should be established. The decision to have a two-question referendum angered the pro-devolution forces in Scotland. In retrospect, however, it can be presented as an astute move in that large votes in favour of change would make it difficult for any future Westminster government opposed to devolution to reverse such a change. Caution on devolution also had the advantage of reassuring erstwhile Conservative supporters to whom Blair's electoral appeal was pitched.

In the event, of course, the 1997 election produced an unprecedented Labour landslide. Despite Major's attempt to repeat his 'defend the Union' strategy of 1992, the Conservatives were routed in both Scotland and Wales: no Conservative MPs were elected in either country. The new government moved quickly, and legislation was set in place for the conduct of new devolution referendums, in Scotland on 11 September 1997, and in Wales a week later.

The Referendum Campaigns and Results

Compared with the 1979 referendum, the 1997 Scottish campaign was notable for the high degree of unity displayed by the parties in both the Yes and the No camps. While there were a few 'dissidents' (Tam Dalyell the

Scottish Labour MP who was the author of the notorious 'West Lothian Question' remained opposed, for instance) they were less in evidence than in 1979 and much less vocal. Cross-party organizations were established to co-ordinate campaigning but again, in contrast to 1979, there were only two major campaigns of this kind.

The main group working for a Yes vote was *Scotland Forward*. Already being planned before the 1997 general election, *Scotland Forward* built on the cross-party consensus of the Constitutional Convention, drawing support from Labour and Liberal Democrats. Its major coup came in the summer of 1997, when the SNP decided that it would throw its weight behind the campaign. To a remarkable extent, *Scotland Forward* presented a united front: on the whole, the parties managed to set aside their differences and worked together towards a common end.

In contrast, the No campaign was less well organized. Once again, there was one main campaign group – *Think Twice*. Unlike *Scotland Forward*, however, *Think Twice* was largely a one-party affair. To a much greater extent than its organizers liked to admit, it was a Conservative-dominated body. While this had become increasingly inevitable as the other parties had moved behind devolution, it was hardly a good omen in a country where the Conservatives had been so recently and decisively routed. Not only that, but compared with the Yes campaign, *Think Twice* was a late starter, not getting off the ground until after the 1997 general election. The lack of time available inhibited effective campaign planning but, in any case, the referendum was widely expected to result in a very clear Yes majority, at least on the first question. It seems likely that many potential opponents of devolution believed that there was little point in expending energy fighting against the prospect of certain defeat. This may well have been a factor behind the general silence from the Scottish business community on the devolution issue, in contrast to 1979 when there had been an active business-based anti-devolution campaign.

As in Scotland, the campaign in Wales was fought through two main umbrella groups – *Yes for Wales*, which campaigned for the assembly, and *Just Say No*, which campaigned against – although, as in Scotland, the parties themselves took on the bulk of the practical campaigning. Labour, Plaid Cymru and the Liberal Democrats threw their weight behind the Yes campaign, while the Conservatives supported the No campaign. However, whereas intra-party dissension had been almost absent in Scotland, it was an important aspect of the campaign in Wales (see McAllister, 1998b). A number of Welsh Labour MPs and activists, particularly in the south Wales valleys, were vocal opponents of their own government's proposals.

The Scottish referendum result demonstrated that devolution – or at least opposition to the constitutional status quo – was indeed the settled will of the Scottish people. On a respectable 60.4% turnout, a large majority (74.3%) endorsed an Edinburgh parliament, and a smaller, but still impressive (63.5%) majority voted to give the new body tax-varying powers (see Table 1). Although there were some regional variations in the result, majorities in all parts of Scotland supported a parliament and only in a few peripheral areas (Orkney, Shetland and Borders) were majorities opposed to tax-varying powers.[4]

If the main result in Scotland had never been seriously in question, the referendum in Wales was always bound to be a close-run thing, hence the government's decision on the timing of the two votes. But even with the momentum of Scotland's vote behind it during the final week, the Yes campaign in Wales faced an uphill struggle. Turnout in Wales was ten percentage points lower than in Scotland and the eventual majority of votes in favour of an assembly was by the narrowest of margins (50.3%). The geography of the 'Yes' vote also suggests a country divided. In no part of Wales did the Yes vote reach 60%. Along the border, in the South Wales valleys, and even in the capital, majorities voted against the measure while the highest votes in favour were recorded in Welsh-speaking north west Wales.

TABLE 3
DIFFERENTIAL TURNOUT AND VOTING IN THE REFERENDUMS (%)

| | | Survey results | |
	Actual vote	Voters	Non-voters (intended vote)
Scotland			
Q. 1 (Parliament)			
Yes	74.3	77	80
No	25.7	23	20
(N)		(1859)	(389)
Q. 2 (tax powers)			
Yes	63.5	66	52
No	36.5	34	48
(N)		(1837)	(334)
Wales			
Yes	50.3	50	36
No	49.7	50	64
(N)		(420)	(169)

A straightforward comparison of the Scottish and Welsh results suggests enthusiasm for devolution in Scotland and apathy (with a large minority opposed) in Wales. Comparing the results with 1979 suggests, however, that the Welsh result can be interpreted as a striking success for the Yes campaign. A very heavy defeat for devolution in 1979 (by four to one) had been turned into a narrow victory (with a higher turnout) in 1997.

The result of the Scottish referendum was not significantly affected by differential turnout. Data from our survey of Scottish electors show that on the first referendum question non-voters were, if anything, more likely to have voted Yes than those who did vote (see Table 3) although they were less enthusiastic about giving the new parliament tax-varying powers than were those who voted. In Wales, however, the equivalent exercise reveals that those who did not vote but who did express a view on the referendum question were almost twice as likely to have voted No as to have voted Yes: the relatively poor turnout in Wales seems to have helped the Yes camp.

Identities and Voting in the Referendum

Why were Scottish voters so positive, and Welsh voters so lukewarm in their support for devolution? Clearly, voters used the referendums to express their opinion on the issue at hand. In itself this is not very informative, however, since a referendum which failed this test would hardly be worth the effort! However, the particular structure of the Scottish vote did allow for an unusual degree of 'finesse' in the expression of opinions which was not open to Welsh voters. The two-question ballot allowed voters to choose three major combinations of votes: Yes to a parliament and Yes to tax powers (supported by 66% of voters); Yes to a parliament and No to Tax powers (11%); and No to both proposals (23%). A fourth option was also possible, No–Yes, but only a very small number of voters (5 in our survey of 2335) seem to have chosen it. As Table 4 shows, Yes–Yes voters were the most enthusiastic about change, Yes–No voters were in favour, but not so strongly so; and No–No voters were almost all opposed. Scottish voters seem to have used the second question in part as a device for indicating the depth of their commitment to devolution.

TABLE 4
REFERENDUM VOTE BY STRENGTH OF SUPPORT FOR SCOTTISH PARLIAMENT (%)

	Strongly Favour	Favour	Neither	Against	Strongly Against
Yes–Yes	94	73	15	1	0
Yes–No	6	25	23	1	0
No–No	+	2	62	99	100
(N)	(766)	(476)	(52)	(211)	(147)

Note: + = less than 1%.

Beyond their opinions on the issue concerned, what guided voters' decisions? As noted above, there are few clear clues as to what factors will influence British voters in referendums. The cues that operate to create relative predictability in election voting need not apply. Here we propose to examine referendum voting in the light of three key identities – class, nation and party. We first present simple cross-tabulations showing the relationship between each set of identities and votes in the referendums before incorporating all three into a multivariate model.

Class identity was clearly associated with voting choice.[5] Table 5 shows that a majority (large in Scotland, narrow in Wales) of those who identified themselves as working class voted Yes. Voting No was much more likely among the self-ascribed middle class: in Wales, a clear majority of this group voted No, while in Scotland, a large minority did so (and a narrow majority voted No on the tax question).

TABLE 5
CLASS IDENTITY AND REFERENDUM VOTE (%)

	Middle Class	Working Class	No class Identity
Scotland			
Yes–Yes	46	74	63
Yes–No	12	10	13
No–No	43	15	25
(N)	(285)	(843)	(666)
Wales			
Yes	41	52	58
No	59	48	42
(N)	(97)	(271)	(53)

There is little doubt that from 1979 to the 1990s there was an increase in the strength of Scottish identity among Scots voters (see Bennie *et al*, 1997: 132–3). Moreover, voters' sense of national identity has been clearly associated with their preferences on the constitutional issue and their party choice (ibid.: 140). Although there is less survey evidence, we might expect the same to be true of Wales, but with the added complications that there is a large non-Welsh minority and a division between Welsh speakers and non-Welsh speakers. Given the nature of the issue at stake in the referendum – and the explicit appeals to national symbols and emotions made by pro-devolution campaigners – it would be surprising if voting in the referendum were not strongly influenced by voters' sense of national identity, and the data in Table 6 confirm this expectation. In Scotland, the more exclusively Scottish voters felt, the more likely they were to vote Yes–Yes. A mere 18% of those who felt British-only voted Yes–Yes, but the proportion rose, to fully 89%, of those who felt Scottish-only. The corollary also holds: the more Scottish voters felt, the less likely they were to vote No–No: only 4% of the 'exclusively Scottish' did so, compared to 69% of the 'exclusively British'. It is worth noting however, that the existence of a sense of

Scottishness, while an important influence on support for devolution, was not in itself sufficient to guarantee such support. Support for the Yes–No option, meanwhile, was rather more even across the various groups: between 8% and 15% of each national identity 'type' voted a split ticket.

A similar linear relationship between national identity and vote occurred in Wales, with the most strongly Welsh identifiers being the most likely to vote Yes (65% did so), and the least strongly Welsh being the least likely to do so (22%). Since a larger proportion of Wales' population than of Scotland's was not born there and a sense of Welsh identity is correspondingly weaker, the relationship between national identity and referendum vote goes some way towards explaining the much closer referendum vote in the Principality. However, it is also striking that the most strongly Welsh group was markedly less pro-devolution than the equivalent group in Scotland. National identity notwithstanding, Welsh voters were less enthusiastic about devolution than were Scots. In part, this is due to the cross-cutting cleavage of language within Welsh society. Turnout was higher among Welsh-speakers than among non-Welsh speakers (74% as compared with 57% in the CREST survey). And among those who voted, 66% of Welsh-speakers voted Yes, while only 45% of Welsh-born non-Welsh speakers did so.

TABLE 6
NATIONAL IDENTITY AND REFERENDUM VOTING (%)

	S/W not Brit	More S/W than Brit	Equal S/W and Brit	More Brit than S/W	Brit not S/W	Other/ None
Scotland						
Yes–Yes	89	75	42	21	18	63
Yes–No	8	12	15	8	13	12
No–No	4	14	43	71	69	24
(N)	(491)	(640)	(526)	(48)	(55)	(41)
Wales						
Yes	65	63	43	31	23	68
No	35	37	57	69	78	32
	(75)	(114)	(133)	(36)	(48)	(15)

Note: S/W = Scottish/Welsh.

As we have seen, the major campaign groups in the referendums were closely associated with the major parties, albeit with some dissension in Labour's Welsh ranks. To the extent that voters were guided by their party loyalties, therefore, the signals were clear in Scotland, though rather more muddied for Welsh Labour supporters. It is hardly surprising to find, therefore, that partisanship was an important influence on voters' choices (see Table 7). In both Scotland and Wales Conservative identifiers were strongly opposed to devolution while supporters of the nationalist parties delivered huge majorities in favour. We might speculate that those (relatively few) nationalists who voted No probably did so either because they feared that devolution would be an impediment to achieving full independence or (in Wales) were unhappy about the weakness of the proposed assembly (see McAllister, 1998b).[6] In Scotland, Labour supporters also voted heavily in favour of constitutional change but Liberal Democrats, although they did give majority support on both referendum questions, were less than enthusiastic – despite their party's historic commitment to home rule. This may reflect the fact that Liberal Democrat voters are frequently more concerned with opposing other parties than with the policy positions of their own party (see, for example, Curtice, 1996). In Wales, a large majority of Liberal Democrats voted against devolution despite their party's clear position in favour but the most important contrast with the Scottish data is that only 59% of Labour identifiers voted Yes compared with 93% voting Yes to the first question in Scotland and 85% voting Yes to both.

TABLE 7
PARTY IDENTIFICATION AND REFERENDUM VOTE (%)

	Conservative	Labour	Lib Dem	SNP/PC	None/other
Scotland					
Yes–Yes	8	85	55	90	53
Yes–No	11	8	19	7	18
No–No	81	7	26	3	29
(N)	(253)	(715)	(112)	(292)	(413)
Wales					
Yes	10	59	29	93	67
No	90	41	71	7	33
(N)	(96)	(213)	(31)	(55)	(12)

The impact of party identification can be examined in more detail by taking account of strength of identification. This is done in Table 8. Although the numbers on which the percentages are based are very small in some cases (especially for Wales) the figures are revealing. In all cases except one (Plaid Cymru) strength of party identification has the expected effect – the stronger the attachment to a party the greater the proportion of respondents which voted in line with the party's position on devolution. Among 'not very strong' Conservatives in Scotland, for example, 68% voted No–No but this rose to an overwhelming 97% of those with a very strong attachment to the party. On the other hand, 93% of 'very strong' Labour identifiers voted Yes–Yes compared with 73% of those who were 'not very strong' supporters. Most Liberal Democrat identifiers have a 'not very strong' attachment to the party and among these only a bare majority voted Yes–Yes, which goes some way to explain the relatively low overall figure for Liberal Democrats noted above. In Wales, it is striking to note that a majority of weak Labour identifiers actually voted No, contrary to party policy and despite a strong campaign by the Labour leadership to secure a substantial Yes vote. Welsh Labour's splits on devolution were clearly not confined to politicians and party activists.

TABLE 8
STRENGTH OF PARTY IDENTIFICATION AND VOTE (%)

	Conservative			Labour		
	VS	FS	NVS	VS	FS	NVS
Scotland						
Yes–Yes	0	8	11	93	87	73
Yes–No	3	7	21	5	8	10
No–No	97	85	68	2	5	17
(N)	(30)	(136)	(82)	(173)	(378)	(155)
Wales						
Yes	0	4	28	64	63	41
No	100	96	72	36	37	59
(N)	(18)	(48)	(29)	(66)	(108)	(39)

	Liberal Democrat			SNP/Plaid		
	VS	FS	NVS	VS	FS	NVS
Scotland						
Yes–Yes	83	56	51	97	88	86
Yes–No	0	26	15	1	9	8
No–No	17	19	34	1	3	6
(N)	(6)	(43)	(59)	(70)	(148)	(65)
Wales						
Yes	100	28	28	100	82	100
No	0	72	73	0	18	0
(N)	(1)	(17)	(12)	(21)	(24)	(10)

Note: VS = very strong; FS = fairly strong and NVS = not very strong.

A Multivariate Model

The three types of identity that we have examined are themselves strongly inter-related. Thus Scots who think of themselves as working class are more likely to identify themselves as Scottish and less likely to support the

Conservatives than are middle-class Scots. To disentangle the relationships between these identities and referendum voting, we conducted logistic regression analyses of Yes voting in Scotland and Wales (focusing in the Scottish case on the first vote, relating to the establishment of a parliament). The dependent variable has been coded 1 if the respondent voted for a parliament, and 0 if they did not. The independent variables are national identity, class identity and party identification (although we do not use strength of identification in the analysis – as we have noted, some of the categories involved have a very small number of cases). As is conventional with categorical variables in regression models, one category from each is included in the constant term and serves as a comparison. So in the case of the national identity variable, those who felt 'Scottish/Welsh not British' serve as the comparison group, for party it is Conservative identifiers and for class it is working class: the coefficients for the other categories tell us how much more (a positive coefficient) or less (a negative coefficient) each category was to vote Yes than the comparison group with the other two variables being held constant.

The regression equations are set out in Table 9 and they reveal striking differences between Scotland and Wales, as well as some similarities. Class identity was not significant at all in either country, once national identity and party identification is taken into account. On the other hand, party affiliation made a significant difference to voting in both countries. Compared to those who saw themselves as Conservative supporters, voters who identified with the other parties were more likely to vote in favour of devolution. For instance, Labour supporters in Scotland were over 30 times more likely to vote Yes than were Scottish Conservatives, holding class and national identity constant.[7] Welsh Labour supporters were less likely to vote Yes than their Scottish counterparts, but even so, they were still 12 times more likely to do so than were Welsh Conservatives. In both countries, Liberal Democrats were also more likely to vote Yes than Conservatives and, not surprisingly, those identifying with the Nationalist Party were the most likely of all to vote Yes (very few, indeed, did not do so). These patterns could be interpreted as meaning that, to a considerable extent, voters followed the leads given by their parties (and where the party was itself divided, as with Welsh Labour, this was reflected in the voting choices of Labour identifiers). On the other hand it could be suggested that, in Scotland at least, the stances taken by the parties on devolution merely ensured that they were in line with the stances of their supporters. It was not so much that the parties gave cues about how to vote in the referendum but rather that their campaigning reflected and emphasized the prevailing opinion among their supporters.

TABLE 9
ACCOUNTING FOR REFERENDUM VOTING: LOGISTIC REGRESSION MODELS

	(Yes vs No) Scotland	Wales
Class identity (comparison = Working class)		
Middle class	-0.16	0.43
Other/None	0.06	0.39
Party identification (comparison = Conservative)		
Labour	3.57**	2.53**
Liberal Democrat	2.29**	1.10*
Nationalist	3.72**	4.32**
Other/none	1.94**	3.01*
National identity (comparison = S/W not Brit)		
More S/W than Brit	-1.23**	0.24
Equally S/W and Brit	-2.39**	-0.25
More Brit than S/W	-3.03**	-0.77
Brit not S/W	-3.23**	-1.16*
Other/None	-1.74**	0.50
Constant	0.94	0.15
-2 log likelihood	1950.93	556.32
Model improvement	757.28	140.22
Significance	0.00	0.00
% correctly classified	85.90	72.64

Note: **   = significant at $p < 0.01$; * = significant at $p < 0.05$

The most striking feature of the multivariate analysis, however, is the very different impacts of national identity on the Scottish and Welsh votes. In Scotland, national identity was an important independent determinant of voting. The less Scottish a respondent felt, the less likely they were to vote for a parliament. Thus, compared to the most Scottish group and taking class and party into account, those who felt 'more Scottish than British' were 3.4 times less likely to vote Yes (although they were still, of course, very likely to vote Yes, the 'exclusively Scottish' were even more likely to do so). At the other end of the scale, voters who felt 'British not Scottish' were 25 times less likely to vote Yes than were the 'exclusively Scottish'. To a considerable degree, then, voting in the Scottish referendum was polarized along lines of national identity. The overwhelming victory for the 'Yes' camp rested on the very high levels of identification with Scotland among Scottish voters: 95% of voters in our sample felt some sense of Scottishness. For 63%, that identification was more important than their identification with Britain, and for a further 29% their sense of Scottishness had the same importance as their sense of Britishness.

The contrast with Wales is marked. National identity was a much less important factor underlying the Welsh vote. Only the least 'Welsh' group differed significantly from the most Welsh: they were about three times less likely to vote Yes. Even among those who felt some sense of Welshness, then, there were differences of opinion about the merits of devolution, and those differences were not particularly affected by strength of attachment to the nation. Nor does the Welsh language emerge as an important factor. When we repeated the Welsh analysis with the inclusion of a variable measuring whether respondents could speak Welsh, it proved insignificant once party identification was controlled.[8]

Conclusion

The Scottish and Welsh referendums offer lessons for how future referendums are likely to be fought and decided. Political parties were important agents. The 'umbrella' campaign organizations were short-lived and did not establish themselves as distinctive major actors in the campaign. Inevitably such organizations cannot produce a campaigning machine out of nothing and they relied heavily on the parties to do most of the campaigning. Crucially, the leaderships of all the major parties made their position on the devolution issue very clear and campaigned vigorously in support of the party line. The survey results reported here suggest that, to a considerable degree, the parties were successful in mobilizing their supporters (especially their strongest supporters) although more so in Scotland than in Wales. To the extent that future referendums are held on issues that clearly divide the parties we can expect to see party loyalty again emerging as a factor influencing voting. Where parties are internally divided on an issue (as Labour was in Wales), their leaders risk losing support from normally loyal voters.

The devolution referendums ushered in potentially far-reaching constitutional changes in the nature of the United Kingdom. The mandates conferred by the two ballots were very different, however. National identity acted as a unifying force in favour of constitutional change in Scotland but failed to do so in the more complex Welsh social and linguistic environment. The pattern of voting in Wales suggests that in politically important ways it is a divided society. It is tempting to conclude that, in contrast, the Scottish result demonstrated that devolution was indeed the 'settled will' of the Scottish people. What was 'settled', however, was that Scotland's position in the UK had to change. There remains a substantial body of opinion that sees devolution as simply a first step and favours further change – to independence. Within Scotland, the constitutional issue will remain unsettled for the foreseeable future.

ACKNOWLEDGEMENT

The referendum survey of the Scottish electorate was part of a larger study of the referendum supported by the ESRC (grant no. R000237374) which we are happy to acknowledge.

NOTES

1. On the EC referendum see Butler and Kitzinger, 1976; on the 1979 Scottish referendum see Bochel *et al.*, 1981; and on UK referendums in general see Bogdanor, 1994.
2. The Neill Committee report on party finance, published late in 1998, did, however, make recommendations relating to television coverage during referendum campaigns, aimed at achieving a 'level playing field'.
3. The Scottish data derive from a postal survey of the electorate, which we ourselves undertook immediately after the referendum (2,335 respondents). The Welsh data are from a largely face-to-face survey undertaken by the Centre for Research into Elections and Social Trends (CREST) which had 686 respondents. These data were made available through the ESRC Data Archive.
4. For a full analysis and discussion of the Scottish results see Pattie *et al.* (1998).
5. The results for measures of 'objective' class are similar to those reported in the Table 5.
6. This must remain a speculation since there are too few cases for more detailed analysis.
7. The coefficients are logits. They can be converted into relative odds by taking their natural antilogarithm.
8. In this analysis there was, in particular, a marked degree of collinearity between speaking Welsh and support for Plaid Cymru. We also incorporated variables indicating the geographical location of respondents in terms of the 'three Wales model' mentioned above, but again these proved to be not significant.

REFERENCES

Balsom, Denis, P.J. Madgwick and D. Van Mechelen (1983) 'The Red and the Green: Patterns of Partisan Choice in Wales', *British Journal of Political Science*, 13: 299–325.

Balsom, Denis (1985) 'The Three Wales Model' in J. Osmond (ed.) *The National Question Again: Welsh Political Identity in the 1980s*, pp.1–17. Dyfed: Gomer.

Bennie, Lynn, Jack Brand, and James Mitchell (1997) *How Scotland Votes,* Manchester: Manchester University Press.

Bochel, John, David Denver and Allan Macartney (1981) *The Referendum Experience: Scotland 1979,* Aberdeen: Aberdeen University Press.

Bogdanor, Vernon (1980) 'The 40 Per Cent Rule', *Parliamentary Affairs*, 33: 249–63.

Bogdanor, Vernon (1994) 'Western Europe' in David Butler and Austin Ranney (eds) *Referendums Around the World: The Growing Use of Direct Democracy,* pp.24–97. Washington: AEI Press.

Borland, John, Ralph Fevre and David Denney (1992) 'Nationalism and Community in North West Wales', *The Sociological Review*, 40, 49–72.

Brown, Alice, David McCrone and Lindsay Paterson (1996) *Politics and Society in Scotland,* London: Macmillan.

Butler, David and Uwe Kitzinger (1976) *The 1975 Referendum*, London: Macmillan.

Curtice, John (1996) 'Who votes for the centre now?' in D. MacIver (ed.) *The Liberal Democrats*, pp.191–204, Hemel Hempstead: Prentice Hall.

Field, William (1997) *Regional Dynamics: The Basis of Electoral Support in Britain*, London and Portland, OR: Frank Cass.

Fisher, Justin (1997) 'Third and Minor Party Breakthrough?' in A. Geddes and J. Tonge (eds) *Labour's Landslide*, pp.53–67, Manchester, Manchester University Press.

Jones, Barry (1997) 'Wales: A Developing Political Economy', in Michael Keating and John

Loughlin (eds), *The Political Economy of Regionalism*, pp.388–405. London amd Portland, OR: Frank Cass.

Kellas, James (1980) *Modern Scotland* (2nd edition), London: George Allen and Unwin.

Kellas, James (1973) *The Scottish Political System*, Cambridge: Cambridge University Press.

McAllister, Laura (1998a) 'The Perils of Community as a Construct for the Political Ideology of Welsh Nationalism', *Government and Opposition*, 33: 497–517.

McAllister, Laura (1998b) 'The Welsh Devolution Referendum: Definitely, Maybe?', *Parliamentary Affairs*, 51: 149–65.

Miller, William L. (1981) *The End of British Politics? Scots and English Political Behaviour in the Seventies*, Oxford: Oxford University Press.

Mitchell, James (1996) *Strategies for Self-Government: The Campaigns for a Scottish Parliament*, Edinburgh: Polygon.

Pattie, Charles, David Denver, James Mitchell and Hugh Bochel (1998) 'The 1997 Scottish Referendum: An Analysis of the Results', *Scottish Affairs*, 22: 1–15.

The Absence of War?
New Labour in Parliament

Philip Cowley

Party cohesion has been a marked feature of British parliamentary life since the end of the nineteenth century. Party votes – those in which 90 per cent or more of the members of one party vote one way, facing 90 per cent or more of the members of the other principal party – were the norm by the end of the century (Lowell, 1926). Cohesion became ever greater in the twentieth century. Voting in the period from 1945 to 1970 was characterized by extraordinarily high levels of party cohesion (Norton, 1975). From 1970 onwards, however, things changed. Members of Parliament (MPs) in the three parliaments of the 1970s voted against their own side on more occasions than before, in greater numbers and with greater effect (Norton, 1975, 1980). Having previously claimed that party cohesion was 'so close to 100 per cent that there was no longer any point in measuring it' (1969: 350–1), Samuel Beer was now to talk of the 'rise of Parliament' (1982: 181; also see Schwarz, 1980).

Such rebellious behaviour continued through the 1980s and into the 1990s. Even with the large majorities enjoyed by Conservatives in the 1980s, government MPs proved willing to defeat the government (Norton, 1985). Mrs Thatcher's governments suffered one clear defeat in each parliament: on the immigration rules in 1982, on the Shops Bill in 1986 (Bown, 1990; Regan, 1990), and on the National Health Service and Community Care Bill in 1990. There were also rebellions and government defeats in standing committee (Melhuish and Cowley, 1995; Cowley, 1998). The limited number of the defeats was primarily a matter of parliamentary arithmetic: MPs continued to be willing to defeat the government but found the size of the majorities too great in all but a small number of cases (Cowley and Norton, 1998).

When the parliamentary arithmetic changed in 1992, rebellions were suddenly much more significant. The Major government suffered four defeats as a result of its own backbenchers rebelling and avoided others only by a mixture of threats, concessions and procedural manoeuvres (Cowley and Norton, 1999). Between 1992 and 1997, the behaviour of the Conservative Parliamentary Party was vital. It effected several changes in policy – either through defeats or through the threat of defeat – and was the focus of media attention. The Conservatives lost their reputation for unity, a reputation they had long-possessed, largely (though not solely) because of the perceived behaviour of their MPs (Crewe, 1996; Cowley, 1997).

Before the 1997 election, the real possibility of a Labour government prompted renewed interest in the behaviour of Labour MPs, not only among academics and journalists (Blevin and Day, 1996; Cowley *et al.*, 1996, Richards, 1996; Riddell, 1996; also see Bale, 1997), but also within the party's own ranks (see Cowley *et al.*, 1996: 1–2). Such interest was understandable, for the behaviour of the Parliamentary Labour Party (PLP) was (and is) an issue of great importance. The PLP fulfils two vital functions – one legislative, the other political – for the government. In political terms, it is a focus of attention for the national media. In legislative terms, it could (and should) be the bulk vote that delivers the programme of the government. If that bulk vote splits, then promised (or hoped for) legislation may not be delivered. Loose cannons, therefore, are dangerous, whether they are in the division lobbies of the House of Commons or the Millbank television centre, broadcasting their opinions to the nation.

The size of Labour's 1997 majority – the biggest since 1935, and Labour's biggest ever – may make government defeats unlikely (though not impossible), but it does not mean that Tony Blair can be blasé about the opinions of his parliamentary party. Even failed rebellions have the potential both to influence policy and to be an embarrassment. And Labour MPs have done both aplenty in the past. Labour's parliamentarians have 'form'. They have, traditionally, been more troublesome than the Conservatives, especially when in government: the three previous periods of Labour government since the war have all seen significant (and increasing) levels of rebellion.

So what – if anything – has happened? This article is an analysis of the behaviour of Labour MPs in the first session of the 1997 parliament. Have they continued to rebel, in line with their historical record? Or has harmony replaced strife? Has there been an absence of war?

Methodology

The voting procedures in the House of Commons score highly in terms of transparency (Rekosh, 1995: 229–39, 294–5). That is important in terms of democratic accountability – since electors can see how their elected representatives have voted – and it is also invaluable in terms of scholarship: the published records of divisions (that is, votes) yield a mass of what David Truman (1959) has termed 'hard data'.

Yet the data are not perfect. Printing errors (such as the names of MPs being mixed-up) are not frequent but neither are they rare. Some errors are obvious (such as when a minister votes against their own government, for example), but others have to be resolved by checking with the MP concerned. As a result of these checks, three 'rebellions' by Labour MPs – recorded in Hansard but disputed by the MPs – have been removed from the data for this parliament. Hansard recorded Phil Woolas (Oldham East and Saddleworth) as voting against the government in only the third division of the parliament during the debate on the Queen's Speech. This would have been a brave act for any newly-elected government MP, but, in fact, Hansard had confused Phil Woolas with Phil Willis, the Liberal Democrat MP for Harrogate and Knaresborough. Similarly, although Hansard recorded Dan Norris (Wansdyke) as voting for a Liberal Democrat reasoned amendment on the Second Reading of the Social Security Bill on 22 July 1997, and Russell Brown (Dumfries) as voting against the Third Reading of the Bank of England Bill, both claim that these 'rebellions' are simply Hansard mistakes.

A further drawback of divisions in the House of Commons is that, unlike in some legislative chambers, abstentions cannot be formally recorded.[1] The whips may formally sanction an absence from a vote, it may be accidental, or it may be deliberate. There is no information on the record that allows us to establish, at least not systematically, the cause of absences. We cannot therefore necessarily read anything into non-voting. For the purpose of systematic analysis over time, therefore, we have to rely on the votes cast.

The article examines the votes cast by Labour MPs in the 380 divisions of the first session of the parliament. The focus of the article is on dissenting votes, that is, those occasions when one or more Labour members vote against their own party whip or the apparently clear wishes (sometimes implicit) of their own front bench. This is the definition employed in earlier research (Norton, 1980, x). And as in previous research, excluded from the analysis are votes on matters of private legislation, private members' bills, matters internal to the House of Commons, and other free votes.

The Rebellions

There have been a total of 16 separate rebellions by Labour MPs thus far this parliament.

The first rebellion came at the Second Reading of the European Parliamentary Elections Bill on 25 November 1997. One Labour MP, Jamie Cann (Ipswich) voted against the Bill, believing that it breached 'the traditional accountability of member to constituency'.[2] The Bill saw a second small revolt on 24 February 1998, when two Labour MPs – Austin Mitchell (Great Grimsby) and Andrew Mackinlay (Thurrock) – voted for an amendment to extend the right to vote in European Elections to Gibraltarians.

The Social Security Bill saw a total of three rebellions on 10 December 1997. Two of these rebellions were minor, involving one and five Labour MPs respectively, the latter taking place on Third Reading.[3] The second of the three rebellions, however, saw some 47 Labour MPs vote against a reduction in lone-parent benefit (along with a considerable number of deliberate abstentions).[4] This was to be the largest Labour rebellion of the session.[5]

The second sizeable Labour rebellion occurred over military action against Iraq on 17 February 1998. A total of 23 Labour MPs – including the two tellers – voted against the government on a motion that 'fully support[ed] the resolve of the Government to use all necessary means to achieve an outcome consistent with [the Security Council] resolutions'.[6]

The issue of education has attracted rebellions on two separate bills. The Schools Standards and Framework Bill saw two MPs – Tony Benn (Chesterfield) and Jeremy Corbyn (Islington North) – dissent on 24 March 1998. The Teaching and Higher Education Bill saw two rebellions.[7] The first, on 8 June, saw 34 Labour MPs – including the two tellers – vote for an amendment, which would have retained maintenance grants for students from low-income families. There were also a number of abstentions.[8] The second, on 1 July 1998, saw just one MP, Dennis Canavan (Falkirk, West), vote against his party whip.

The Human Rights Bill saw one small rebellion on 2 July 1998, when Jeremy Corbyn (Islington North), supported a Liberal Democrat clause on the guaranteeing of non-discrimination. Six days later, the Report Stage of the Competition Bill saw 25 Labour MPs vote for a backbench amendment on newspaper ownership.

There were four rebellions following the recall of parliament to discuss the Criminal Justice (Terrorism and Conspiracy) Bill. The first, objecting to the timetable motion, saw 16 Labour MPs rebel. The second saw 19 vote in favour of a reasoned amendment at Second Reading. The third, on an amendment moved by Chris Mullin that would have required the audio recording of suspects, was supported by 29 MPs. And the fourth, concerning the Bill's application to conspiracy to commit offences outside the United Kingdom, saw 18 rebel. The four rebellions together involved a total of 37 Labour members, of whom eight rebelled on all four votes.[9]

The final rebellion of the session came on 11 November 1998, when Dennis Canavan voted with the Opposition against over-turning a Lords amendment which would have allowed the Scottish parliament to have decided its own representation.

The Rebellions in Context

These 16 rebellions mean that there were rebellions by Labour MPs in just four per cent of divisions in the first session of the parliament. In absolute terms, this is clearly not a high level of dissent: it means that slightly fewer than one division out of every 20 saw a rebellion – no matter how small – by a Labour MP. The others saw complete cohesion.

Of more interest, though, is to view the rebellions in relative terms. How does the behaviour of Labour MPs in the first session of this parliament compare to that of government MPs in previous parliaments? Table 1 shows the frequency and size of rebellions by government MPs in the first sessions of all the post-war parliaments.

TABLE 1
REBELLIONS BY GOVERNMENT MPs IN FIRST SESSIONS 1945–98

Parliament	N	As % of divs	Max	As % of MPs	Mean	As % of MPs
1945	**10**	n.a.	**32**	**8**	**15**	**4**
1950	**1**	n.a.	**7**	**2**	**7**	**2**
1951	2	n.a.	22	7	12	4
1955	7	n.a.	22	6	4	1
1959	17	n.a.	13	4	3	1
1964	**0**	**0**	**0**	**0**	**0**	**0**
1966	**9**	n.a.	**59**	**16**	**15**	**4**
1970	7	n.a.	39	12	10	3
1974F	**8**	n.a.	**76**	**25**	**35**	**12**
1974O	**54**	n.a.	**145**	**45**	**29**	**9**
1979	32	6	48	14	8	2
1983	76	16	42	11	7	2
1987	61	12	38	10	8	2
1992	**93**	**23**	**41**	**12**	**13**	**4**
1997	**16**	**4**	**47**	**11**	**14**	**3**

n.a.= data not available

Note: The parliament of February 1974 had only one session. Bold indicates a Labour government.

There were fewer rebellions in the 1997 session than in the first sessions of six of the post-war parliaments (those of 1959, October 1974, 1979, 1983, 1987 and 1992). Indeed, the comparison between this session and the first session of some of the more recent parliaments is striking. The first session of every parliament from October 1974 onwards has seen noticeably more rebellions. By this stage of the 1992 parliament, for example, government (Conservative) MPs had rebelled on 93 occasions, almost six times as often as Tony Blair's MPs.

This appears to support those who argue that Labour MPs are being particularly timid at the moment. However, two pieces of evidence point to an opposite conclusion. First, there have been more rebellions in the first session of this parliament than in the first sessions of eight of the post-war parliaments (those of 1945, 1950, 1951, 1955, 1964, 1966, 1970 and February 1974). In crude arithmetic terms, then, Labour MPs thus far this parliament have been more rebellious than government MPs in the majority of the previous post-war parliaments. To be sure, most (but not all) of these parliaments are before the 1970s, when the cohesion of parliamentary parties began to loosen, but it is still evidence that suggests that any claim that Labour MPs are now highly cohesive needs to be clear about its time-frame. Labour MPs are currently rebelling less frequently than MPs in recent parliaments, but seen over a longer perspective there is nothing particularly unusual about their behaviour.

Second, whether we consider the size of the largest rebellion (the fourth column in Table 1) or the mean size of all the rebellions in the first session (column six), we find that Labour MPs are now rebelling in greater numbers than government MPs in many of the previous parliaments. The 47 MPs who rebelled over lone-parent benefits constitute a larger rebellion than any by government MPs in the first session of all but four post-war parliaments (those of 1966, February and October 1974 and 1979). And only four parliaments (1945, 1966, and the two of 1974) have seen larger mean rebellions in the first session.

However, when considering the size of any rebellions, one needs to bear in mind that there are currently far more government MPs around than usual: the 418 Labour MPs elected in May 1997 constitute the largest parliamentary party since 1935. We can take this into account by expressing the size of rebellion as a percentage figure (as in columns five and seven of Table 1). Seen in this way, the largest rebellion (at 11 per cent of the PLP) is larger or the same as the largest rebellion in the first sessions of eight post-war parliaments, and is only marginally smaller (by 1 percentage point) than the largest rebellion in a further two. The mean rebellion (at 3 per cent) is as big or bigger than in eight of the post-war parliaments and smaller than in six.

Thus it would be wrong to portray Labour MPs as having been especially timid in this first session. To be sure, they are rebelling infrequently (and less frequently than government MPs in most of the more recent parliaments) but when they do rebel they are rebelling in numbers (or at least in numbers which are on a par with, or greater than, the rebellions seen in most recent parliaments).

It may also be that the first session of a parliament – particularly the first session of a parliament following a change in government – is atypical of the rest of the parliament. Table 2 shows the relationship between rebellions in the first and other sessions of all post-war parliaments.

TABLE 2
RELATIONSHIP BETWEEN FIRST AND OTHER SESSIONS 1945–97

Parliament (number of sessions)	Number of rebellions in first session	Number of rebellions in parliament	Mean number of rebellions per session
1945 (4)	10	79	20
1950 (2)	1	5	3
1951 (4)	2	11	3
1955 (4)	7	12	3
1959 (5)	17	120	24
1964 (2)	0	1	1
1966 (4)	9	109	27
1970 (4)	7	204	51
1974F (1)	8	8	8
1974O (5)	54	309	62
1979 (4)	32	159	40
1983 (4)	76	203	51
1987 (5)	61	198	40
1992 (5)	93	174	35

Note: The parliament of February 1974 had only one session. Bold indicates a Labour
        government.

As can be seen, in most parliaments the first session sees a lower than
average number of rebellions. Only in four parliaments (those of 1955,
1983, 1987 and 1992) has the first session been more rebellious than the
sessions in the rest of the parliament. In all the others – save for February
1974, where there was only one session in the parliament – the first session
has been less rebellious than the rest of the parliament. Importantly, this is
true of *all* the first sessions following a change of the party in government
(again, excluding February 1974: that is, 1945, 1951, 1964, 1970 and 1979).
It is also true of *every* period of Labour government.

While there is no guarantee that this PLP will behave as PLPs (and
Conservative parliamentary parties) have in the past, the data strongly
suggest that this first session of the parliament has been atypical of what is
to come: not only are future sessions of this parliament likely to see further
dissent, therefore, but they are likely to see disproportionately more dissent.

Who are the rebels?

Taken together, the 16 rebellions have involved a total of 78 Labour MPs
(around 19 per cent of the parliamentary party).[10] This figure is slightly
lower than for the more recent parliaments: by (roughly) this stage in the
1979 parliament, for example, 30 per cent of government (Conservative)
MPs had rebelled. The figures for the three parliaments that followed were

39, 37 and 22 per cent respectively. Yet this figure is important, because it suggests that the tendency (or ability) to rebel is not to be found solely among a small handful of the party. Rather, almost one in five of the PLP (or around one in four of the backbenchers) have already shown that they will, if necessary, defy their whips.

This is not to argue that these 78 MPs will be persistent rebels. We have not identified 78 rebels waiting for causes: some of these MPs may cast no further dissenting votes this parliament. But it remains a useful corrective to those who believe that Labour's MPs now behave like Daleks.[11]

Of the 78, most have not rebelled frequently: 27 have cast just one dissenting vote, another 41 have cast between 2 and 5 dissenting votes, and 10 have cast more than 5. Table 3 lists these top ten dissenters. Jeremy Corbyn and Dennis Canavan head the list, both of whom have so far cast a total of 11 votes against the party line.

TABLE 3
TOP TEN LABOUR REBELS IN THE 1997 PARLIAMENT

Name	Number of dissenting votes
J. Corbyn (Islington North)	11
D. Canavan (Falkirk West)	11
J. McDonnell (Hayes and Harlington)	9
D. Skinner (Bolsover)	8
T. Benn (Chesterfield)	8
L. Jones (Birmingham Selly Oak)	7
J. McAllion (Dundee East)	7
A. Wise (Preston)	7
T. Dalyell (Linlithgow)	6
B. Grant (Tottenham)	6

What characteristics – if any – define these rebels? Three are of particular interest: the cohort differences, the gender differences, and the extent to which the rebels have 'form'.

Cohort Differences

Before the last election, Tony Blair placed great emphasis on the extent to which new Labour MPs would be New Labour MPs. He told the *New Statesman* (5 July 1996):

> the new intake of MPs in 1992 were of a very high calibre. And they supported the need to modernise, on the whole. I think that the next intake will do so even more.

If Blair is right, we should find less dissent among newly-elected MPs than among those who had entered the Commons before the 1997 election; and we should also find less rebellion from those who entered at the 1992 election than before.

And indeed, the new intake *is* less rebellious than those with prior service. Of the 184 new MPs – that is, who were elected in 1997[12] – 23 (13 per cent) rebelled at least once in the first session. Of these, 13 – listed in Table 4 – have rebelled on more than one occasion. By contrast, of the 235 MPs elected before 1997, 55 (23 per cent) have rebelled at least once, of whom 38 have done so twice or more. The difference between the two groups is statistically significant (p<0.01).

TABLE 4
MOST REBELLIOUS NEW MPs IN THE 1997 PARLIAMENT

Name	Number of dissenting votes
J. McDonnell (Hayes and Harlington)	9
A. Cryer (Keighley)	5
H. Best (Leeds North West)	5
K. Pollard (St Albans)	4
K. Hopkins (Luton North)	4
J. Cryer (Hornchurch)	3
R. Marshall-Andrews (Medway)	3
M. Caton (Gower)	2
I. Gibson (Norwich North)	2
B. Iddon (Bolton South East)	2
T. McWalter (Hemel Hempstead)	2
I. Stewart (Eccles)	2
M. Wood (Batley and Spen)	2

Furthermore, of the 163 MPs first elected before the 1992 election, 42 (26 per cent) have rebelled, compared to 13 of the 65 (20 per cent) elected at the 1992 election (although the differences are not statistically significant). Thus, in line with Blair's claim, those elected in 1997 are less rebellious than those elected in 1992, who are, in turn, less rebellious than those elected before 1992 (see also Norris, 1998).

Two factors potentially complicate this analysis. First, there is the possible effect of socialization on dissent; and second, there is the possible distortion caused by the scale of Labour's victory.

Socialization

The pressures on new MPs may make their behaviour in their first parliamentary session atypical. The newly-elected may always be less likely to rebel than their peers. If so, those elected in 1997 may appear to be loyal now, but their behaviour may change later. However, evidence from previous parliaments does not support such a view. Table 5 shows the percentage of newly-elected MPs to have rebelled in the first session of the last four parliaments and compares it to incumbent MPs. The table gives an overall figure along with separate figures for the two main parties.[13]

TABLE 5
REBELLIOUSNESS OF NEW AND INCUMBENT MPs, BY PARLIAMENT AND PARTY, 1979–97

	Incumbents %	Newly-elected %
1979		
Conservative	23	54
Labour	62	85
Both	41	66
1983		
Conservative	34	54
Labour	48	77
Both	39	60
1987		
Conservative	37	36
Labour	43	56
Both	39	48
1992		
Conservative	23	17
Labour	54	70
Both	36	48

Of the 12 pairs of figures, in only one case – those Conservative MPs first elected in 1992 – are the newly-elected less likely to rebel than the incumbents. Indeed, quite the reverse: in the past, newly-elected MPs have been *more* likely, often much more likely, to rebel than the incumbents. Thus it seems unlikely that newly-elected MPs are being more loyal merely as they find their feet at Westminster.

The problems of a large majority

The second complication is caused by the size of Labour's majority. The scale of Labour's victory brought in many MPs who were not expected by their party (and often by themselves) to win their seats. These MPs – named the 'unlikely lads' by one of their number – were not as carefully vetted by the party in advance, and their election brought fears within the party hierarchy that they might cause trouble within parliament (see Draper, 1997: 8).[14]

This does not yet appear to be happening on a significant scale. Of the 23 rebels who won their seats at the 1997 election, six 'inherited' Labour seats (that is, the seat for which they were elected was one already held by Labour), seven won 'key seats', and ten came in unexpectedly. Thus of the 44 MPs who inherited, 14 per cent have rebelled; of the 80 who won key seats, 9 per cent have rebelled, and of the 60 who came in unexpectedly, 17 per cent have rebelled. Those elected in the key seats, then, appear to be the most loyal; those elected unexpectedly, the least loyal. However, the differences are not statistically significant. Moreover, those who inherited – and about whose victory Labour could have been most certain – are almost as rebellious as those who came in unexpectedly. At present, then, the presence of a group of 'unlikely lads' and lasses on the Labour benches is having little effect on the levels of dissension.[15]

Gender Differences

The most striking single feature of the 1997 Labour intake was the presence of so many women MPs (see, for example, McDougall, 1998). The most striking feature of the rebellions so far this parliament, however, has been the lack of women, especially newly-elected women, among those rebelling.

In each of the five main rebellions during the first session women were consistently under-represented among the rebels. For example, 8 per cent of women MPs rebelled over lone-parent benefit, compared with 12 per cent of men. Over Iraq the figures were 3 per cent and 6 per cent; over student grants, they were 6 per cent and 9 per cent; over newspaper ownership, 5 and 6 per cent; and over terrorism they were 8 and 9 per cent. In total 21 per cent of male Labour MPs have rebelled so far this parliament, compared to 10 per cent of female Labour MPs (a difference that is significant at $p < 0.01$).

However, the real difference is not between men and women but between newly-elected women and (almost) everyone else. There is, for example, practically no difference between the behaviour of incumbent men (24 per cent of whom have rebelled) and incumbent women (22 per cent of whom have rebelled). Of the 119 newly-elected men, 21 (18 per cent) have rebelled; but of newly-elected women, just two – Ann Cryer and Christine Butler – have broken ranks so far. They constitute just 3 per cent of newly-elected female Labour MPs (with the difference between them and newly-elected men being significant at $p < 0.01$). This loyalty has attracted media comment, much of it hostile to women (see for example Purves, 1997; Mitchell, 1998; Watkins, 1998), of which the most hostile was Brian Sedgemore's comparison of the women with the Stepford Wives (*The Times*, 7 February 1998).

This high level of loyalty among newly-elected women is one of the reasons why newly-elected MPs overall appear so loyal (see above). Newly-elected men are also more loyal than incumbents, but around half of the difference between the 1997 intake and all others is explained by the large number of very loyal female members.

What explains this? Given that so much of the parliament has yet to come, and given that the overall number of rebellions is now low, it is probably better not to attempt to analyse this difference in too much detail. It may be that these differences will even out after more votes. However, it is worth briefly rejecting three explanations as clearly erroneous.

First, this is not a pattern seen before with women MPs. If anything, in the past, women members have been slightly more rebellious than their male counterparts. In every parliament since 1979, women MPs have been – slightly – more likely to have rebelled than male MPs. The same is true when examining only the behaviour of women Labour MPs. And, as noted above, those women who were in the Commons before 1997 are currently behaving no differently from their male counterparts. This suggests that any explanation for the gender difference needs to look at this particular batch of women MPs and their circumstances rather than at women *qua* women.

Second, it is unlikely to have been caused by the use of all-women shortlists, the system of gender quotas which Labour employed during the selection process in order to raise the number of women candidates in winnable seats. It has been argued that this process brought into parliament MPs who, because they had not been subject to the full rigours of an open competition for their candidature, were not up to the job.[16] Ann Widdecombe, for example, has complained of the 'docility and absence of ability' displayed by many of the new women MPs (*Sunday Times*, 4 October 1998). She has linked this directly to the use of all-women shortlists, arguing that:

Serious politicians arrive in the House already battle-hardened... Blair's Babes have arrived with starry eyes and a pager, shielded by positive discrimination from any real competition. They nod in unison behind the front bench... Some of the dear little souls have even whinged that Madam Speaker is too hard on them and indeed has caused more than one to burst into tears. Can anyone imagine Bessie Braddock, Barbara Castle or Margaret Thatcher dissolving at a ticking off from the Speaker?

The problem with this line of argument is that only about half of the newly-elected Labour women MPs were selected from all-women lists (Criddle, 1997); and there is no evidence of a difference between those so selected and those not. The newly-elected Labour women MPs are not rebelling, no matter how they were selected. Shortlists, then, are not the explanation.

Third, it also seems unlikely that the type of seat for which the women are sitting causes the difference. As noted above, there were no significant differences in propensity to rebel between MPs representing different types of seat. In other words, controlling for type of seat makes no difference to the conclusion.

Whatever happened to Blair's Bastards?

In 1996 a paper was published with the rather scurrilous title *Blair's Bastards* (Cowley *et al.*, 1996). Based on analysis of rebellions in the last parliament (up to May 1996), the paper attempted to identify those MPs then on the Labour benches who were likely to cause trouble for any incoming Labour government. It was dismissed by the Labour Party as 'academic nonsense' (*Sunday Telegraph*, 23 August 1996), a badge worn with some pride by at least one of its authors. The paper identified 38 Labour MPs (six of whom are no longer in the Commons) who had rebelled against the party line on at least 20 occasions. Table 6 lists the number of dissenting votes cast in the last parliament by the other 32, as well as showing the number of dissenting votes cast by the same MPs so far this parliament.

All but two of the MPs in that list rebelled in the first session: the 30 rebel MPs identified in *Blair's Bastards* are just 7 per cent of the PLP, but they amount to almost 40 per cent of those who rebelled. They thus form the core of any parliamentary rebellion, especially as they tend to have rebelled more often than other rebels: of the ten most rebellious MPs, all except two were identified in *Blair's Bastards*. The two are: John McDonnell (who was not an MP in 1992) and Tam Dalyell, who cast 13 dissenting votes in the last parliament, placing him outside the 38 most rebellious MPs. And the list included Alice Mahon, Malcolm Chisholm and Neil Gerrard, all of whom resigned from the government over the issue of lone-parent benefits. Some of the press coverage of Chisholm's resignation presented his discontent as surprising (see, for example, *The Times*, 11 December 1997): in fact, as Table 6 shows, he was the (joint) 25th most frequent dissenter in the last parliament. Rather than being nonsense – academic or otherwise – the list appears to have been a very good predictor of MPs' behaviour.

TABLE 6

NUMBER OF DISSENTING VOTES CAST IN 1997 PARLIAMENT BY MPs IDENTIFIED IN
BLAIR'S BASTARDS AS THE MOST REBELLIOUS IN THE 1992 PARLIAMENT

Rank	Name	1992	1997
1	D. Skinner	121	8
2	H. Barnes	80	2
3	J. Corbyn	72	11
4	A. Mahon	55	3
5	D. Canavan	52	11
jnt 6	T. Lewis	49	3
jnt 6	K. Livingstone	49	4
8	A. Simpson	45	3
9	A. Wise	44	7
jnt 10	T. Benn	41	8
jnt 10	A. Bennett	41	2
12	H. Cohen	40	2
13	N. Godman	39	2
14	T. Davis	37	0
15	B. Michie	35	2
jnt 16	B. Grant	34	6
jnt 16	L. Jones	34	7
18	D. Abbott	32	4
19	L. Smith	30	3
jnt 20	R. Campbell	26	2
jnt 20	D. Davies	26	1
jnt 20	N. Gerrard	26	3
jnt 23	G. Dunwoody	25	3
jnt 23	D. Winnick	25	2
jnt 25	J. Austin	24	2
jnt 25	M. Chisholm	24	1
jnt 25	J. Marshall	24	1
jnt 25	A. Mitchell	24	2
29	J. McAllion	23	7
30	J. Cann	22	1
31	M. Connarty	21	0
32	I. Davidson	20	2

Conclusion

So early into the parliament it would be unwise to make too many firm
observations (let alone any predictions) about the behaviour of Labour's
mass of MPs. Parliamentary behaviour is not a constant: much can and does
change from session to session, depending on the issues of the day and the
government's handling of them (Cowley and Norton, 1998). However, three
broad conclusions can be identified, both because they are of intrinsic
interest, and because they may be pointers – however rough – to the rest of
the parliament. First, Labour MPs are currently rebelling infrequently, in
both absolute terms, and by comparison to most of the recent parliaments.
However, there is nothing exceptional about their behaviour when

compared to all post-war parliaments, and when they do rebel they are doing so in respectable numbers. Second, newly-elected MPs are the most loyal, with newly-elected women even more loyal – quite staggeringly so – than newly-elected men. And third, there are few surprise names among those who choose to rebel, especially those who choose to rebel frequently: most could be (and were) identified by their behaviour in the last parliament.

ACKNOWLEDGEMENTS

The research for this article was funded by a grant from the University of Hull's Research Support Fund. This largesse enabled me to pay Mark Stuart to do all the hard work, something for which I am very grateful. The article also draws on research on previous parliaments funded by the ESRC (R000 23 5320). Earlier versions of the article were delivered to the EPOP Conference in Manchester in September 1998 and to seminars at the Universities of Essex and Hull in November 1998. The author is grateful for the comments of all participants.

NOTES

1. Recent proposals to allow recording of abstentions met with a positive reaction from parliamentarians. See HC 779 (1998).
2. Letter to author.
3. The rebellion on Third Reading also almost certainly saw a number of abstentions, including Alan Simpson, Neil Gerrard and Maria Fyfe.
4. *The Times* (12 Dec. 1997) claimed 25 deliberate abstentions, of whom they identified ten: Julie and Rhodri Morgan, George Galloway, Chris Mullin, Harry Cohen, Diana Organ, William Rammell, Tony McWalter, John Naysmith and Huw Edwards. *The Guardian* (11 Dec. 1997) listed 13, of whom Gerald Steinberg, Andrew Bennett, Lawrence Cunliffe and Jim Marshall are in addition to those listed in *The Times*.
5. In an article in *The Times* on 4 Aug. 1998 ('Why I Feared Frank'), Peter Lilley claimed that the revolt involved 'more than 100 Labour MPs – bigger than any revolt John Major ever faced'. This is an erroneous claim for two reasons. First, because one can only arrive at a figure of more than 100 by adding together the 47 who voted with the 57 who did not, something that for reasons explained in the text is a wholly fatuous exercise. And second, because even without including abstentions, John Major faced three rebellions of greater size, all during the passage of the Firearms (Amendment) Bill, the largest of which saw 95 Conservative MPs vote against their whips.
6. The figure of 23 includes Mohammad Sarwar, suspended from the PLP, and casting just his eighth vote in the House since his election.
7. In addition, there was a rebellion on 8 June – over the so-called 'Scottish anomaly' – which saw no dissenting votes but a number of abstentions. The BBC News On-Line report gave the number of abstainers at 13, including Ken Livingstone, Tony Benn, Jeremy Corbyn, Audrey Wise and Lynne Jones.
8. The BBC News On-Line report gave the number of abstentions at 15.
9. They were Dennis Canavan, Jeremy Corbyn, Tam Dalyell, Lynne Jones, John McAllion, John McDonnell, Kevin McNamara and Dennis Skinner.
10. This figure includes Mohammad Sarwar.
11. See, for example, *The Sunday Times,* 29 March 1998. The simile is correct in only one sense: just like Labour, the Daleks usually lost.
12. This includes Douglas Alexander, the winner of the Paisley South by-election, but excludes Peter Temple-Morris.
13. The overall figure excludes members of third and minor parties.

14. Also see 'Millbank's Danger List of Rebels', *Sunday Times,* 23 Nov. 1997, which claimed that Labour had identified 20 'suspect' MPs.
15. Excluding the unexpected victors, some 10 per cent of newly-elected MPs have rebelled. Including them raises the figure by just three percentage points.
16. Indeed, this author was (mis)quoted as saying something similar when this research was first reported in the media. See *The Observer,* 20 Sept. 1998.

REFERENCES

Bale, Tim (1997) 'Managing the Party and the Trade Unions', in Brian Brivati and Tim Bale (eds) *New Labour in Power,* pp.159–78. London: Routledge.
Beer, Samuel (1969) *Modern British Politics,* London: Faber & Faber.
Beer, Samuel (1982) *Britain Against Itself,* London: Faber & Faber.
Blevin, J. and A. Day (1996) 'Poll Shock: New Labour Candidates Take Left turn', *Tribune,* 26 April.
Bown, Francis A.C.S. (1990) 'The Shops Bill', in Michael Rush (ed.) *Parliament and Pressure Politics,* pp.213–33. Oxford: Oxford University Press.
Cowley, Philip (1997) 'The Conservative Party: Decline and Fall', in Andrew Geddes and Jonathan Tonge (eds) *Labour's Landslide,* pp.37–50. Manchester: Manchester University Press.
Cowley, Philip (1999) 'Cohesion or Chaos? The Conservative Parliamentary Party', in Peter Dorey (ed.) *The Major Premiership.* London: Macmillan.
Cowley, Philip and Philip Norton (1998) 'Rebelliousness in the British House of Commons', unpublished paper presented to the Third Workshop of Parliamentary Scholars and Parliamentarians, Oxford.
Cowley, Philip and Philip Norton (1999) 'Rebels and Rebellions. Conservative MPs in the 1992 Parliament', *British Journal of Politics and International Relations* 1: 84–105.
Cowley, Philip and Philip Norton with Mark Stuart and Matthew Bailey (1996), *Blair's Bastards: Discontent within the Parliamentary Labour Party,* Research Papers in Legislative Studies 1/96 (University of Hull)
Draper, Derek (1997) *Blair's Hundred Days,* London: Faber & Faber.
Crewe, Ivor (1996) '1979–1996', in Anthony Seldon (ed.) *How Tory Governments Fall,* pp.393–451. London: Fontana.
Criddle, Byron (1997) 'MPs and Candidates', in David Butler and Dennis Kavanagh, *The British General Election of 1997,* pp.186–209. London: Macmillan.
HC 779 (1998), The Sixth Report from the Select Committee on Modernisation of the House of Commons, 'Voting Methods', London: The Stationery Office.
Lowell, A.L. (1926) *The Government of England,* London: Macmillan (Vol.2).
McDougall, Linda (1998) *Westminster Women,* London: Vintage.
Melhuish, David and Philip Cowley (1995) 'Whither the New Role in Policy Making? Conservative MPs in Standing Committees 1979 to 1992', *The Journal of Legislative Studies* 1: 54–75
Mitchell, Austin (1998) 'Why I Am Sick of Women MPs', *Independent on Sunday,* 18 Jan.
Norris, Pippa (1998) 'New Labour, New Politicians? Changes in the Political Attitudes of Labour MPs 1992–1997', in A. Dobson and J. Stanyer (eds) *Contemporary Political Studies 1998,* pp.766–80. Nottingham: Political Studies Association (Vol.2).
Norton, Philip (1975) *Dissension in the House of Commons 1945–74,* London: Macmillan.
Norton, Philip (1980) *Dissension in the House of Commons 1974–1979,* Oxford: Clarendon Press.
Norton, Philip (1985) 'Behavioural Changes', in Philip Norton (ed.) *Parliament in the 1980s,* pp.22–47. Oxford: Blackwell.
Purves, L. (1997) 'Blair's Babes in the Wood', *The Times,* 2 Dec.
Regan, Paul (1990) 'The 1986 Shops Bill', *Parliamentary Affairs,* 41: 218–35
Rekosh, E. (1995) (ed.) *In the Public Eye: Parliamentary Transparency in Europe and North America,* Washington, DC: International Human Rights Law Group.

Richards, S. (1996) 'Politics', *New Statesman,* 13 Dec.
Riddell, Peter (1996) 'The Ins and Outs of Power', *The Times,* 25 March.
Schwarz, John E. (1980) 'Exploring a New Role in Policy-Making: The British House of Commons in the 1970s', *American Political Science Review* 74: 23–37.
Truman, David (1959) *The Congressional Party: A Case Study,* New York: John Wiley & Sons.
Watkins, Alan (1998) 'A Bloodthirsty Lot, the Women in the House', *Independent on Sunday,* 22 Feb.

MPs and Europe: Enthusiasm, Circumspection or Outright Scepticism?

David Baker, Andrew Gamble and David Seawright, with Katrina Bull

The issue of Europe has undermined the unity of both major parties over recent decades, and it shows few signs of disappearing from the political agenda so far this parliament. Questions of EMU, common foreign and security policy, and home affairs and immigration continue to divide opinion, in both the major parties. This article – which draws on the results of a survey sent to all 659 MPs in mid-1998 – allows us empirically to test the views of the parliamentary elites on Europe.

The research builds on two previous surveys which have examined the views of Conservative and Labour MPs on European integration (see Baker *et al.*, 1995, 1996a, 1996b, 1997). (Both datasets are deposited with the Data Archive at the University of Essex). The new survey adds another dataset at a particularly important time. It allows us to examine the views of the large influx of new Labour MPs, widely believed to be very pro-European, as well as to see whether the remaining Conservative MPs are as eurosceptic as is commonly thought. It also allows us to measure the views of the large Liberal Democrat representation in the Commons, the largest since 1929, and for the first time large enough to be meaningfully surveyed.

Conducting the Survey

The investigation was based upon a postal survey of all 659 MPs, conducted in the middle months of 1998, using an updated version of earlier surveys conducted in 1994 and 1996 (ESRC R000231298 and ESRC R000221560 respectively). The 1998 questionnaire (R000222397) contained 55 attitude questions on various aspects of European integration. Both the issues chosen for investigation and the nature of the questions asked were derived from analysis of a wide range of published views of politicians on Europe, and from a series of unattributable interviews, lasting between 20 minutes and an hour, conducted before the survey with leading parliamentarians representing a known and politically balanced range of opinion across the main parties.

The overall response rate to the questionnaire was 39 per cent. Broken down by party, as in Table 1, the response rate was 33 per cent from Labour MPs (a considerable achievement given that Labour MPs are routinely reminded on their pagers not to answer *any* questionnaires), 42 per cent from Conservatives, and 73 per cent from the Liberal Democrats. As a result of this differential response rate, our respondents contained nine per cent fewer Labour MPs than in the Commons as a whole, while the Conservatives and Liberal Democrats were slightly over-represented (by four and six per cent respectively). None of these differences are of a magnitude to cause us to doubt the reliability of our findings.

TABLE 1
RESPONSE RATE

	N	As % of parliamentary party	As % of respondents	% of Commons	Difference
Labour	138	33	54	63	-9
Conservative	70	42	29	25	+4
Liberal Democrat	34	73	13	7	+6

Results of the 1998 Survey

The analysis in this article will focus exclusively on the three main parties. No attempt has been made here to sub-divide the data to show the differences between back- and frontbench attitudes to the questions asked, both because too few Labour frontbenchers (five in total) replied and because all the Liberal Democrat respondents were frontbenchers, given the limited number of MPs available to cover such duties.

The wide range of issues covered by the questionnaire can usefully be examined under six headings. The first asked parliamentarians their views on the quality of the European debate in the UK.

The European debate

As Table 2 shows, clear majorities in all three parties believed that there was a paucity of informed debate on Europe in both the electorate and the media. In both cases, the Liberal Democrats were the most critical (unanimously so concerning the electorate), while the Conservatives were the most likely to be satisfied with the level of the debate in the media. The former probably reflects the Party's traditional difficulties in getting even its own core support to be sufficiently pro-European for its leadership's liking (see

Curtice and Clarke, 1998). The latter may reflect the fact that much of the press in the United Kingdom takes a eurosceptic stance (although despite this, over three-quarters of Conservatives also said they were dissatisfied with media coverage of the issue).

Majorities of Conservative and Liberal Democrat respondents believed that the issue was well debated within their own parties. A similar view was, however, not taken by most Labour respondents: over half (53 per cent) said that there was a paucity of informed debate within the party. This was anticipated in general remarks made during our preliminary interviews with Labour MPs in the spring of 1998. Several argued that the leadership was tightly controlling the agenda of discussion on Europe within the party, leaving no space for proper internal debate on the issue.

TABLE 2
ATTITUDES ON THE QUALITY OF THE EUROPEAN DEBATE

There is a paucity of informed debate on Britain's role in Europe in...

	Strongly agree/ agree %	Neither %	Strongly disagree/ disagree %
(a) my party.**			
Labour	53	12	35
Conservative	21	14	65
Liberal Democrat	17	10	73
(b) the electorate.**			
Labour	88	3	8
Conservative	88	6	6
Liberal Democrat	100	0	0
(c) the media.			
Labour	80	6	14
Conservative	76	10	23
Liberal Democrat	84	13	3

Note: In Tables 2 to 7, * indicates that chi-squared is significant at the 0.05 level; ** indicates that it is significant at the 0.01 level.

Sovereignty, institutional and constitutional matters

The responses to the questions investigating parliamentarians' views on sovereignty and institutional and constitutional matters (shown in Table 3) clearly reveal the extent of Conservative euroscepticism. Of the three parties, Conservative MPs gave the most eurosceptic responses to all five questions, often by a long way. This is clearest in response to 3.3, where 69 per cent of Conservative respondents believed parliament should have supremacy over EU law, a statement that effectively rejects the Treaty of Rome. The corresponding figures for Labour and the Liberal Democrats were 13 and 12 per cent respectively. A full quarter of Conservative MPs want withdrawal from the EU, and over 60 per cent gave sceptical responses to the four other questions.

The Liberal Democrats emerge as the least sceptical. They have the lowest percentage of parliamentarians giving a sceptical response to four of the questions (being level with Labour on the fifth), and the number giving a sceptical response does not rise above 13 per cent. Labour, too, appear predominantly pro-European, if not quite as enthusiastic as the Liberal Democrats. Just three per cent favour withdrawal, and the percentage giving a sceptical response never rises above 29 per cent. Labour and the Liberal Democrats are therefore close together on these issues. In response to all five questions, the majority of Labour and Liberal Democrat respondents gave a diametrically opposed answer to the majority of Conservative respondents.

TABLE 3
ATTITUDES ON SOVEREIGNTY, INSTITUTIONAL AND CONSTITUTIONAL MATTERS

	Strongly agree/ agree %	Neither %	Strongly disagree/ disagree %
3.1 Sovereignty cannot be pooled.**			
Labour	22	17	61
Conservative	61	6	33
Liberal Democrat	6	16	78
3.2 Britain should withdraw from the EU.**			
Labour	3	1	96
Conservative	26	11	63
Liberal Democrat	3	0	97
3.3 An act of Parliament should be passed to establish explicitly the ultimate supremacy of Parliament over EU legislation.**			
Labour	13	20	67
Conservative	69	7	24
Liberal Democrat	12	6	81
3.4 The Commission should lose the right to initiate legislation.**			
Labour	29	19	52
Conservative	61	10	29
Liberal Democrat	10	17	73
3.5 The Council of Ministers should be the supreme institution in the EU.**			
Labour	29	15	56
Conservative	72	10	18
Liberal Democrat	13	10	77

However, the data also reveal noticeable splits within Labour and the Conservatives. As well as the Conservative split on withdrawal (3.2), there are also sizeable divisions over the pooling of sovereignty (3.1) and the role of the Commission (3.4). Labour MPs were also split over the Commission (although in the opposite direction to the Conservatives) and over the Council of Ministers (3.5), suggesting a battle ahead if too much power is seen to be lost by the Westminster parliament. The Liberal Democrats, however, showed a remarkable degree of cohesion on all five questions.

TABLE 4
ATTITUDES ON MONETARY POLICY

	Strongly agree/ agree %	Neither %	Strongly Disagree/ disagree %
4.1 Britain should never permit its monetary policy to be determined by a European Central Bank.**			
Labour	20	15	65
Conservative	66	9	25
Liberal Democrat	13	10	77
4.2 Britain should never rejoin the ERM.**			
Labour	11	19	70
Conservative	64	6	30
Liberal Democrat	7	10	83
4.3 Membership of the Euro is crucial for Britain's future prosperity.**			
Labour	65	19	16
Conservative	13	16	71
Liberal Democrat	87	7	7
4.4 Joining the Single Currency will signal the end of the UK as a sovereign nation.**			
Labour	10	7	83
Conservative	66	6	28
Liberal Democrat	3	7	90
4.5 It is essential that there should be a national referendum before the UK enters a single currency.*			
Labour	80	7	13
Conservative	97	2	2
Liberal Democrat	71	16	13
4.6 A single currency will institutionalize neo-liberal economic policy in Britain.			
Labour	23	27	50
Conservative	27	28	45
Liberal Democrat	27	38	35

Note: Not all rows sum to 100% due to rounding.

Monetary policy

Those questions on monetary policy that asked respondents for their views on the ERM, the Single Currency and the EU Central bank, largely confirmed the findings of the earlier statements (see Table 4). In each of the first four questions, the majority of Conservative respondents gave sceptical responses, while the majority of Labour and Liberal Democrat respondents gave euroenthusiast responses, with the Liberals Democrats being slightly more enthusiastic than Labour. For example, 65 per cent of Labour MPs and 87 per cent of Liberal Democrat MPs believe that membership of the Euro is crucial for Britain's future prosperity, compared to just 13 per cent of Conservatives (4.3).

Similarly, just as before, the data reveal the Liberal Democrat respondents to be largely united in their views, while the other two parties contain sizeable dissenting minorities on some issues. The Conservatives split over the ERM (4.2) and single currency (4.4), while both Labour and the Conservatives split over the European Central Bank (ECB) (4.1). Such dissident minorities could pose a long-term threat for party management on Europe, especially if any future ECB took unpopular decisions on levels of interest rate and employment.

The final two questions in this section provoked slightly different responses. Clear majorities of all three parties supported the need for a referendum before Britain entered the single currency (4.5), with the Conservatives being the most in favour. By contrast, responses to the question on the possible institutionalization of neo-liberal economic policies by any future common currency (4.6) caused real divisions of opinion: all three parties split into three sizeable groups. Given the inter-party differences of opinion that are clear on most other issues, this may be an indication of that survey conductor's nightmare: that MPs of all parties chose to interpret 'neo-liberal' in different ways, thereby confusing the issue.

National security

Questions on matters of national security reveal a slightly different pattern to many of those issues previously discussed, as Table 5 shows. As before, the Conservative respondents were by far the most sceptical of the three parties, with 80 per cent or more choosing a sceptical response to all three questions. At its strongest, in the case of Qualified Majority Voting (QMV) in foreign and defence policy, 90 per cent were opposed. And, as before, the Liberal Democrats were the most enthusiastic, with majorities adopting an enthusiastic stance on all three questions (although almost a third of Liberal Democrat respondents opposed QMV in foreign and defence policy).

The difference comes with Labour. The three questions produced clear divisions within Labour's ranks. On balance, Labour was slightly more enthusiastic than sceptical, but only just: the sceptical grouping within Labour's ranks on these issues is only marginally smaller than the enthusiasts. And, equally importantly, all three questions revealed a sizeable grouping – around a quarter of Labour respondents – who responded that they neither agreed nor disagreed with the statements. This could indicate problems of question wording, but this is unlikely given that it appears not to have been a problem for respondents from other parties. It is more likely to represent a group of undecided Labour MPs, who could yet fall on one side or other of the debate.

The statements on issues of national security thus present us with two insights into MPs' views on Europe. First, that while Labour is usually closer to the Liberal Democrats than to the Conservatives (indeed, that remains true in this case), the distance between the parties can differ depending on the type of issues under examination. When it comes to issues of national security, Labour is noticeably less euroenthusiastic than on issues of sovereignty or monetary policy. And second, it is not just that Labour are less enthusiastic: they are also split. Issues of national security, then, have the potential to cause problems of party management for Labour.

TABLE 5
ATTITUDES ON NATIONAL SECURITY

	Strongly agree/ agree %	Neither %	Strongly disagree/ disagree %
5.1 Britain should block the use of QMV in the areas of foreign and defence policy.**			
Labour	36	22	42
Conservative	90	1	9
Liberal Democrat	32	10	58
5.2 A single European Army would undermine rather than underpin the security of the UK.**			
Labour	33	28	39
Conservative	83	7	10
Liberal democrat	13	29	58
5.3 Britain should not participate in the lifting of borders as specified in the Schengen agreement.**			
Labour	33	23	44
Conservative	87	4	9
Liberal Democrat	7	13	80

Budgetary matters

Table 6 deals with the monetary costs of the EU to its member nations, costs that are going to rise for the richer nations such as Britain during any future enlargement or growth in central institutions like the ECB. Once again, Conservative scepticism is confirmed, both on any increase in structural funds (where 60 per cent take a sceptical stance) and especially on the enlargement of the budget (to which 91 per cent are opposed). Majorities of both Labour and Liberal Democrat MPs support the need for an increase in structural funds, but both are badly split over the need for any enlargement of the EU's budget. Both parties split into three almost equal groups (with roughly a third adopting a sceptical stance, a third being enthusiastic, and a third being neither). Yet again, therefore, we see that Labour's generally euroenthusiastic stance has its limits. Importantly, so too do the Liberal Democrats. This is the first issue to show that even the very euroenthusiast Liberal Democrats can split over Europe, given the right issue.

TABLE 6
ATTITUDES ON THE BUDGET

	Strongly agree/ agree %	Neither %	Strongly disagree/ disagree %
6.1 The EU's budget should be enlarged.**			
Labour	36	28	36
Conservative	6	3	91
Liberal Democrat	39	32	29
6.2 An increase in structural funds is essential for EU enlargement.**			
Labour	67	19	14
Conservative	29	11	60
Liberal Democrat	74	16	10

Economic policy

The Liberal Democrats also split over questions on EU economic policy, as shown in Table 7. By contrast, the Conservatives were again united in response to all three statements; and in all three cases, they adopted an opposed position to the majority of Labour respondents. These three statements were also interesting because of what they reveal about the beliefs of New Labour. For example, 35 per cent either agreed with or were neutral towards statement 7.1, which suggests that EU job creation requires a reduction in employer's social costs. Even question 7.2, which argued that Labour market inflexibility was chiefly responsible for unemployment, saw 27 per cent of Labour respondents either in agreement with or unconcerned by this statement. But one of the most interesting indications of New Labour's change in economic perspective can be seen in the answer to 7.3 – 'Public ownership is irrelevant for the achievement of social justice' – where 26 per cent actually agreed and 15 per cent remained uncommitted. This line of argument should not be pursued too far. In all three cases, the majority of Labour respondents adopted a more traditional stance – rejecting the need to reduce social costs, not seeing inflexible Labour markets as the cause of unemployment, and seeing public ownership as relevant for social justice – but the size of the dissenting minorities is a sign of how far Labour has travelled along the path of economic orthodoxy.

TABLE 7
ATTITUDES ON ECONOMIC POLICY

	Strongly agree/ agree %	Neither %	Strongly disagree/ disagree %
7.1 A reduction in social costs placed on the employer is essential for job creation in the EU.**			
Labour	18	17	65
Conservative	94	3	2
Liberal Democrat	32	26	42
7.2 Inflexibility in European labour markets is the principal cause of unemployment.**			
Labour	10	17	73
Conservatives	87	3	10
Liberal Democrat	26	16	58
7.3 Public ownership is irrelevant for the achievement of social justice.**			
Labour	26	15	59
Conservative	88	9	3
Liberal Democrat	49	19	32

A Cohort Effect?

Our two previous surveys revealed a powerful cohort factor at work within Britain's two governing parties. By focusing on certain issue statements common to both the 1994 and 1996 surveys, we showed that the Conservative Party at Westminster was moving inexorably towards a more eurosceptic position, while Labour was moving in the opposite direction (Baker *et al.*, 1997). The change in attitudes occurred at different times in different parties. In the Labour Party, the sea-change came after the catastrophic election defeat in 1983, for which Labour's anti-European policy was partly blamed. In the Conservative Party the arrival in parliament in 1979 of a disproportionately large number of free-market, nationalist MPs marked the beginning of a more sceptical thinking on Europe.

The size of Labour's landslide election victory contributed to a huge turnover in the composition of the Commons: of the 659 MPs elected in 1997, 260 entered the Commons for the first time. These MPs will be crucial to the future ideological direction of the parties. We now examine their views, and in Tables 8 and 9 compare them to the previous cohorts.

TABLE 8

CONSERVATIVE COHORT DIFFERENCES

	Strongly agree/ agree %		Neither %		Strongly disagree/ disagree %	

8.1 An act of Parliament should be passed to establish explicitly the ultimate supremacy of Parliament over EU legislation.

	Strongly agree/ agree %		Neither %		Strongly disagree/ disagree %	
1959–74	80	(27)	0	(13)	20	(60)
1979–92	64	(61)	7	(18)	29	(21)
1997	80		7		13	

8.2 Joining the Single Currency will signal the end of the UK as a sovereign nation.

1959–74	70	(37)	10	(7)	20	(56)
1979–92	61	(55)	7	(9)	32	(36)
1997	73		0		27	

8.3 The key to closing the 'democratic deficit' is strengthening the scrutiny by national parliaments of the EU legislative process.

1959–74	70	(69)	0	(21)	30	(10)
1979–92	84	(84)	11	(7)	5	(9)
1997	93		0		7	

8.4 Britain should block the use of QMV in the areas of foreign and defence policy.

1959–74	100	(80)	0	(13)	0	(7)
1979–92	89	(88)	2	(7)	9	(5)
1997	87		0		13	

8.5 A single European Army would undermine rather than underpin the security of the UK.

1959–74	90	(60)	0	(13)	10	(27)
1979–92	82	(78)	9	(11)	9	(11)
1997	80		7		13	

Note: In Tables 8 and 9, by-election entrants have been grouped with the next general election cohort.

Table 8 shows the responses given by Conservative MPs to five questions – the five where in our previous work we discovered the greatest amount of inter-cohort difference – broken down by their entry cohort. The table is a sceptic's delight and an enthusiast's nightmare.

The new intake of Conservative MPs is extremely eurosceptic: 73 per cent agreed that the single currency meant the end of the UK as a sovereign nation state. Indeed, this figure of 73 per cent is the lowest sceptical response to the five issues in Table 8: 80 per cent believe an act should be passed to challenge the Treaty of Rome (8.1) and that a single European army would undermine the UK's security (8.5); 87 per cent would like to see QMV blocked for foreign and defence policy (8.4); and an astonishing 93 per cent view the 'democratic deficit' as being a lack of scrutiny by national parliaments (8.3).

These figures are far higher than those given in our previous survey of Conservative MPs in 1994, as shown by the figures in parentheses in Table 8. Had the responses seen in 1994 been repeated in 1998, we would have clear evidence of an on-going cohort effect: those elected in 1997 would have been more sceptical than those elected between 1979 and 1992 who would, in turn, have been more sceptical than those elected between 1959 and 1974.

However, what is striking about Table 8 is that this did not happen. The responses from the earlier cohorts who responded in 1998 are far more sceptical than figures for the same cohorts in 1994. For example, in 1994, 27 per cent of those elected between 1959 and 1974 said that they wanted an act to challenge the supremacy of EU legislation (8.1); by 1998, that figure had almost trebled to 80 per cent. Something similar – if less pronounced – happened with the 1979–92 cohort.

Unfortunately, because this is not a panel survey – one that tracks the views on the same individuals over time – we have no way of knowing whether this transformation is the result of conversion (of MPs changing their minds) or replacement (of the more euroenthusiastic Conservatives having been disproportionately 'weeded out' by the electoral turnover on 1 May 1997). But whatever the cause, the effect is pronounced. As a result, although the 1997 cohort are very eurosceptic, they are in many cases not much more eurosceptic than their colleagues elected from the earlier parliaments. Indeed, in some cases (8.4 and 8.5, for example) they are the least eurosceptic grouping.

Some caution is needed with these figures. Given the size of the Conservative parliamentary party, analysis of any one cohort – even one as large in relative terms as those elected in 1997 – is problematic. The N for the 1997 Conservative respondents is 15 and just 10 for the 1959–74 cohort. Yet even with this caveat in place, the overall conclusion appears clear: the eurosceptic movement of the Conservative parliamentary party speeded up after the 1997 election, both because the new MPs were themselves eurosceptic and because the body of existing MPs became more sceptical.

With Labour, our findings are slightly more complicated. The difference between the first two cohorts remains clear. We do find some differences between the responses given by each cohort in 1994 and now, but none of the differences alters the basic finding: as we found in 1994 (again, the figures in brackets in Table 9), those elected in or before 1983 were far more inclined to take a sceptical position than those elected after the commitment to withdrawal from the EU was ditched.

TABLE 9

LABOUR COHORT DIFFERENCE

	Strongly agree/ agree %		Neither %		Strongly disagree/ disagree %	

9.1 An act of Parliament should be passed to establish explicitly the ultimate supremacy of Parliament over EU legislation.

1950–83	22	(29)	8	(6)	70	(65)
1987–92	8	(7)	11	(25)	81	(68)
1997	13		31		56	

9.2 Joining the Single Currency will signal the end of the UK as a sovereign nation.

1950–83	26	(33)	11	(3)	63	(64)
1987–92	11	(11)	8	(6)	81	(83)
1997	9		6		85	

9.3 The key to closing the 'democratic deficit' is strengthening the scrutiny by national parliaments of the EU legislative process.

1950–83	79	(79)	6	(12)	15	(9)
1987–92	61	(69)	22	(17)	17	(14)
1997	69		21		10	

9.4 Britain should block the use of QMV in the areas of foreign and defence policy.

1950–83	41	(56)	18	(10)	41	(34)
1987–92	36	(37)	17	(15)	47	(48)
1997	36		26		38	

9.5 A single European Army would undermine rather than underpin the security of the UK.

1950–83	33	(38)	22	(18)	45	(44)
1987–92	28	(16)	23	(31)	49	(53)
1997	36		33		31	

But the third cohort – those elected in 1997 – do not behave in such a predictable way; and with 70 Labour MPs from this cohort responding to our survey, we feel greater confidence in the level of their representativeness. On one question (9.2) the 1997 intake are more enthusiast than their colleagues from the 1987–92 intake, on one (9.4) they are exactly the same, and on three (9.1, 9.3 and 9.5) they are less enthusiastic. What does this mean? And how can we explain it?

In broad terms, it seems clear that the new Labour cohort are not hugely more euroenthusiastic than their immediate predecessors, nor are they noticeably more sceptical. And on the crucial question of joining the single currency (9.2) there has been a further euroenthusiastic shift: just 9 per cent of our 1997 intake believed that this momentous decision will lead to the end of the UK as a sovereign nation state. So, while the 1997 intake have not added to the momentum of Labour's ideological shift nor have they reversed it.

The opposition to the idea of a single European army has actually hardened in this Parliament (9.5) along with support for scrutiny by Westminster of the EU legislative process (9.3). There might be a reasonable explanation for this. Tony Blair has never offered unqualified enthusiasm for Europe; his comments are always tempered with important caveats. This attitude of enthusiasm qualified with circumspection was best expressed in his speech to the Friedrich-Ebert Stiftung on 30 May 1995 where Blair stated that elite political opinion should not be allowed to get ahead of public opinion, as he claimed it did at the time of Maastricht. In the same speech he outlined Labour's policy of opposition to a European army but advocated greater use of cooperation between European forces. Blair's stance may offer one explanation for the way the 1997 intake split into three when asked about the idea of a single European army.

Conclusion

Both major parties have significant minorities opposed to the party line on Europe, especially on issues that deal with fundamental questions of national sovereignty and interdependence. On the key issue of full-blown euroscepticism – withdrawal – those Conservative respondents agreeing (26 per cent) or uncommitted (11 per cent) constitute a very significant minority in the parliamentary elite. In the case of our Labour respondents, some of the New Labour ideas on market-driven solutions to economic problems clearly divide the party significantly. The left-of-centre attitudes to social and economic questions found in the last survey (Baker *et al.*, 1996b) appear to have diminished; but Labour MPs remain rather cautious about offering extra powers to elected EU institutions. On the whole, the Liberal Democrats are confirmed by this survey as the most pro-European party but even they appear divided on some economic and constitutional questions.

The lessons for Tony Blair are that he can push a fairly aggressive pro-European line in government without the risk of opening up major division and dissent within his parliamentary elite (although the same can certainly not be said within the British press). William Hague's general attack on the Single Currency and the associated loss of British sovereignty also appears to chime well with the attitudes of a clear majority of our Conservative respondents. But in both cases issues like the Single Currency continue to produce sizeable minorities out of tune with the respective party leaderships.

What does the future hold in store? Much will depend on what happens when the Euro starts, and how it interacts with recent global financial difficulties. If the Euro is a success then there will be strong pressure for Britain to join, and for the government to hold a referendum soon after the next general election. If Labour wins that election, dependent on a good performance and the margin of victory, it is likely also to win the referendum, aided by majority business and trade union support, with senior Tories joining the 'yes' campaign. The only major cloud on this horizon would be the British press. Labour's leadership well remembers the famous front page of the *Sun*, which referred to Mr. Blair's possible pro-European intentions asking whether he was 'the most dangerous man in Britain'.

The European issue made life impossible for John Major. William Hague will not be allowed to walk away from it either. In the event of the Tories winning the next election then their hands are presumably tied, even if they come to see that joining the Euro is essential. Either way, the Labour anti-European faction is unlikely to make much headway. The major headache for Hague is how he is now going to stop his local parties deselecting pro-European MPs before the next election. The Thatcherite Right is clearly swinging behind Portillo who is poised to challenge for the leadership if Hague loses the next election. Portillo is promoting the line of 'No to the Euro on principle'. Hague's position for all its apparent toughness is really a development of Major's, designed to hold the party together, if at all possible. Significantly, if Portillo's line was ever adopted the pro-Europeans might well be forced to leave. Many of the less prominent may well leave anyway.

The intriguing thing from our data is that although the party members have resoundingly backed Hague by more than 5:1, support from the MPs for his line is much less overwhelming. In our survey they are split 2:1 on Europe. That suggests there is a lot of deselection to do if the Right continues to press on this issue or, as our 1997 cohort data indicates, many of the new candidates will be ultra-sceptics themselves in any case. Most observers (including the *Sun*, which pronounced it an 'ex-party') are incredulous. But the calculation of the Tory Right is that a campaign to save the pound will prove deeply popular. The stakes are very high – if they are wrong the party could be out of office for a long time, and Portillo (or someone like him) may well have Disraeli's job of getting the party to accept the situation and rebuild its appeal.

ACKNOWLEDGEMENTS

The Members of Parliament Project survey team would like to express their thanks to the MPs and academics who sponsored the survey. Without their support the response rates would have been much lower. They are: Roger Casale, Jimmy Hood, James Plaskitt, Bill Rammell (Labour);

Peter Bottomley, Julie Kirkbride (Conservative); Nick Harvey, David Heath (Liberal Democrat); John Swinney (Scottish National Party); David Marquand, Martin Holmes (Oxford University); Philip Norton (Hull University); and Pippa Norris (Harvard University). We would also like to take this opportunity to express our thanks and gratitude to Philip Cowley for his insightful comments on this work.

REFERENCES

Baker, David, Andrew Gamble and Steve Ludlam (1995) 'Backbench Conservative Attitudes to European Integration', *Political Quarterly* 66: 221–33.

Baker, David, Andrew Gamble, Imogen Fountain and Steve Ludlam (1996a) 'The Blue Map of Europe: Conservative Parliamentarians and European Integration', in C. Rallings, D. Farrell, D. Denver and D. Broughton (eds), *British Elections and Parties Yearbook* 1995, pp.51–89. London and Portland OR: Frank Cass.

Baker, David, Andrew Gamble, Steve Ludlam and David Seawright (1996b) 'Labour and Europe: A Survey of MPs and MEPs', *Political Quarterly* 67: 353–71.

Baker, David, Andrew Gamble, Steve Ludlam and David Seawright (1997) 'The 1994/96 Conservative and Labour Members of Parliament Surveys on Europe: The Data Compared', paper presented to the American Political Science Association. Washington, August 28–31.

Curtice, John and Scott Clarke (1998) 'The Liberal Democrats and European Integration', in D. Baker and D. Seawright (eds), *Britain for and against Europe*, pp.88–107. Oxford: Oxford University Press.

Nowhere to Run...?
British MEPs and the Euro

Roger M. Scully

We were never *really* the forgotten front – though it may have seemed to be so sometimes (Lord Mountbatten, South East Asia, 1944).

The issue of 'Europe' has established itself as one of the hardy perennials of British politics. More than 25 years after the UK entered the European Union (EU),[1] and over 45 years since the British began their troubled relationship with the integration process by opting out of its first, hesitant manifestation, Europe remains an issue of great partisan contention. The UK has long since gone 'into Europe', but Europe has also gone into the very core of UK politics, with no diminution in its ability to raise passions across the political elite. The salience of the issue has even survived considerable re-positioning by both major parties over the last decade. Indeed, debates have become, if anything, sharper, as the prospect of Economic and Monetary Union (EMU) has loomed – with a single currency (the Euro) replacing national currencies in most EU states. In recent years, Conservatives have witnessed Europe in general, and the Euro in particular, contribute to the downfall of both Margaret Thatcher and John Major, and cause considerable problems for their newest leader, William Hague. Equally apparent has been the potential for the issue to splinter the heterogeneous Blairite coalition: the *Sun* newspaper, for one, converted from staunch Conservative support towards an endorsement of New Labour, nonetheless evinces little enthusiasm for swapping its former rhetoric of 'Up Yours, Delors!' for an appreciation of the possible benefits of closer European integration. Ignoring the European issue in British party politics today is akin to ignoring an elephant in your living room.

It is, then, at least a minor paradox that the group of British politicians most directly and consistently engaged with Europe have been widely ignored. The UK's Members of the European Parliament (MEPs) operate on the 'forgotten front' of British party politics, receiving minimal media attention or public recognition. Only individuals whose renown was established prior to becoming a MEP – like Barbara Castle, or Northern Ireland's two long-standing members, John Hume and Ian Paisley – have escaped this anonymity; even major British figures in the parliament such as Lord Plumb and Pauline Green remain largely unknown to the wider populace.[2] The lack of public attention has, for the most part, been matched by the scholarly community. While some studies have touched on British MEPs' political attitudes (Baker and Seawright, 1998), others considered the manner of their election (Butler and Westlake, 1994), and one even analysed their careers in Strasbourg and Brussels (Westlake, 1994), these exceptions to the rule leave much that is unknown. Given this neglect, it is perhaps unsurprising that one former British member could comment that 'we were always seen as the fifth wheel'.

There are, however, good reasons to believe that the marginal status of MEPs is changing. Over recent years the European Parliament (EP), and thereby its membership, has become much more powerful. Progressive transfers of policy competence from national governments to the Union have been accompanied in recent treaties by a considerable growth in the EP's prerogatives, with the 1997 Amsterdam Treaty giving the chamber full 'co-decision' rights over most major EU laws (Corbett et al., 1995; Scully, 1997a, b, n.d.). Though some still labour under the delusion that the EP remains a 'multi-lingual talking shop' (see, for example, The Independent, 14 June 1998), the chamber has become a highly important arena within which political parties pursue their policy aims. As one current Conservative member observes, the EP has become 'just another front in the political battle that British political parties have... They have councillors, they have MPs and they have MEPs, and they're all integrated in the same system and all essentially doing the same work on different battlegrounds'.

As well as contributing directly to achieving a party's aims by influencing policies over which the EP has significant powers, MEPs are also increasingly recognized for their ability to make a more indirect contribution, as a source of expertise on the complexities of European politics (Raunio, 1998). Many MEPs serve on one of their chamber's specialist policy committees, where most of the parliament's real work is done (Corbett et al., 1995). The expertise that committee membership instils (Bowler and Farrell, 1995), as well as a more general educative effect resulting from immersion in the European political environment, equips MEPs to be highly valuable sources of information across the ever-increasing portion of government policy-making with an important EU dimension. This point was explicitly acknowledged by Labour subsequent to its May 1997 election, with the formalization of a system (originating during the party's period in opposition), under which a substantial number of European Parliamentary Labour Party (EPLP) members were appointed as European parliamentary private secretaries to Labour ministers (see also Spiers, 1997).

In short, national parties have an increasing number of reasons to enhance links with their European representatives, and there are some signs of British parties now doing so. Nonetheless, while the relationship between parties and MEPs has grown in significance, scholars still have much to learn about it. The purpose of this article is to advance our understanding of this relationship and its connection to the broader European debates within British parties. The chosen approach is a case study of a major parliamentary vote held in May 1998. At issue was the granting of approval by the EP for the completion of EMU to begin the following January. The vote, therefore, concerned a topic that was both of immense importance for the EU and also the subject of considerable political controversy in Britain. In these circumstances, what sort of political pressures operate on MEPs, who bridge national and European politics, and what response do these pressures yield? Drawing on quantitative analysis of the vote and on numerous in-depth interviews, the article examines why British MEPs took the positions they did, and addresses two further questions. First, what does the vote on the Euro tell us more generally about European debates and divisions within the major parties? And second, how does the examination of this issue helps inform scholars about the relationship between parties and their European representatives? The findings presented indicate that Britain's MEPs are not the uniformly pro-European grouping that caricature might suggest, and reinforce the point that European parliamentarians, though operating in a unique political setting, experience pressures common to many others in their national parties.

British MEPs and the Euro

> In my view it's the most important issue of all; it's the one that makes or breaks the show... Where it leaves Britain is another matter, but monetary union is the most ambitious economic policy ever attempted in history. Whatever else it is, it's not banal! (Conservative MEP, April 1998)

Over the weekend of 1–3 May 1998, the EU took a momentous decision. With approval from the requisite institutions, it was agreed that the final stage of EMU would begin in January 1999 among 11 of the 15 EU countries. Even for those countries not participating – the UK, Denmark, Sweden and Greece – it was an event that could not be ignored. This was certainly true for the UK, the largest EU state not joining the Euro-zone. As incumbent of the rotating Union Presidency Britain had the awkward job of overseeing a venture from which it was itself excluded, albeit of its own volition. Much had been made by the Blair government of its positive attitude to the EU and of how its Presidency would demonstrate the leadership role in Europe, which this attitude helped Britain to assume. That the most important event during Britain's stewardship was to be the launching of a monetary union minus the UK thus caused some short-term embarrassment. Of longer-term political significance, continued British procrastination over EMU – John Major's 'wait-and-see' approach having been amended to the Blair/Brown 'prepare and decide' (whether to join after January 1999) formula – was underpinned by a widespread awareness that monetary union had the potential to cause serious partisan divisions.

One group of UK politicians, however, was required to take a public position. The 87 British MEPs, along with their 539 colleagues, were invited at a special Brussels plenary session of the EP on 2 May to endorse the agreement concluded the previous day by national governments. Though symbolic of the chamber's growing voice within the Union, the parliamentary vote had only limited significance in formal constitutional terms: under treaty article 109j, the EP was required to be 'consulted', but national governments were not required to abide by any opinion of the parliament. Nonetheless, many members were aware that a substantial anti-Euro vote, signifying divisions in the EU, would be viewed negatively in the financial markets and might damage the new currency's future stability.[3]

British MEPs, however, had perhaps even more at stake in the vote than others. Unlike most of their counterparts, the domestic background for UK representatives was one of considerable partisan division over EMU's merits. They also faced an additional pressure, caused by the UK government's intention to change the system for EP elections in Britain, replacing 84 mainland single-member districts with 11 multi-member regional lists. MEPs who wished to return to the chamber after the elections in June 1999 would have to endure a new candidate selection process, in which parliamentary behaviour on high-profile issues like EMU might be scrutinized. With candidate selection in the major parties occurring shortly after the Euro vote, it was unclear how members should interpret these domestic factors, or how their interpretations might interact with personal attitudes.

Would pro-integration members, for instance, endorse a deal that excluded Britain from a major advance in European unity? As one member put it: 'I am delighted that it is about to happen, [but] I am deeply distressed that Britain is not going to be a part of it at the beginning.' Would such MEPs support monetary union hoping that success would lead to subsequent British membership? Alternatively, would more sceptical MEPs oppose monetary union outright, or take the view that other EU members should experience the consequences of their folly? Moreover, whatever their personal views, would members be affected by the debates within their national parties and the re-selection process which many would be facing? One Conservative member was clear about how he expected the major parties' representatives to behave:

> If on the Labour side there aren't divisions, that should be even more extraordinary than that there shouldn't be divisions on the Conservative side, because those who are most vigorously opposed both to the economics and the politics of monetary union, that I know in the Parliament, are on the Labour side.

A more systematic understanding of members' views can be drawn from the recent research of David Baker and colleagues (see, for example, Baker and Seawright, 1998). Their surveys of national and European parliamentarians from both major parties include several questions on EMU. Among Labour MEPs, their 1996 poll found strong support for monetary union. Only 14 per cent of respondents (N=26) endorsed ('strongly agree'/ 'agree') the propositions that 'EMU is unrealisable' and that 'EMU is undesirable', with 79 per cent rejecting ('strongly disagree'/ 'disagree') both. A similar division of opinion (18 per cent to 78 per cent) prevailed against the idea that EMU meant 'the end of the UK as a sovereign nation', while a still substantial majority (61 per cent to 21 per cent) rejected the statement, with which a left-of-centre audience might be expected to sympathize, that the UK 'should never permit its monetary policy to be determined by an independent European central bank'. These answers indicate a strong consensus among Labour MEPs in favour of the Euro – greater, certainly, than existed then among Westminster MPs surveyed.

Tapping into the attitudes of Conservative MEPs in 1998 is more difficult since they were surveyed just prior to the 1994 EP elections. The reported results thus include responses from some MEPs (N=22) who were not returned, as well as a sample of EP candidates (N=41), many of whom did win election to the new parliament. The party's European representatives in the 1989–94 EP overwhelmingly favoured EMU (even more than the post-1994 Labour contingent), but new candidates in 1994 were much closer to the prevailing Euro-sceptical trend in the national party: more than 50 per cent believed that 'EMU is not desirable'. As one former member comments, 'The current Conservative group in the European parliament is much more Euro-sceptic than at any time when I was there. I mean, most of the pro-Europeans have gone.' Nonetheless, given that MEPs in 1994 were almost uniformly pro-EMU, and that very few EP candidates in the 1994 sample subsequently entered the parliament, the post-1994 body of Tory MEPs should still have strongly pro-Euro attitudes.

Whatever their views, it is undoubtedly true that many British MEPs would have preferred not to have to take a stand on the issue in May 1998. As one Labour member commented (shortly afterwards):

I abstained on the single currency. Now I might have voted against if it wasn't for the list [that is, the forthcoming re-selections based on PR], but I thought in the light of that it was better if I abstained... There's a climate of fear in the EPLP at the moment, really, if people are going to be honest.

Similarly, one Conservative member, prior to the vote, discussed the problems for those facing re-selection battles:

There were one or two reports in this month where... I voted in a way, which I thought might avoid creating a fuss... But the great question will be that of 1 to 2 May – the voting on monetary union. And there I can see... that colleagues will find it very difficult to resolve, and each will have to resolve it for themselves.

Unfortunately for this member, and for others caught in similar dilemmas, there was literally 'nowhere to run' on May 2. They had to take a position of some sort.

The Vote

Across the parliament as a whole, the Euro-agreement won substantial backing. A total of 468 MEPs (75 per cent of the parliament's total membership) voted 'Yes', compared to 64 (10 per cent) who voted 'No', with 24 (4 per cent) registering an abstention.[4] But what about British members?

TABLE 1
VOTING ON THE EURO AGREEMENT BY PARTY (UK MEMBERS ONLY)

VOTE	Labour	Cons	Lib-Dem	SNP	Others*	Total
Yes	49	2	2	1	2	56
No	2	3	–	–	1	6
Abstain	3	9	–	–	–	12
Absent	6	4	–	1	2	13
Total	60	18	2	2	5	87

Note: * These include Northern Ireland's three members (Ian Paisley, John Hume and James Nicholson), and Ken Coates and Hugh Kerr, who both left the Labour group in 1998.

As Table 1 shows, even among the British the Euro deal was strongly supported – by 56 of 74 participating members. This appears to reflect the overwhelming preponderance of Labour MEPs in the UK contingent, and their strong support for the Euro. However, the stark Conservative divide, despite their representation also being (the 1994 surveys suggest) pro-EMU, indicates the need for further investigation of the voting patterns and what lies behind them.

Probing further: quantitative analysis

As a first step in understanding why MEPs voted the way they did, it is important to establish whether the apparent 'party' difference shown in Table 1 is directly attributable to differences between Conservative and Labour MEPs or is an artefact of other influences on behaviour. To investigate this possibility, a multivariate analysis of the voting patterns was conducted, with several independent variables specified.

A variable was included measuring length of service for each member, to test whether the more experienced might differ from newer entrants; perhaps because they had more time to 'go native' by being socialized into pro-European beliefs. The variable measures the number of years spent in the chamber; as in previous studies (Arnold, n.d.; Mughan *et al.*, 1997), the variable is logged to allow for likely diminishing returns the longer the time spent in the chamber.[5] The age (in years) of each member is included to test for any 'generational' effect: whether younger members represent a new political generation with different attitudes on this issue from their seniors. Biographical information on MEPs – drawn from standard reference works – was utilized to examine the impact of their prior political experience: specifically, whether they had ever been Westminster MPs, something which might be posited to instil greater attachment to national institutions and national sovereignty. The variable was coded as a dummy, taking the value '1' if the member had previously been a National parliamentarian, '0' otherwise. A control variable for gender (coded '0' for male, '1' for female) was also included, as were dummy variables for members from the two major parties, and for those from England, Scotland and Wales. The former set of dummies directly measure any 'party effect'; the latter explore whether behaviour might differ between the constituent nations of the UK. The 'base' categories (for which no dummy variable was entered) were Northern Ireland for nationality, and Other Parties.

The dependent variable was coded '2' if an MEP supported the Euro-agreement, '0' if they voted against, and '1' if the member registered an abstention. OLS regression estimates are reported in Table 2.[6]

The results fail to indicate any impact for several putative causal factors. In line with research on other major EP votes (Scully, 1998), the findings here do not show longer-serving MEPs 'going native'. Although some members' attitudes may change over time, experienced MEPs do not disproportionately support measures of closer integration. Nor does previous national parliamentary experience appear to have conditioned behaviour in the vote. The age and gender variables manifest, at most, mild influence, albeit in expected directions: older members are more cautious about radical changes like EMU, while women view it more favourably (see also Mughan *et al.*, 1997). However, neither coefficient attains statistical significance.

TABLE 2
OLS REGRESSION ESTIMATES (STANDARD ERRORS) FOR UK MEPs' BEHAVIOUR ON EURO VOTE

Variable	Coefficient (std. error)	*p*-value
Years as MEP (logged)	0.04 (0.11)	0.74
Age (years)	-0.01 (0.01)	0.21
Gender	0.18 (0.16)	0.27
National parliamentarian	-0.08 (0.31)	0.80
Labour	-0.16 (0.28)	0.56
Conservative	-1.02 (0.28)	0.00
English	-0.16 (0.24)	0.50
Scottish	1.01 (0.58)	0.08
Welsh	0.77 (0.60)	0.21
(Constant)	2.55 (0.47)	0.00

Adjusted R^2 = 0.35
N = 74

Two important behavioural influences can, however, be identified. The nationality variables show Scottish MEPs to be more supportive of the Euro agreement than other UK members. This finding is interesting given the 'Old Labour' image of the Scottish Labour Party: the Euro agreement, which requires independence for the European central bank and tight fiscal discipline from participant countries, would seem calculated to arouse hostility from traditionalist Labour members. But the result matches the tone of recent Scottish political debate, where the Nationalists have made a pro-EU (and pro-Euro) stance a major element of their electoral appeal. By far the strongest predictor of behaviour, however, remains party. Notwithstanding their basically supportive attitudes, Conservative MEPs were much more likely than others not to support the EMU deal. This being so, it suggests the need for further, qualitative investigation of the voting patterns.

Probing further: Labour MEPs

In the parliamentary debate preceding the Euro vote, the first speech was by

British Chancellor Gordon Brown, in his capacity as Council of Ministers' President-in-Office. Brown's positive tone on the Euro was echoed later by Pauline Green, who commented that 'The careful preparations being made mean that those of us who support British membership – of whom I am one – will be able to conduct a campaign for a Yes vote [in a future UK referendum] with some confidence'. Strong support for the Euro among Labour MEPs – scoring 81.5 on a standard index of voting cohesion[7] – was therefore seen by many as a positive endorsement of EMU and the possibility of future British membership.

Where it occurred, opposition to the Euro agreement was rooted in suspicion or hostility to EMU. Taking advantage of MEPs' prerogative to explain their votes – done subsequent to votes, usually in writing, and entered into the official record – four of the five active Labour dissidents (two voting against, three abstaining) defended their actions by arguing monetary union to be 'fatally flawed' (Michael Hindley), or even 'ill-conceived, undemocratic and economically disastrous' (Tom Megahy). Similarly one abstainee, Stan Newens, asserted that 'Much more needs to be done to counter growing unemployment and poverty', while another, Shaun Spiers, though prefacing his remarks with praise for the UK Presidency, stated that 'The single currency project has been driven by faith, not reason', before lamenting: 'I fear, however, that it will result *either* in recession and unemployment in the less competitive Member countries, *or* in a huge increase in the EU's powers and budget, against the wishes of our citizens. I could not welcome either outcome.'

Among Labour members supporting the deal, however, genuine approval of EMU, mixed with the desire (whether from genuine loyalty or apprehension at the consequences for re-selection) to support the party line, and not oppose a deal brokered by their government. As one Labour MEP said, 'We're in government, and so, therefore, with government comes responsibility. And the responsibility to ensure that you're not embarrassing your own government.'

While it is impossible to specify the precise mixture of these motives behind 'Yes' votes, the following testaments from four EPLP members (or, as it termed itself until the late-1980s, the British Labour Group) identify some salient calculations:

> I'm not coming back, so it doesn't matter, but I like to think it wouldn't have affected me anyway, but who knows – but certainly, those who want to get on the list, or high up enough on the list to have any chance of winning, are not going to do anything that in any way appears to rock the boat or seem to be against the party, and the line from Downing Street was that 'you vote for this'. So it was a brave soul who voted against it.

It's interesting that there should be that unity of purpose. It wasn't the case a year ago. I think in a sense there is a greater acceptance within the Labour Party's ranks of the inevitability and desirability of belonging to the Euro zone... However, there's also another factor, and that's the impending selection process, and nothing concentrates members' minds more than the possibility of unemployment...it encouraged members to think in a positive way!

The Euro vote wasn't difficult, wasn't problematic... I mean, we've got a few old die-hards, but...I didn't see that as problematic at all.

I think probably there was among many people a sense of inevitability. It may have been, and I wouldn't be too sure about this, an awareness that stepping out of line before our particular type of selection system for next year's election might not be the most sensible career move.

What can be said for certain is that while EPLP opponents of EMU estimate their strength at around one-third of the 1994–99 membership,[8] the evidence from the Euro vote does nothing to contradict the 1996 survey which indicated this to be a significant over-estimate. Although their numbers were likely swelled in the vote by other pressures, a substantial majority of Labour MEPs favour EMU, and European unity more generally. The days of the EPLP being an isolated anti-integration minority in the EP now seem long past. With its national MPs apparently also disinclined to rebellion over the EU (Cowley, 1999), the Labour government would seem relatively immune from the sort of Europe-related parliamentary conflicts which bedevilled recent Conservative governments. Serious disputes are more likely to concern the party's recent adherents in the news-media.

The Conservatives

Conservative MEPs have often been regarded as more pro-European than their national counterparts: Mrs Thatcher described them as a 'residue of Heathism' (Thatcher, 1993: 749). While some members acknowledge this image, and others even reinforce it,[9] they are not a uniformly pro-European bloc immune from the politics of their national party. The Euro vote demonstrated this clearly. While the centre of gravity of the divisions may differ in the EP, here, as elsewhere, the Conservatives are deeply divided over EMU. Despite intensive discussions prior to the vote among Conservative MEPs, they realized that no consensus was attainable.[10] The whip eventually agreed among the group was to abstain, but this was doomed to being ignored by at least some. As one member recounted shortly afterwards:

It was quite clear that we had two members – John Stevens and Lord Plumb – who were definitely going to vote for the single currency, but who could have agreed to abstain if everyone was going to abstain. What they were not prepared to do – and I think they had every cause and justification for – was to do so and there be an asymmetry if those opposed were saying 'we will not abstain come what may'. Once the decision was made by some to oppose – two with a fair degree of consistency and honour, and one without any integrity whatsoever – the die was cast.

Nor was this division merely a function of the specific circumstances of the Euro vote. At least two members interviewed indicated that they would have *opposed* British entry if that had been at issue; by contrast, another stated that '*if* the Labour government had said that we were going to join the single currency on 1 January 1999, I would have supported them'. Given these divisions, and with many members facing the uncertainties of a new selection process, it is unsurprising that for fully half of Tory members, discretion – via abstention – proved the better part of valour. Indeed, despite constituting less than 3 per cent of the EP's membership, British Conservatives contributed over 37 per cent of those abstaining on the Euro vote. This decision gave the Tories an Index of Agreement score of 44.5 – much lower than Labour, but probably still a significant over-estimate of the genuine unity in the group. That their MEPs achieved little unity on this issue – and that merely, in essence, an agreement to be undecided – says much about continuing Conservative difficulties in building a more united party on major European questions.

One member concisely summarizes the experience of these difficulties for an individual MEP:

I think there is particularly for Conservatives in the European Parliament, mainly in the last few years...a series of very difficult political decisions that you have to make. Now you could say they're not important, but they are important in terms of what you're trying to do in the EP. And everyone *does* come to a difficult conclusion on that because they are balancing up loyalty to the party, their own views, their own views of their own career, what they think are their moral obligations to their constituents or whatever it is, and they sum all those things up and come to different conclusions. And that does, I think, within the EP, create a sense of every man or woman for him or her-self.

It is likely that Conservative representation in the EP will move further towards the more sceptical viewpoint of the current party leadership after the 1999 elections. But it is far from clear that this will entirely resolve their

MEPs' problems. The chamber works on consensus-building: as one Tory MEP observes, 'You don't get anything done in isolation in the European parliament.' More sceptical Conservatives may simply find themselves increasingly marginal within the parliament, unable to advance their party's policy agenda. Bridging the national and European arenas was difficult for many Conservatives on the Euro vote; it will probably continue to be so for the party's European representatives on other matters for some considerable time.

Implications: European Parliamentarians and 'Europe'

It's a bit of a snap-shot of British politics in many respects. If you ask the question 'What is Europe about? What kind of Europe do we want?' in the two major parties, you're really asking a much more fundamental kind of question, which is 'What kind of *Britain* do you want?' It's really the same question. I think the reason why the Conservatives are so divided is this fundamental failure to bring together, to stitch together, these two different ends about what they think Britain is about: is it about the past, or about the future? (Labour MEP, July 1998)

The outcome of the May 1998 EP vote on the Euro is interesting and significant in itself: finding out how MEPs behaved over this historic advance in Europe's economic integration. The central argument of this article, however, is that analysis of the behaviour of UK MEPs in this vote is also able to convey wider lessons – about both the ongoing European debates within the British parties, and the relationship between national parties and their European representatives. Precisely because of the importance and controversy of the Euro vote's subject matter, it highlighted aspects of both these issues with an unusual degree of clarity.

It was shown above how the behaviour of UK MEPs on the Euro vote was overwhelmingly a function of partisan differences. This finding matches much previous work on the EP, showing substantial party cohesion in most votes in the chamber (Raunio, 1996). But differences on this occasion were not primarily a function of attitudinal distinctions between representatives of different parties: rather, they were grounded in differences between the national parties. The findings here thus support other work indicating that in major EP divisions, a national party's position can exert considerable influence over its European representatives (Hix and Lord, 1996; Gabel and Hix, n.d.). While the median MEP in most parties may be significantly more pro-European than the equivalent national parliamentarian, it does not follow from this that MEPs blindly pursue a pro-integration agenda immune from domestic political influences.

In addition, the findings of this case-study support other work suggesting that debates on Europe do not appear likely to be the basis for visceral divisions among Labour Party representatives in the near future. Labour's MPs do not appear greatly excited by the issue, while their MEPs are in sympathy with the national government's generally positive approach to the EU. While this absence of conflict is undoubtedly beneficial for the party internally, a generally neglected benefit of the party's consensus on Europe is the degree to which it also helps the party's MEPs advance its policy agenda within the mainstream of debates in the EP. Divisions on Europe are much more deep-rooted in the Tory party: among the party membership, in the national parliament *and* in their EP representation as well. That the balance of forces seems to be moving in a generally sceptical direction, including among the party's MEPs, may offer the basis for a new European consensus within the party. However, such a direction also risks minimizing the contribution Conservative European parliamentarians can make to advancing the policy goals of a party which, out of power at home, has few other such avenues open to it.

ACKNOWLEDGEMENTS

This article draws on 30 non-attributable interviews conducted by the author with serving or former MEPs. The author would like to thank them all for giving so generously of their time and assistance, as he would Martin Bond of the European Parliament London Office, and Philip Cowley and Paul Webb who both provided helpful comments.

NOTES

1. For the sake of consistency, I follow the now established convention of referring throughout to the European *Union*, even when discussing matters which pre-date the formal establishment of the Union in 1993.
2. Lord Plumb was President (Speaker) of the EP from 1987–89. Pauline Green has been leader of the Socialist group in the chamber since July 1994 – nonetheless, her possible candidature for the office of Mayor of London has received wide scepticism on the grounds of her low public profile.
3. I thank several members for conveying this point to me.
4. MEPs may register an abstention during a vote: this is distinct from the practice in the House of Commons where abstention means not participating in the division. Percentages in the Euro division referred to include all votes plus members (70, or 11 per cent, of the total membership) who did not participate.
5. Linear specifications of the model, run as a check, resulted in minimal differences to the results reported here.
6. The use of OLS might be questioned, given that dependent variable's categories form an ordinal rather than interval-level scale. However, as ordered-logit models produced almost identical results, this article reports the more familiar and easily interpretable regression findings.
7. This measure, the standard means of estimating voting cohesion in the EP, is computed by excluding absent MEPs, and then calculating the 'highest modality minus the sum of the

other two modalities', multiplying this figure by 100, and then dividing this figure by the total number of votes cast (Raunio, 1996: 125).

8. One anti-Euro Labour MEP suggested, 'on EMU, I suppose 20 members more or less share my views, so it's about 2–1', although he went on to observe that 'in the Socialist group it would be about 10–1 against'.

9. One Conservative member commented on his motivation for becoming an MEP that 'the party in this country was moving in a more Euro-sceptic direction, and I wanted to do what I could to prevent that happening in Brussels or Strasbourg'.

10. Information supplied by several members.

REFERENCES

Arnold, Laura (n.d.) 'Legislative Activity and Effectiveness in the U.S. Senate: Reaping the Rewards of Seniority'. Unpublished paper, Ohio State University.

Baker, David and David Seawright (1998) *Britain For and Against Europe*. Oxford: Oxford University Press.

Bowler, Shaun and David Farrell (1995) 'The Organizing of the European Parliament: Committees, Specialization and Co-ordination', *British Journal of Political Science* 25: 219–43.

Butler, David and Martin Westlake (eds) (1994) *British Politics and European Elections, 1994*. London: St. Martin's Press.

Corbett, Richard, Francis Jacobs and Michael Shackleton (1995) *The European Parliament, Third Edition*. London: Longman.

Cowley, Philip (1999) 'The Absence of War? New Labour in Parliament', in J. Fisher, P. Cowley, D. Denver and A. Russell (eds) *British Parties and Elections Review Volume 9*, pp.154–70. London and Portland OR: Frank Cass.

Hix, Simon and Christopher Lord (1996) 'The Making of a President: The European Parliament and the Confirmation of Jacques Santer as President of the Commission', *Government and Opposition* 31: 62–76.

Gabel, Matthew and Simon Hix (n.d.) 'The Ties that Bind: MEP Voting Behaviour and the Commission President Investiture Procedure'. Unpublished paper, London School of Economics.

Mughan, Anthony, Janet M. Box-Steffensmeier and Roger M. Scully (1997) 'Mapping Legislative Socialization', *European Journal of Political Research* 32: 93–106.

Raunio, Tapio (1996) *Political Group Behaviour in the European Parliament*, University of Tampere Doctoral Dissertation.

Raunio, Tapio (1998) 'Beneficial Cooperation or Mutual Ignorance? Contacts between MEPs and National Parties'. Unpublished paper, University of Helsinki.

Scully, Roger (1997a) 'The European Parliament and the Co-Decision Procedure: A Re-Assessment', *Journal of Legislative Studies* 3: 58–73.

Scully, Roger (1997b) 'The European Parliament and Co-Decision: A Rejoinder to Tsebelis and Garrett', *Journal of Legislative Studies* 3: 93–103.

Scully, Roger (1998) 'MEPs and the Building of a Parliamentary Europe', *Journal of Legislative Studies* 4: 91–107.

Scully, Roger (n.d.) 'Reaching the Summit? The European Parliament and the Amsterdam Treaty'. Unpublished paper, Brunel University.

Spiers, Shaun (1997) 'Relations between the Government and the European Parliamentary Labour Party', in S. Tindale and E. Barrett (eds) *Britain in Europe: Initiatives for the 1998 Presidency*, pp.89–98. London: Institute for Public Policy Research.

Thatcher, Margaret (1993) *The Downing Street Years*. London: HarperCollins.

Westlake, Martin (1994) *Britain's Emerging Euro-Elite? The British in the Directly Elected European Parliament, 1979–1992*. Aldershot: Dartmouth.

Young People and Contemporary Politics: Committed Scepticism or Engaged Cynicism?

Dominic Wring, Matt Henn and Mark Weinstein

Growing concern about public disaffection with the British political process and its institutions has manifested itself in a number of ways. While some have addressed the apparent decline in electoral participation, others have sought to assess and understand the motivations and interests of specific groups within the population such as women and those belonging to ethnic minorities (see for instance, Saggar, 1997; Peake, 1997). Recently, attention has also begun to focus on young people's engagement with the political process. This concern was borne out by a campaign launched in the run-up to the 1997 General Election. Backed by a cross-party alliance, the music industry initiative *Rock the Vote* urged young people to make sure they were entered on the electoral register so that they might exercise their democratic rights (Martin and Street, 1997: 33–8). Symbolically the campaign's May 1996 launch event took place at the prestigious Ministry of Sound club in London's West End. In promoting itself *Rock the Vote* attempted to reinforce the idea that, collectively, the youth vote could play a potentially important role in British politics.

This perception, on the part of politicians, that young people are increasingly politically important was evidenced by their activity during the election campaign. During that campaign, the victorious Labour Party made a concerted effort to target youth with a specially produced promotional video and advertising in magazines and even nightclubs (Wring, 1997).[1] Similarly, following their defeat, the Conservatives opted to elect William Hague as their new leader in a clear vote of confidence in youth over experience. Hague, in a bid to make his age part of his appeal, talked of a 'fresh start', wore a baseball cap and attended the Notting Hill carnival.

Young People and Political Participation

The Political 'Know-nothings'?

During the 1997 General Election a number of prominent journalists criticized young people for their apparent detachment from the democratic process. Taken together these commentaries have helped to cement a popular conception of the nation's youth as lazy, disinterested and apathetic. Writing in *The Times*, Nigella Lawson suggested that those young people who complained of feeling marginalized and disenfranchised from the political system:

> should be treated with contempt... Look here, dimbo, I want to say: by refusing to vote you are disenfranchising yourself. It's no good moaning about which ever party gets in later and claiming that it's not your fault as you didn't vote for them: it will be your fault, absolutely your fault. (*The Times*, 9 April 1997)

Continuing in much the same vein, Polly Toynbee dismissed many youths as 'airheads' and 'know-nothings': 'They are the don't vote, won't vote, don't give a damn, and they're smug and self-righteous about it too' (*The Independent*, 28 April 1997). Moreover, *Evening Standard* columnist Anne Applebaum denounced those young people who 'naturally blame politicians for their apathy' for being 'intellectually lazy' (*Evening Standard*, 20 March 1997). Comments such as these have led Axford and Huggins to conclude that the nation's media have been complicit in creating an image of a youth population self-consciously cultivating its own 'designer cynicism' (Axford and Huggins, 1997).

Aside from journalistic commentaries, the perception that young people are politically alienated is reinforced by their apparent reluctance to go to the polls. During the run-up to the 1997 elections there was public concern about the predicted low turnout of the youth vote – The *Financial Times* reported that only just over 50% of first-time voters were likely to use their vote (*The Financial Times*, 7 April 1997). On polling day itself Gallup reported that only 57% of 18 to 24-year-olds said they would definitely vote, compared with 86% of people in the 45 to 64 age group (King, *Daily Telegraph*, 1 May 1997). The figures would appear to confirm a trend. In the previous national election of 1992, only 61% of 18 to 24-year-olds voted, compared with a general turnout of 77.7% (Butler and Kavanagh, 1997: 254). In 1997 the latter figure was 71.4%, the lowest poll since the war. This would suggest a further decline in the number of young people voting (MORI/Rock the Vote, quoted in *London Youth Matters,* 1997).

Heath and Park's research looks specifically at those young people who were born during the 1960s and socialized during the late 1970s and 1980s. While they reject the notion of a materialistic generation, often characterized as 'Thatcher's children', they *do* conclude that this 1980s generation 'appear to be less interested in politics' than any of the other age groups they questioned (Heath and Park, 1997: 6).

In their detailed examination of electoral turnout, Crewe, Fox and Alt suggest that the relationship between age and participation is relatively straightforward. Put simply: 'the younger an elector, the less likely he or she will vote regularly' (Crewe *et al.*, 1992: 23). Regular turnout appears to increase with length of residence, age, marriage and a variety of other factors that involve people in national and personal networks. Most importantly Crewe and his colleagues emphasize the distinction between the 'alienated abstainer', who, they assert are 'a minuscule minority of the electorate as a whole', and the more common 'apathetic abstainer' (Crewe *et al.*, 1992: 26). It would appear that it is apathy and indifference that keep people away from the polls. This assertion finds some support from the work of Bynner and Ashford, authors of a study based on a longitudinal survey of several 16 to 20-year-olds living in four different areas of the UK (Bynner and Ashford, 1994:2). They identify several explanations for youth disaffection and detachment from the political process. These include young people's negative experience of the education system and early departure from it, as well as their low level of attainment and poor employment prospects (Parry *et al.*, 1992: 84). Bynner and Ashford conclude that while apathy is commonly associated with educational failure among pre-16s, not voting is connected to a broader range of circumstances and feelings.

Writing in 1996, Helen Wilkinson concluded there was evidence of a 'historical political disconnection' among young people in Britain (Wilkinson, 1996: 242). In the following year this alleged apathy of youth was a major theme of a report from the think-tank Demos by Mulgan and Wilkinson. In this report the authors went on to tie this disconnection to other forms of detachment, specifically the youth population's apparent 'unwillingness to obey the law, to play by the rules, or to pay for the needs of others' (Mulgan and Wilkinson, 1997: 218). They theorize that the origins of this disconnection may lie in a more general decline of trust in society's core institutions combined with a frustration borne of unfulfilled ambitions. Nevertheless Mulgan and Wilkinson recognize that young people *do* care about certain political issues such as environmentalism and animal rights. It is surprising then that the same authors conclude their report with a series of rather mechanistic solutions including recommendations for longer voting periods in elections, polling stations in places like cinemas, and even compulsory voting 'to ensure that young people do indeed exercise their rights' (Mulgan and Wilkinson, 1997: 220).

An Engaged Cynicism

In their extensive study of democratic participation, Parry, Moyser and Day make explicit the relationship between political efficacy, cynicism and participation by arguing that cynicism makes less of an impact on participation than a low level of efficacy. Furthermore they contend that, if anything, political cynics tend to be *more* active. Interestingly they also suggest that:

> to a very large extent, it would appear that participation occurs as a response to some event or issue which has immediate consequences for a person's own life... for the ordinary man or woman in the street, the predominately local issues of the environment and planning head the list (Parry *et al.*, 1992: 262–3).

Apart from Parry and his colleagues' work there is a growing body of scholarship challenging the notion that those disengaged from formal politics are somehow necessarily detached from the wider democratic process. For their part Roker and Player question the preoccupation with youth participation in conventional politics, most obviously through the ballot box. Having gathered data from a multi-area school survey of 14 to 16-year-olds, the authors challenge the image of young people as alienated, disaffected and selfish (Roker and Player, 1997: 11). Significantly they uncovered a high level of voluntary and campaigning activity among the young people they interviewed with respondents typically not regarding what they were doing as necessarily 'political'.

Similarly in her ethnographic study, Kum Kum Bhavnani raises the possibility that the young people she talked with could have provided instances of activity which they themselves may not have defined as 'political' but which could be placed within the domain of politics. In a series of enlightening passages it is quite clear that, for Bhavnani's subjects, 'politics' as represented by parties and politicians simply does not connect with their everyday lives in any meaningful way. Of the views expressed in her interviews, three keep reappearing: 'politics is boring...politics is difficult to understand, and...there was no point in voting' (Bhavnani, 1994: 139). In another study of young people Gaskin, Vlaeminke and Fenton also found that while their subjects tended to 'show a distinct alienation from mainstream politics' these people also saw work with 'voluntary organisations as a route to social and political action' (Gaskin *et al.*, 1996).

When it came to formal politics Roker and Player attempted to gauge their sample's interest by asking which party they felt closest to: only 29% actually identified a party, with the remaining 71% responding either 'not sure' or 'none' (Roker and Player, 1997). In 1997, the election year, an Industrial Society sponsored report found that a minuscule 2% of those 12 to 25-year-olds surveyed had an affinity with any political party (Industrial Society, 1997: 13). Figures such as these have sometimes been used to characterize young people as being disengaged from society and politically illiterate. London Youth Matters, an umbrella organization representing a myriad of groups in the capital, contend that critics have been too ready to use limited data to attack a youth population which has become a 'soft target for those wanting to jump on the moral bandwagon...a scapegoat generation' (London Youth Matters, 1997: 4).[2]

Disengagement from formal politics is by no means a new phenomenon. A similar theme can be found in the earlier literature, particularly during the 1970s when scholars such as Marsh used survey data to argue that people regarded politics as 'a remote and unresponsive system run by cynical and aloof politicians' (Marsh, 1977: 115). A similar line of analysis underpins Bynner and Ashford's more recent survey of young people's attitudes: when questioned one third of respondents thought politicians were only in politics for their own benefit; upwards of a sixth believed that it did not make any difference which party was in power; and a fifth endorsed the view that 'none of the political parties would do anything for me' (Bynner and Ashford, 1994).

Aside from the academic commentaries on youth citizenship, several sectional interest organizations have devoted time and resources to the subject. This preoccupation reflects a wider public concern. The TUC's 1996 publication, *Testament of Youth*, portrays widespread apathy about the political process among the nation's young in the context of concerns about low pay, poor training and declining trade union membership. A specially commissioned Gallup survey, on which their report is based, suggested that only 40% of 18 to 24-year-olds were certain or very likely to vote in the 1997 general election. The report also quoted an earlier NOP survey for the TUC in which 69% of young people say that politicians understand either 'not very well' or 'not at all' 'what working life today is really like' (TUC, 1996). Similarly, the 12 to 25-year-olds questioned as part of the Industrial Society backed 2020 Vision Programme regarded politicians as 'pointlessly argumentative, out of touch with young people, untrustworthy and uncaring, and obsessed with economic policy at the expense of social policy' (Industrial Society, 1997: 13).

Though most of the literature suggests politicians cannot be trusted, young people still appear to have faith in representative democratic government. As Heath and Topf have pointed out, there is a critical difference between people's attitudes towards parties (and the politicians who lead them) as distinct from the democratic process (Heath and Topf, 1987). This demarcation is consistent with Axford and Huggins' characterization of young people as 'disenchanted democrats' (Axford and Huggins, 1997: 2). Furthermore, recognizing the interest that young people *do* have in a broader conception of 'politics', Wring, Henn and Weinstein have supported the idea of lowering the age of assent to 16 in an attempt to bring more young people into the democratic process (Wring *et al.*, 1998: 15).

1997: A Turning Point in Youth Socialization?

Curtice and Jowell report that the concluding years of Conservative rule were marked by a widespread sense of falling confidence in politicians and the political system they represent. Significantly, while they identify a very low regard for the system and its custodians, they do not suggest that this declining confidence has led to a more alienated electorate (Curtice and Jowell, 1997: 92).[3] On the contrary, they find relatively high levels of public self-confidence. Furthermore, they suggest that those who have lost confidence in the political system seemed to be responding by wanting to change it rather than withdrawing from it. Linked to this they found a 'growing tolerance of unconventional political action by others' (Curtice and Jowell, 1997: 94).

Having re-interviewed respondents following the 1997 General Election, Curtice and Jowell also suggest that the poll result may have, albeit temporarily, increased some of the electorate's sense of hope and optimism about the future (Curtice and Jowell, 1997: 106). It is a mood the New Labour government has been keen to promote. Critically, ministers have attempted to demonstrate their willingness to listen to different groups. Britain's youth, in particular, have been well courted.[4] Indeed this follows on from statements made by Tony Blair prior to the election, notably the one in which he declared he would rather young people participate and vote against Labour than not at all (*The Guardian*, 15 August 1997). That said, Blair, not to mention his main opponents, did appear to have other preoccupations; as Kimberlee notes 'most of the election campaign centred around the concerns of middle-aged homeowners in the key marginal constituencies' (Kimberlee, 1998: 89). When politicians did address issues of concern to young people they tended to do so 'too often from their parents' perspective' (Leonard and Katwala, 1997: 112).

Blair's rhetoric about a 'Young Country' did appear to strike a chord with the electorate and especially youth. Within a year of Labour's election victory the new government did however find itself in conflict with sections of the younger population angered by new policy initiatives on education, employment, drugs and other matters. Formerly supportive music artists articulated this disappointment. In one dramatic intervention a member of the group Chumbawamba drenched John Prescott with water at an awards ceremony.[5] A month later the *New Musical Express* (NME) published damning commentaries on Labour's performance from many of those who had supported the party's election campaign (NME, 14 March 1998).

Government supporters appeared worried by the NME article. Several helped launch a counter offensive with one former candidate offering the riposte: 'That a collection of spoiltbrat, coke-snorting millionaire pop stars with the attention span of a goldfish have decided they've had enough of the Labour Government should cause no lost sleep' (Paul Richards, *The Guardian*, 16 March 1998). Whatever their effect on opinion comments from both sides, together with the media debate that followed, helped promote the idea that young people's concerns were no longer peripheral to the political agenda.

Research Design

This study was designed to yield a representative sample of first time voters across Nottinghamshire. We focused exclusively on 'attainers', defined as men and women who were 18 years old at the time that the electoral register was compiled (October 1997) and 17-year-olds who would be eligible to vote by the time that the electoral register came into force (February 1998). These attainers are clearly identified on electoral registers. Of course, not every attainer would be captured by this method – indeed, approximately 14% of 18 to 19-year-olds are not registered to vote, which compares with only 2% of those aged 50 or above (Arber, 1993: 81). Nonetheless, the vast majority of our target group was eligible for inclusion through this method.

Our intention in limiting our study to attainers was twofold. First, they would have no *formal* experience of participating in elections, and therefore have had no opportunity of expressing party preferences through voting, or of casting their verdict on the political parties and all that they stand for. In this sense, these attainers are relatively inexperienced politically compared to older people,[6] and as such they provide a fascinating target group for study in terms of their perception of politics, parties and politicians in Britain.

Second, in research terms, attainers are a relatively unique target group. Most social and political surveys that examine the views of young people tend to combine their views with older youths. Hence, attainers will be analysed as part of an 18 to 24 (or 18 to 25)-year-old group (see for instance Parry *et al.*, 1992: 156), or included in studies of students, typically alongside respondents with an increasingly mature age profile as Higher Education is opened up to new entrants.

Nottinghamshire was chosen because it represents the archetypal local economy in transition. There has been a decline in heavy industry within the county as epitomized by the collapse of the local mining industry. Similarly, there has been a shift of investment from power generation, textiles and engineering and into new technology based and service industries. In turn this has led to a marked change in shape of the labour market with an increasingly middle class, white-collar professional group as well as pockets of high and long-term unemployment. According to the local authority, the number of jobs within the county declined by 5% between

1991 and 1995, while male earnings fell to 13% below the national average, with youth unemployment of particular concern (Nottinghamshire County Council, 1996). Nottinghamshire is also interesting because it has been relatively marginal in local and national political terms throughout the 1980s. Indeed it has a post-war electoral history as a largely settled adversarial two-party political system, although it is now a predominantly 'Labour' area (Young et al., 1997: 499). Thus, in terms of the views of its young attainers, Nottinghamshire is likely to serve as a useful barometer for the country as a whole.

We used a random sampling method, stratified by the eight local authority districts in the county, and with respondents drawn from the electoral register. Of the 7,958 attainers across the county, it was decided to include 5,000 young attainers, a 63% sample. Respondents were mailed a questionnaire direct to their home address in mid-June 1998. Given that the purpose of the study was to determine those factors that acted as a disincentive for young people to become engaged in politics, we recognized the possibility that only the more 'political' young people in our sample might respond. With this in mind, we decided to enter respondents into a prize draw, with £100 of compact disk/cassette tape vouchers provided by the Nottinghamshire County Council. While increasing the general response rate, it was anticipated that we would encourage the participation of those young people who were driven primarily by the possibility of winning the prize draw, and thus offer a more accurate representation of the youth population as a whole.[7]

The actual size of the sample gained was 1,597 from the 5,000 attainers included in the study, a response rate of 32%. This response rate can be put into context by comparing it with the voting turnout for the county as a whole, and for each of the eight local authority districts. We would expect of course that people are more likely to participate in elections (where their vote has some influence over local decision-making) than in our survey (where their response does not). We found that, contrary to our expectations, there was only a marginal difference between the two. Furthermore, our survey contains only the views of 17 and 18-year-olds. As young people are less likely to vote in elections than older age-groups, we can assume that if we had voting details for this age group, the turnout would be considerably lower, and therefore closer to our survey response rate. Our overall response of 32% is only marginally less than the percentage turnout for the last countywide council elections (1993) when the turnout for all voting adults was 35.9%.

Results

This study has attempted to gain an understanding of how young people relate to political institutions and processes. Respondents were asked for their opinions of politicians and political parties. Furthermore the survey gathered replies to a set of more wide-ranging questions concerning the sample's more general attitudes, or civic orientation, to politics. In one item respondents were encouraged to identify the topic of most concern to them, thereby giving some definition and substance to the salient issues as well as what young people believe politics to be essentially about. Aside from this, respondents were also questioned about how much they discussed the subject, their levels of activity and their consumption of local media.

Political Engagement

Our research reveals evidence that, far from being apolitical and apathetic, young people *are* interested in political issues. First, we found that there was a clear majority of people (over 80%) who discuss politics with friends and family (see Table 1). When asked about national politics, nearly two-thirds (60%) of respondents replied that they had *some* or more interest in the topic; few admitted to having *none at all* (14%). There was, however, less engagement with local issues: just over two fifths (41%) said they had at least some interest, approximately twice the number who had none (21%).

TABLE 1
ATTAINERS POLITICAL ENGAGEMENT (%)

	A great deal	Quite a lot	Some	Not very much	None/ not at all
Generally speaking, how often would you say that you talk about politics with your friends or family?	3	13	31	35	19
How much interest do you normally have in national politics?	5	19	37	26	14
How much interest do you normally have in local politics?	2	8	32	38	21

The interest respondents had in politics manifested itself in various ways. When asked what they thought was the most important issue,[8] respondents who replied tended to focus on education, followed by international matters, the environment, general politics, economics and other topics in that order (see Figure 1 below). The responses were generally well thought through, and typically the young participants within the survey recorded quite detailed and sophisticated answers. Furthermore, we received only one sardonic response, '*England to win the World Cup*'; given President Chirac's immediate poll ratings boost in the aftermath of France's victory in the football competition this year, perhaps this is not such a non-political indicator after all.

FIGURE 1
AGENDA OF YOUTH CONCERNS

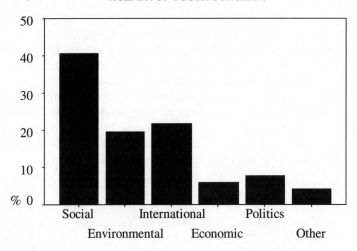

Confidence in the Political Process

Young people clearly have a strong commitment to the democratic process. Three-quarters of those included in the survey stated that it was important to vote in national elections (76%), and perhaps surprisingly given the low turnout in recent contests, two-thirds claimed the same for local elections (64%). Significantly, twice as many attainers admitted they strongly agreed when asked about the former (33%) as against the latter type of contest (19%). Only a fraction responded that voting in both national (3%) and local (4%) elections was not important. This apparent faith in the electoral process is reinforced by the low figure for those who expressed the view that 'voting is a waste of time' (5%) and the high number who disagreed (74%) with this contention (see Table 2).

TABLE 2
PERCEPTION OF IMPORTANCE OF VOTING (%)

How much do you agree or disagree with each of the following statements?

	Strongly agree	Agree	Neither	Disagree	Strongly disagree
Important to vote in national elections	33	43	21	2	1
Important to vote in local elections	19	46	31	3	1
Voting is a waste of time	2	3	22	46	28

Reflecting the fluctuating levels of turnout in different polls, 22% replied that they did not know whether they would vote in the next national election, rising to 36% when the question was asked of local contests and 42% in relation to the European parliamentary race (see Table 3). A small minority claimed that they would not participate in general (9%) or local (10%) elections at all, with nearly twice as many intending to abstain in the next poll for the European parliament (21%). These results suggest that young people are not naively over-generalizing their support for elections. They are discriminating supporters of the democratic process, with considerably fewer recognizing an importance in voting at European elections compared to local or national contests. This may be due to the perceived remoteness of the European parliament from their lives.

TABLE 3
INTENTION TO VOTE, AND PARTY IDENTIFICATION (%)

	Yes	No	DK
Do you intend to vote in the next parliamentary general election?	70	9	22
Do you intend to vote in the next local election?	55	10	36
Do you intend to vote in the next European parliamentary election?	37	21	42
If you do intend to vote (in the next parliamentary general election), do you know which party you will vote for?	41	59	
If you do intend to vote (in the next local election) do you know which party you will vote for?	36	64	
If you do intend to vote (in the next European parliamentary election), do you know which party you will vote for?	20	80	

Of those who intended to vote in a national election, only 41% knew which political party they would support, as against a clear majority (59%) who did not. The figures for local elections were similar, with slightly less (36%) reporting that they knew who they would support as against nearly two-thirds who did not (64%). The degree of uncertainty was even more noticeable for the European elections, with only 20% admitting to knowing which party they would vote for compared with over four-fifths who did not (80%). This trend perhaps bares out the marked tendency for greater shifts of allegiance among those going to the polls for elections to the European parliament. Nevertheless, there is still evidence of potential and substantial young voter volatility in the non-European contests.

Political Activism

Perhaps predictably, given their relative youth, the attainers were rather inexperienced politically (see Table 4). Only a fraction admitted to having joined a political party (1%) in the past. When asked whether they might ever consider becoming a member, only 7% of respondents thought they were likely to do so. A majority of two-thirds (66%) replied that they thought it unlikely, but another 27% admitted they did not know, suggesting they were open to persuasion in the future. Though a minority, there appears to be a sufficient number of members and potential joiners to service political parties and thus enable them to survive with at least a rudimentary structure.

TABLE 4
POLITICAL ACTIVISM (%)

	Yes	No
Have you ever joined a political party?	1	99
Have you ever written to your Member of Parliament?	10	90
Have you ever written to your local councillor?	7	93
Have you ever joined a campaign group?	11	89
Have you ever signed a petition?	83	17
Have you ever given money to a campaign?	46	54
Have you ever taken part in a march or demonstration?	14	86

Just over a tenth of respondents (10%) said they had written to their MP. Marginally more agreed they were likely to do so in the future (14%) against a substantial proportion who said that this was unlikely to happen (41%). Similarly, relatively few (7%) admitted to having written to any local councillors with nearly twice that (10%) agreeing they were likely to do so in the future as against two-fifths who were not (40%).

The pattern of dislocation from formal politics is continued when respondents were asked for their opinion of politicians. Only a minority (19%) agreed that politicians *cared for young people like themselves* with over double that (39%) saying they did not, and a comparable number (43%) not knowing one way or the other. Similarly under a fifth (17%) disagreed with the contention that *once elected, politicians lose touch,* suggesting substantial scepticism, even cynicism, with formal politics, parties, and their elected representatives. This is borne out by the significant minority (47%) who supported the statement, though just over a third (36%) admitted to having no decisive opinion on the matter. Larger majorities agreed with other assertions which were roundly critical of parties, notably the statement that *parties are interested in votes not opinions* (52%) and that *it doesn't matter who is in power, things go on much the same* (51%) as against dissenters on these topics (18% and 28% respectively).

Somewhat surprisingly, however, when asked whether they thought *politicians were all the same,* nearly half (48%) dissented from this view as opposed to a sceptical quarter of the sample who agreed with the statement (27%) and those who had no opinion either way (25%).

TABLE 5
YOUTH PERCEPTION OF FORMAL POLITICS (%)

How much do you agree or disagree with each of the following statements?

	Agree	Neither	Disagree
Politicians care about young people like myself	19	43	39
Politicians are all the same	27	25	48
Once elected, politicians lose touch with people pretty quickly	47	36	17
Parties are only interested in people's votes, not in their opinions	52	30	18
It doesn't matter which party is in power, in the end things go on much the same	51	21	28

Other Indicators of Political Activism

When asked whether they had ever joined a campaign group, those who had were in a clear minority (11%), though, as we have seen, this was substantially more than the small number who had belonged to a party. Marginally more admitted that they were likely to join one in the future (13%), though the most sizeable group (39%) said they did not know. The reticence of many to commit themselves to a group did not mean they were unwilling to participate in some way or another and, in fact, could be interpreted to suggest that they were open-minded about this idea. A substantial majority (83%) said they had signed a petition and only a minority ruled this out in the future (5%). Nearly half (46%) admitted to having given money to a campaign in the past, and 14% of respondents had participated in a march or demonstration. Interestingly, only a third (31%) said they were unlikely or extremely unlikely to participate in this type of direct action in the future.

Respondents were asked a series of questions on specific single-issue campaigns. Besides differing aims, these initiatives have used a variety of advertising media and awareness-raising techniques. Nevertheless, all were of some interest to young people. The first of these, a health campaign called *Drugs Abuse Resistance Education* (*DARE*), was originally pioneered in Nottinghamshire between 1993 and 1996.[9] Similarly *Stick it in the Box*, a council initiative to increase youth turnout, was launched throughout the county in anticipation of the 1997 local and Westminster elections.[10]

The other two campaigns were run on a national basis prior to the last General Election in 1997. These were *Operation Black Vote*, which aimed to increase electoral participation among ethnic minority voters, and the *Rock the Vote* initiative mentioned earlier in this article. The latter slogan, devised for a campaign pioneered in the United States during the run-up to the 1996 presidential race, was adopted by the British music industry as a means of increasing young voter registration and awareness before the 1997 election. The first national campaign of its kind, it enjoyed the sponsorship of several celebrity patrons together with a relatively high presence in the media regularly consumed by youth (Cloonan and Street, 1997: 33–8).

Asked whether they knew about any of these campaigns, just over a fifth (21%) recognized *Stick it in the Box* as against a majority who did not (74%). Surprisingly, perhaps, nearly all of the respondents (96%) said they had heard of *DARE*. In comparison, only 9% of survey respondents admitted to having heard of *Rock the Vote* as against the overwhelming majority (88%) who had not. The numbers who had heard of *Rock the Vote* were only marginally more than the 7% who said they knew of the lower-profile and, by its nature, more specialized *Operation Black Vote* campaign.

The higher recognition rates for the local campaign initiatives suggest that regional rather than national organizations may be in a better position to communicate with young people. This point is arguably reinforced by respondents' own non-national media use. Questioned about their weekly viewing and listening habits, more than three-quarters (78%) admitted to viewing local/regional news programmes at least twice a week. While the numbers who never listened to local/regional news on the radio formed a sizeable minority (20%), over half (51%) tuned in twice or more every week. Most respondents also read the local/regional press at least once or more every week (83%) as against barely one in 20 (6%) who never do so.

Conclusion

Contrary to the perception of some media commentators, the survey has assessed the attitudes of young, potential first-time voters and uncovered a group with an interest in political issues if not the formal institutions associated with them. It has been argued that there is a civic orientation among the young to the democratic process, but an antipathy to formal, professional politics. This trend is most marked when significant numbers of respondents confessed to having been involved in minimal, politically related activities such as giving money, petition-signing, and even attendance at demonstrations. These approaches perhaps reflect the sample's concern with issues relating to the environment, education and international affairs.

It was seen that respondents divided into two smaller groups of the activist and the alienated, aside from a clear majority who may appear less motivated but displayed important signs that they were engaged with the democratic process. This was most clear when a large proportion of those questioned expressed some desire to take part in elections. The commitment was especially marked in the case of national and local contests, if not that of the European parliament. Significantly, the apparent concern with regional politics was further borne out by other results. When asked about their media use, most respondents watched, listened or read local news sources on a regular basis. Added to this, more agreed that they had heard of the regionally based campaigns than the similar national initiatives aimed at them.

ACKNOWLEDGEMENTS

We would like to acknowledge the financial support from Nottingham County Council, and in particular the input from Alistair McGrady of the Council's Policy and Information Department.

NOTES

1. Labour went as far as placing adverts in club toilets with stickers bearing the legend 'Now wash your hands of the Tories', D. Wring, 'The Media and the Election', in Geddes and Tonge (1997).
2. The report goes on to provide evidence from a range of organizations documenting young people's experience of crime, unemployment and poverty, and their lack of skills, qualifications and opportunities to account for their 'fractured' experiences. The document quotes data and statistics from, among others, the Volunteer Centre UK, TUC, British Youth Council, BBC, Youth Aid, and NACRO.
3. Only 22% of the electorate trust governments to put the interests of the nation above that of party; 28% agree with the statement that *'parties are only interested in people's votes, not their opinions'*, and over a quarter of the population now strongly agree that *'political parties and MPs are out of touch with the needs of the electorate'*.
4. See, for example, Peter Mandelson's argument that the Labour Party is different and can make a difference. 'A lifeline for youth', *The Guardian*, 15 Aug. 1997.
5. Chumbawamba vocalist Danbert Nobacon claimed that he did it 'on behalf of single mothers, pensioners, sacked dockers, people being forced into "workfare", people who will be denied legal aid, students who will be denied the free university education that the entire front bench benefited from, the homeless and all the underclass that are now suffering at the hands of the Labour government'.
6. This is not to suggest that these attainers are politically naive. Elections are certainly the most commonly used means for participating in politics in Britain. But these young people will have experienced politics indirectly through the mediation of journalists and broadcasters. In addition some of them may have taken part in politics by joining campaigns, movements and party youth wings or carried out political acts through other informal means such as petitions, donations and so on.
7. For an overview of the benefits to be acquired for survey response through offering incentives to potential participants, see F. Fowler (1993) *Survey Research Methods, California*, Sage, p.40.
8. We asked an open question: *'Which community, national or international issue are you most concerned about?'* We created six categories from this question. Full details including other technical aspects of the project can be obtained from the authors on request.
9. The campaign was aimed primarily at children aged 9 to 11, typically the younger siblings of the sample surveyed here. While most of the work was done in Nottinghamshire schools, there was also some advertising and media publicity throughout the county (for more details see, G. Empson (1997) 'DARE you be inspected', *Teaching Today*, summer).

10. The campaign, managed by Nottinghamshire County Council, ran throughout April 1997 with the key slogan appearing on hoardings, buses and in newspaper advertisements. In addition 6,000 leaflets were distributed around the county's schools and colleges.

REFERENCES

Applebaum, A. (1997) 'Don't care, won't vote – what a cop out by 'yoof' ', *Evening Standard*, 20 March.
Arber, S. (1993) 'Designing Samples', in N. Gilbert (ed.) *Researching Social Life*. London: Sage.
Axford, B. and R. Huggins (1997) 'Young People and Political Marketing: Untargettable or Sentimental at Heart?', Paper presented to Images of Politics: International Conference on the History and Development of Political Communication on Television, Amsterdam, October 23–5.
Bhavnani, K. (1994) *Talking Politics: A Psychological Framing of Views from Youth in Britain*. Cambridge: Cambridge University Press.
Butler, D. and D. Kavanagh (1997) *The British General Election of 1997*. London: Macmillan Press.
Bynner, J. and S. Ashford (1994) 'Politics and Participation: Some Antecedents of Young People's Attitudes to the Political System and Political Activity', *European Journal of Social Psychology*, 24:2.
Cloonan, M. and J. Street (1997) 'Popular Culture and Politics', *Politics*, 18:1.
Crewe, I., T. Fox and J. Alt (1992) 'Non-voting in British General Elections, 1966–October 1974', in D. Denver and G. Hands (eds), *Issues and Controversies in British Electoral Behaviour*, pp.18–30. Hemel Hempstead: Harvester Wheatsheaf.
Curtice, J. and Roger Jowell (1997) 'Trust in the Political System', in R. Jowell *et al.* (eds). *British Social Attitudes: The 14th report. The End of Conservative Values?* pp.89–106. Aldershot: Ashgate.
Empson, G. (1997) 'DARE You Be Inspected', *Teaching Today*.
Fowler, F. (1993) *Survey Research Methods*, California, Sage.
Gaskin, K., M. Vlaeminke and N. Fenton (1996) *Young People's Attitudes Towards the Voluntary Sector: A Report for the Commission on the Future of the Voluntary Sector*. Loughborough: Loughborough University.
Heath, A. and A. Park (1997) 'Thatcher's Children?', in R. Jowell *et al.* (eds). *British Social Attitudes: The 14th report. The End of Conservative Values?* pp.1–22. Aldershot, Ashgate.
Heath, A. and R. Topf (1987) 'Political Culture', in R. Jowell *et al.* (eds), *British Social Attitudes: the 1987 report. The End of Conservative Values?* pp.51–69. Aldershot: Gower.
Kimberlee, R. (1998) 'Young People and the 1997 General Election', *Renewal*, 6:2.
King, A. (1997) 'Eighteen today and voting for the first time', *Daily Telegraph*, 1 May.
Lawson, N. (1997) 'There's no excuse for not voting', *The Times*, 9 April.
Leonard, M and S. Katwala, (1997) 'It was the young wot won it!' Renewal, 5:314.
London Youth Matters, (1997) *The Kids are Alright? What it's like to be young in London in the 1990s*. London: London Youth Matters.
Mandelson, P. (1997) 'A lifeline for youth', *The Guardian*, 15 Aug. 1997.
Marsh, A. (1977) *Protest and Political Consciousness*. London: Sage.
Martin C. and J. Street (1997) 'Popular Culture and Politics', *Politics*, 18: 1.
Mulgan, G. and H. Wilkinson (1997) 'Freedom's Children and the Rise of Generational Politics', in G. Mulgan (ed.) *Life after Politics: New Thinking for the Twenty-first Century*, pp.213–21. London, Fontana Press.
New Musical Express, (1988) 'Betrayed: The Labour Government's war on you', 14 March 1998.
Nottinghamshire County Council (1996) *Building Together: Strategic Plan 1997–2001*. Nottinghamshire: Nottinghamshire County Council.
Parry, G., G. Moyser and N. Day, (1992) *Political Participation and Democracy in Britain*. Cambridge, Cambridge University Press.
Peake, L. (1997) 'Women in the Campaign and in the Commons', in A. Geddes and J. Tonge (eds) *Labour's Landslide: the British General Election of 1997*, pp.165–78. Manchester: Manchester University Press.

Roker, D. and K. Player (1997) 'Challenging the Image: Young people as Volunteers and Campaigners', *Youth Action*, No.60, Study for The Trust for the Study of Adolescence.

Saggar, S. (1997) 'The Dog that Didn't Bark: Immigration, Race and the Election', in A. Geddes and J. Tonge (eds) *Labour's Landslide: The British General Election of 1997*, pp.147–64. Manchester: Manchester University Press.

The Industrial Society, (1997) *Speaking Up Speaking Out! The 2020 Vision Programme Summary Research Report*. London: Industrial Society.

Toynbee, P. (1997) 'Mrs Thatcher's airhead revenge', *The Independent*, 28 April.

Trades Union Congress (1996) *Testament of Youth: A Manifesto for Young Workers*. London: TUC.

Wilkinson, H. (1996) 'But Will They Vote? The Political Attitudes of Young People', *Children and Society*, 10:3.

Wring, D. 'The Media and the Election', in A. Geddes and J. Tonge (eds) *Labour's Landslide: The British General Election of 1997*, pp.70–84. Manchester: Manchester University Press.

Wring, D., M. Henn and M. Weinstein, (1998) 'Lowering The Age of Assent: Youth and Politics in Britain', *Fabian Review*, 110:4.

Young, M., M. Henn and N. Hill (1997) 'Labour Renewal Under Blair? A Local Membership Study in Middleham', in J. Stanyer and G. Stoker (eds), *Contemporary Political Studies*, pp.495–509. Exeter: Political Studies Association.

Reference Section

As in previous volumes, we provide here a reference section in which assorted information, which is likely to be useful to readers but which takes a good deal of digging out, is collected and presented in a convenient form. The subjects covered are broadly the same as before. Unfortunately for election-watchers there were no parliamentary by-elections during 1998 but we have included details of the results of the 1997 Scottish and Welsh devolution referendums, and the referendums held in Northern Ireland and London in the spring of 1998.

The section begins with a chronology of important political events during 1998, prepared as usual by David Broughton. We then move on to summaries of opinion poll results, giving monthly figures for voting intention in all the main polls, voting intentions in Scotland from System Three and, from Gallup, data on ratings of party leaders, preferences for Prime Minister, approval of the government's record, personal prospective economic evaluations and perceptions of economic competence. There follows a summary of the results of the local elections held in England on 7 May 1998 – the first major test at the polls for the new government.

After the referendum results we provide details of key economic indicators before an extensive section on the political parties, which includes not only details of party officers and addresses, but also data on key internal elections. We conclude with our usual table detailing circulation of national newspapers.

We would like to thank those who have helped in the gathering, checking and preparation of the material in this section, especially David Broughton, Colin Rallings, Michael Thrasher, Mark Stuart, Simon Atkinson and Ben Marshall.

Justin Fisher
Philip Cowley
David Denver
Andrew Russell

1. Chronology of Events 1998

JANUARY

2. The High Court ruled that the 17-year-old son of a Cabinet Minister who had admitted selling illegal drugs could be named, after much speculation in the tabloid press. The naming allowed the Cabinet Minister concerned (Home Secretary Jack Straw) to comment on the matter.

5. The Chancellor of the Exchequer, Gordon Brown, promised a 'national crusade' against unemployment at the launch of the government's New Deal for unemployed young people between the ages of 18–24.

8. The Labour Party expelled two of its members of the European Parliament (Ken Coates and Hugh Kerr) after they continued to criticize the leadership of Prime Minister Tony Blair, particularly with respect to welfare reform plans and the centrally controlled decisions regarding the candidates' list for the European Parliament elections in 1999.

9. The Secretary of State for Northern Ireland, Mo Mowlam, made an unprecedented visit to the Maze Prison near Belfast for direct talks with loyalist prisoners in an attempt to keep the peace process on track.

11. John Wells, satirist, co-writer of the *Dear Bill* letters in *Private Eye*, died aged 61.

12. William Straw, son of Home Secretary Jack Straw, was given a formal police caution after he admitted selling a small amount of cannabis resin to Dawn Alford, an undercover reporter from the *Daily Mirror*.
Eric Sunderland, the chief counting officer in charge of the Welsh devolution referendum in September 1997, admitted that there had been confusion in the way that votes had been counted. He denied that this had affected the result.
The UK and Irish governments unveiled their blueprint for the future of Northern Ireland. The document, *Propositions on Heads of Agreement*, was designed to inject some impetus into the negotiations.

14. Conservative MPs endorsed the proposals of the party's leader William Hague, concerning new procedures for electing the party leader, previously the preserve solely of MPs. They voted overwhelmingly in favour of a one-member, one-vote system among party members.

15. Prime Minister Tony Blair initiated a debate on reform of the welfare state with a speech to Labour Party workers in Dudley in the West Midlands. Blair warned that 'the status quo is not an option. Long-term, principled reform is the way forward'.
   The election agent for Mohammad Sarwar, the suspended MP for Glasgow Govan, was charged with breaking regulations with regard to election expenses.

20. Geoffrey Robinson, the Paymaster-General, was criticized by Sir Gordon Downey, the parliamentary commissioner for standards, for failing to register the £12.5 million off-shore trust of which he was a discretionary beneficiary. This continued the scrutiny of Robinson's financial affairs which had started in late 1997.

29. Prime Minister Tony Blair announced a new inquiry into the events of 30 January 1972 in Londonderry, Northern Ireland when 14 unarmed men were killed by British troops in an incident known as 'Bloody Sunday'. The three-member tribunal of enquiry would sit in public in both London and Northern Ireland and it would have the power to call witnesses.

FEBRUARY

2. A High Court jury found that a director of Camelot, the operator of the National Lottery, had attempted to bribe a rival to drop his bid for the licence. Guy Snowden had sought to bribe Richard Branson. Snowden resigned from the Camelot board immediately and the following day, Peter Davis, the director of OFLOT, the Lottery regulator, also resigned after allegations that Branson had informed Davis about the bribery attempt but that nothing had been done.

5. Prime Minister Tony Blair made it clear that the government had no intention of introducing new legislation to curb the freedom of the press. The move was interpreted as a rebuke for Lord Irvine of Lairg, the Lord Chancellor, who had earlier indicated his support for a press privacy law.

8. Enoch Powell, the former Conservative and Ulster Unionist MP, died aged 85.

15. Opposition MPs called for a public inquiry into the cost of refurbishing the official residence of the Lord Chancellor, Lord Irvine, after the details of the total cost of about £650,000 were revealed. The cost included about £60,000 on wallpaper.

20. Sinn Féin was suspended from the multi-party peace talks in Northern Ireland after the IRA was formally blamed for two murders earlier in the month.

23. Pressure on the Northern Ireland peace talks was intensified when a car bomb exploded outside shops in the mainly Protestant town of Portadown in County Armagh. Four people were injured.

24. The Court of Appeal issued an unusual condemnation of capital punishment as it quashed the conviction of Hussein Mattan, a Somali seaman who had been hanged for murder in 1952. The case was the first to be referred back to the Court of Appeal by the Criminal Cases Review Commission. The Court added that 'capital punishment was not perhaps a prudent culmination for a criminal justice system which is human and therefore fallible'.

26. Stuart Proffitt resigned as a senior executive with the publishers HarperCollins after a row over the publication of *East and West*, the memoirs of Chris Patten, the last Governor of Hong Kong. Allegations were made that censorship of the book was attempted to suit Rupert Murdoch's business interests in China, after it became known that the memoirs were critical of the Chinese authorities.

MARCH

1. An estimated 200,000 people marched through London in one of the largest marches (The Countryside March) seen in the capital for some years. The marchers represented a loose coalition of groups and individuals. The main uniting force was opposition to the private member's bill to ban all hunting with hounds proposed by Michael Foster, the Labour MP for Worcester.

3. The Lord Chancellor, Lord Irvine, appearing before the House of Commons public affairs committee, attempted to justify the £650,000 spent refurbishing his official apartment at Westminster by referring to the need for quality materials rather than 'something from the DIY store'. He felt that the refurbishment was something for which 'future generations would be grateful'.

4. Two men were murdered in a bar in Pontzpass in County Armagh in Northern Ireland. The men, one a Catholic and the other a Protestant, were killed by members of the Loyalist Volunteer Force (LVF).

6. The Lord Chancellor, Lord Irvine, was again criticized when he was accused by MPs of misleading the House of Commons public administration committee when he had answered questions on plans for the reform of the House of Lords.

11. Fifty Labour MPs signed a motion calling on the government to review the role of the Lord Chancellor. They called for the creation of a Justice Department to be headed by a member of the Cabinet.

12. Gerry Adams, President of Sinn Féin, met Prime Minister Tony Blair. Adams declared that Sinn Féin remained 'deeply committed' to the peace process and to securing a 'lasting, endurable settlement for Northern Ireland'.

13. The private member's bill to ban all hunting with hounds, proposed by Michael Foster, the Labour MP for Worcester, was lost as it ran out of parliamentary time.
Ron Davies, Secretary of State for Wales, announced that the new Welsh Assembly would sit in Cardiff after a strong challenge from Swansea. He also announced a design competition for the assembly building.

17. The Chancellor of the Exchequer, Gordon Brown, presented his second budget to the House of Commons. He announced an overhaul of the United Kingdom's tax and benefits system in an effort to encourage work and enterprise, including the introduction of the working families' tax credit.
Former Conservative Cabinet Minister, Jonathan Aitken, was arrested and questioned by police over allegations of perjury and conspiracy to pervert the course of justice. The allegations arose after the collapse of Aitken's libel action against the *Guardian* and Granada TV.

23. The latest round of multi-party peace talks took place in Northern Ireland and included Sinn Féin who returned to the negotiations after being suspended in February.

25. George Mitchell, the former US Senator and chairman of the Northern Ireland peace talks, set a 15-day deadline for their completion. He gave the various parties until 9 April to bring the process to 'a swift and favourable conclusion'.

26. The government presented to the House of Commons its long-awaited green discussion paper on welfare reform entitled *New Ambitions for Our Country: A New Contract for Welfare*. Frank Field, Minister for Welfare Reform at the Department of Social Security, claimed that the document represented the first truly comprehensive review of the welfare state since the Beveridge Report of 1942.

27. Joan Maynard, trade unionist and former Labour MP, nicknamed 'Stalin's Granny', died aged 76.
   Baroness Lestor of Eccles (Joan Lestor), former Labour MP, died aged 66.

28. William Hague, Conservative Party leader, announced that his reforms of the party, under the *Fresh Future* banner, had won the support of 80 per cent of party activists in a postal ballot. The vote was however marred by a low turnout, with only about one-third of the members actually participating.

APRIL

1. John Prescott, the Deputy Prime Minister and Secretary of State for Environment, Transport and the Regions, was cleared by Sir Gordon Downey, the Parliamentary Commissioner for Standards, of impropriety in failing to declare a donation of £28,000 received by a 'blind trust' operated by his office before the May 1997 general election.

10. A multi-party peace agreement (the Good Friday agreement) was signed between the UK and Irish governments and eight political parties at Stormont Castle, Belfast. The agreement was subject to approval by referendums on both sides of the Irish border in May. The agreement would replace the Anglo-Irish agreement of 1985. The cornerstone of the agreement was that the fate of Northern Ireland could only be decided by the votes of the people, based on a new legislature, a new executive body, cross-border links and a British-Irish council. Paramilitary prisoners were to be released within three years and a commitment to achieve the decommissioning of arms was to be affirmed. The agreement was the result of 22 months of negotiation, with the final session lasting 32 hours.

13. Sir Ian McGregor, the former chairman of British Steel and the National Coal Board and a major figure in the 1984–85 miners' strike, died aged 85.

15. The Orange Order rejected the Good Friday agreement, calling for

'clarification' of the issues of policing, prisoners and the decommissioning of arms.

18. David Trimble, the Ulster Unionist leader, won the backing of his party's ruling Council for the Good Friday agreement by 540 votes to 210. Considerable uncertainty had preceded the vote given the rejection of the agreement by the Orange Order and a degree of equivocation among the party's MPs.

19. Denis Howell, Labour Minister of Sport 1964–70 and 'drought supremo' during the summer of 1976, died aged 74.

20. Archbishop Trevor Huddleston, a long-time campaigner against apartheid in South Africa, died aged 84.

22. The lower house of the Irish Parliament, the Dáil, overwhelmingly approved the Good Friday agreement.

25. The Ulster Defence Association (UDA), the largest loyalist paramilitary organization, endorsed the Good Friday agreement and called for a 'yes' vote in the forthcoming referendum.

28. Chris Patten, the former Conservative Party chairman and the last Governor of Hong Kong, was appointed to head an independent commission charged with making recommendations for the future policing of Northern Ireland.

30. The Irish Republican Army (IRA) issued a statement in which they stated that the Good Friday agreement was 'a significant development', praising the role of Sinn Féin and its peace strategy. However, the IRA made it clear that they would not be giving up their weapons.

MAY

2. The Single European Currency, the euro, was officially 'born' in Brussels with 11 European Union member states agreeing to take part from 1 January 1999. Wim Duisenberg was confirmed as the Head of the European Central Bank located in Frankfurt.

3. Foreign and Commonwealth Secretary Robin Cook came under pressure after a report was published in the *Sunday Times* suggesting that the Foreign and Commonwealth Office (FCO) had known that a UK

company, Sandline International, had sent arms to Sierra Leone early in 1998 in contravention of a United Nations arms embargo imposed in October 1997.

6. Foreign and Commonwealth Secretary Robin Cook announced the setting up of an independent inquiry to look into the facts of the Foreign Office's role in the 'arms to Africa' affair, chaired by Sir Thomas Legg, a former permanent secretary in the Lord Chancellor's department.
The government announced that the opening of the new Scottish Parliament would be brought forward from January 2000 to July 1999, following the elections scheduled for May 1999.

7. Local elections were held in England, producing modest gains for the Conservatives and losses for both Labour and the Liberal Democrats compared to contests for the same seats in 1994. Labour remained however the strongest party overall in local government and the Conservatives remain in third place behind the Liberal Democrats. However, voter turnout was only 27 per cent, the lowest since records began in 1947.

. In a referendum in London, government proposals for a directly-elected mayor and assembly were approved by a large majority. The turnout was 34 per cent, producing a 72 per cent majority in favour of the mayor and a new assembly.

10. At a special Sinn Féin conference in Dublin, 331 out of 350 delegates voted in favour of participation in the Northern Ireland assembly elections planned for June and they also called for a 'yes' vote in the forthcoming referendum on the Good Friday agreement.
Lord (Bob) Mellish, Labour Party Chief Whip under the leadership of Harold Wilson 1969–76, died aged 85.

11. Prime Minister Tony Blair dismissed the furore over arms supplies to Sierra Leone as 'hoo-ha', asserting that FCO officials had been right to work for the restoration of the deposed President Kabbah.

17. Lord (Hugh) Cudlipp, the creator of British tabloid journalism after 1945 and chairman of Mirror Group newspapers, died aged 84.

18. The Customs and Excise investigation into the 'arms to Africa' affair concluded that no action should be taken against Sandline International on the grounds that any prosecution would fail and it would not be in the public interest.

21. The government published a White Paper on workers' rights entitled *Fairness at Work*. Controversy broke out over the provisions for union recognition (a simple majority of those voting or at least 40 per cent of those eligible to vote). Prime Minister Tony Blair declared that 'the days of strikes without ballots, mass picketing, closed shops and secondary action are over'.
Former Conservative Cabinet Minister, Jonathan Aitken, was formally charged with perjury, perverting the course of justice and conspiracy to pervert the course of justice.

22. Irish voters on both sides of the border gave their support to the Good Friday agreement signed on April 10. In simultaneous referendums, the first all-Ireland ballot since 1918, the positive vote in favour cleared the way to assembly elections in Northern Ireland in June. The 'yes' vote in the North was 71 per cent and almost 95 per cent in the Republic.

26. The National Executive Committee (NEC) of the Labour Party approved a plan to increase the vetting of the disciplinary record of Labour MPs, with the aim of preventing those deemed to be unsuitable from being re-selected as candidates.

JUNE

1. William Hague, Conservative Party leader, announced a re-shuffle of the Shadow Cabinet. The first re-shuffle since Hague became party leader in June 1997, it involved two new entrants (Ann Widdecombe at Health and David Willetts at Education and Employment) as well as the allocation of different responsibilities for five others. Peter Lilley was appointed deputy leader of the Conservative Party charged with policy formulation, while Michael Ancram was named as the successor to Lord Parkinson as party chairman from October.

4. The seven-member monetary policy committee of the independent Bank of England increased the base UK interest rate by 0.25 per cent, to 7.5 per cent. It was the sixth rise since the May 1997 general election. The increase was heavily criticized by both business and trade unions as likely to tip the UK economy into recession.

5. The government announced the phased closure of the Dounreay nuclear plant in northern Scotland on the grounds that it had no long-term future. Existing re-processing tasks would last until about 2006 after which the de-commissioning of the plant would begin.

The shareholders of Vickers (of which car maker Rolls-Royce was a subsidiary) approved the sale of Rolls-Royce to Volkswagen, Europe's largest car manufacturer. The price of £470 million was substantially higher than an earlier offer from BMW.

10. Sir David English, editor of the *Daily Mail* between 1971 and 1992 and subsequently Chairman of Associated Newspapers, died aged 67.

13. Reg Smythe, cartoonist and creator of Andy Capp for the *Daily Mirror* from 1957, died aged 80.

18. Margaret Beckett, President of the Board of Trade and Secretary of State for Trade and Industry, announced the government's proposals for a national minimum wage. Partly based on the recommendations of the Low Pay Commission, the plan envisaged a minimum wage for those aged 22 or over as £3.60 an hour from April 1999. Estimates suggested that about 2 million people, three-quarters of them women, would benefit from the plan.

20. A list of 27 new life peers was published, including Melvyn Bragg, broadcaster and novelist, Northern Foods chairman Chris Haskins and television executive Waheed Ali who, at the age of 34, became the youngest person ever appointed as a life peer.

21. Peter Temple-Morris, re-elected as a Conservative MP in May 1997, announced that he had joined the Labour Party. Temple-Morris had been suspended from the Conservative Party in December 1997 for opposing the 'eurosceptic' line of the party leadership. Thereafter, he described himself as an 'Independent One-Nation Conservative'.

22. The House of Commons voted by 336 votes to 129 to reduce the age of consent for homosexuals from 18 to 16 to bring the law into line with that applying to heterosexuals.

JULY

1. The New Northern Ireland Assembly met for the first time, with Ulster Unionist leader David Trimble being elected as the First Minister of the power-sharing administration. Seamus Mallon of the SDLP was elected as his deputy.

5. The *Observer* claimed that lobbyists close to the government were using

their contacts to secure preferential access to ministers and to obtain information of commercial value. The two lobbyists most involved, Roger Liddle and Derek Draper, were both closely associated with Peter Mandelson. Draper claimed he was on intimate terms with the '17 people who count' in government circles (most of them not ministers). Three days later, William Hague, Conservative Party leader, accused Prime Minister Tony Blair of surrounding himself with 'feather-bedding, pocket-lining, money-grabbing cronies'.

Tensions rose in Northern Ireland once more with the march of 5,000 Orangemen to the church in Drumcree, near Portadown, for the third time in three years, posing a serious threat to the Good Friday agreement. Johnny Speight, creator of Alf Garnett and *Till Death Us Do Part*, died aged 78.

9. Margaret McDonagh was appointed general secretary of the Labour Party, the first woman to hold the post. She succeeded Tom Sawyer, who was made a life peer in June after being general secretary since 1994.

10. The National Health Service celebrated its fiftieth birthday.

12. General revulsion was expressed when three young boys were killed in a petrol bomb attack on their home in Ballymoney, County Antrim. Calls were made to stop the Drumcree stand-off between Orangemen and the security forces.

15. The House of Commons Standards and Privileges Committee cleared Geoffrey Robinson, the Paymaster-General, of an allegation that he had not declared a payment of £200,000 from a company owned by the late Robert Maxwell, accepting that he had never received the money.

17. Gordon Brown, Chancellor of the Exchequer, presented the government's expenditure plans for the financial years 1999–2000 to 2001–2, providing an aggregate increase in spending of £56 billion on health, education and infrastructure.

22. The House of Lords ignored an overwhelming vote in favour by the House of Commons when it voted by 290 to 122 against a government amendment to reduce the age of homosexual consent from 18 to 16. On July 27, the government confirmed that the amendment would be dropped as a result and it would be introduced as a piece of separate legislation in the next session of parliament.

24.   R.W. (Tiny) Rowland, entrepreneur, former owner of the *Observer* and chairman of the Lonrho corporation 1961–95, died aged 80.

27.   The Cabinet Office issued a new code of conduct regulating contacts between government ministers and lobbyists. Any leaking of confidential information to lobbyists was specifically seen as unacceptable.
       The report of Sir Thomas Legg's inquiry into the 'Arms to Africa' controversy was published. The Foreign and Commonwealth Office was criticized for failures of communication but the most direct criticism was directed at Peter Penfold, the High Commissioner in Sierra Leone. Robin Cook, Foreign Secretary, claimed the report exonerated ministers entirely and that 'modernization' reforms were to be introduced into the FCO.

27–29 Prime Minister Tony Blair carried out the first re-shuffle of his government, dismissing four members of the Cabinet and making a number of changes at junior ministerial level. Those leaving the Cabinet were Harriet Harman (Social Security), Gavin Strang (Transport), David Clark (Chancellor of the Duchy of Lancaster) and Lord Richard (Leader of the House of Lords).
       The most significant of the changes were the move of Peter Mandelson from being Minister without Portfolio in the Cabinet Office to Secretary of State for Trade and Industry; Margaret Beckett from Trade and Industry to Leader of the House of Commons; Nick Brown from Chief Whip to Minister of Agriculture; Stephen Byers to be Chief Secretary to the Treasury, replacing Alistair Darling who took over Social Security; Ann Taylor became the Chief Whip and Jack Cunningham, previously Agriculture Secretary, took on a new role of 'enforcer' in charge of co-ordinating the activities of the various government departments. Baroness Jay became Leader of the House of Lords.
       The most controversial change was the exit from the government of Frank Field, previously Minister of State for Social Security, who resigned after he was refused the post of Secretary of State. In his resignation speech to the House of Commons, Field said that the failure to make progress on fundamental reform of the welfare state stemmed from his lack of executive responsibilities and lack of support from other ministerial colleagues.

30.   Prime Minister Tony Blair presented a report on the performance of the

government in its first year. The document claimed that of the 177 election pledges contained in the 1997 election manifesto, 50 had been carried out, 119 were in hand, and only eight remained still to be tackled. A government White Paper on local government reform was published. It included proposals for directly-elected mayors with executive powers, annual council elections and an end to the 'capping' of council budgets by central government.

The conviction of Derek Bentley, hanged for the murder of a policeman in 1953, was described by the Appeal Court as 'unsafe' and the conviction was therefore rescinded posthumously.

31. The German electronics group, Siemens, announced that it would close its semi-conductor plant on Tyneside by the end of the year, with the loss of 1,100 jobs. The state-of-the-art facility had only been opened by the Queen in April 1997, costing £1.2 billion, including £50 million in government grants. The principal cause was the collapse in the price of computer microchips.

AUGUST

1. David Shayler, a former MI5 officer, was arrested in Paris and detained by the French authorities pending a British request for his extradition to face charges under the Official Secrets Act. Shayler had claimed that MI6, the external intelligence service, had plotted to assassinate the Libyan leader, Colonel Gadaffi.

3. Gus Macdonald, chairman of the Scottish Media Group and head of Scottish Television, was appointed as a Scottish Office Minister responsible for business and industry after being made a life peer. Renewed charges of 'cronyism' were based on the fact that Macdonald was not a Labour Party member nor had he any previous parliamentary experience.

5. The decennial Lambeth Conference of the Communion of the Anglican bishops adopted by a vote of 526 to 70 a resolution that homosexual relations were 'incompatible' with Christian scripture. The vote reflected the strong opposition of African and Third World bishops to any relaxation of traditional Christian teaching on homosexuality.

6. The Labour Party national executive committee decided that there were no grounds for disciplinary action against Derek Draper who had been heavily involved in the 'cash for access' controversy in July.

15. The Northern Ireland peace process was put under further strain when a car bomb planted by a splinter republican group exploded in Omagh, County Tyrone, killing 28 civilians and injuring 220 others. It was the worst single incident in the province since the beginning of the 'Troubles' in 1969. The 'Real IRA' admitted responsibility for the atrocity on 18 August and apologized for the death of the civilians.

19. Bertie Ahern, Prime Minister of the Republic of Ireland, unveiled a series of 'extremely draconian' anti-terrorist measures in the light of the Omagh bombing. This involved the extension of the time available to detain suspects without charge and new offences relating to the withholding of information connected to terrorism.

20. Prime Minister Tony Blair pledged to follow the Irish government in the granting of new powers to the British authorities to help in the hunt for the Omagh bombers.

25. Prime Minister Tony Blair unveiled a package of anti-terrorist measures designed to make it easier to convict people of conspiring within the UK to commit a terrorist offence anywhere in the world.

30. The Labour Party's annual financial report showed that 97 people had made contributions of £5,000 or more to the party in 1997. Those donors included many prominent businessmen. Party membership figures published earlier in the month revealed the first drop since Tony Blair became party leader in July 1994, down to 394,000 members in July 1997 from 405,000 in January.

SEPTEMBER

1. The third Viscount Rothermere, proprietor of Associated Newspapers (publishers of the *Daily Mail* and *Mail on Sunday*), died aged 73.

2–3 The Criminal Justice (Terrorism and Conspiracy) Bill was passed by both Houses of Parliament and received the royal assent the following day. The bill was the government's reaction to the Omagh bombing in August. The bill took just 27 parliamentary hours to reach the statute book. The government met fierce cross-party criticism focusing upon the scope of the bill and the speed with which it was forced through. Prime Minister Tony Blair insisted that the bill was a 'proportionate, targeted response' to the Omagh bombing.

4. Fujitsu announced the closure of its semi-conductor production in the

North East of England, with the expected loss of 570 jobs. The seven-year-old plant cost £350 million and was located in the Sedgefield constituency of Prime Minister Tony Blair.

7. At a meeting with Prime Minister Tony Blair, a delegation from the Trades Union Congress (TUC) urged the establishment of a special task force of ministers, employers and trade unions to combat the increase in manufacturing jobs being lost.

8. The board of Manchester United football club recommended acceptance of a £625 million bid to buy the club by British Sky Broadcasting (BSkyB), part of Rupert Murdoch's News International group. The next day, the Office of Fair Trading opened an investigation into the bid.
The Real IRA, the splinter republican organization responsible for the Omagh bombing in August, announced a 'permanent' ceasefire.

9. Tommy Graham, Labour MP for Renfrewshire West, was expelled from the Labour Party after five charges against him had been proven, following an investigation and his suspension from August 1997. Graham declared that he would seek judicial review of his expulsion.

11. Scottish Secretary Donald Dewar relaunched the Scottish Labour Party as 'Scottish New Labour', publishing a manifesto for the elections to the new Scottish Parliament scheduled for May 1999.

14. The annual TUC conference opened in Blackpool. The main call from the conference was for government action on the recession in manufacturing. In addition, a campaign to fight for a higher national minimum wage than that set by the government was pledged. Income disparities were also highlighted. John Edmonds, the leader of the General and Municipal Boilermakers Union (GMB) declared that 'a company director who takes a pay rise of £50,000 when the rest of the workforce is getting a few hundred is not part of some general trend – he is a greedy bastard'.

15. Eddie George became the first ever Governor of the Bank of England to address the TUC annual conference.

19. Scottish Secretary Donald Dewar was formally chosen as Labour's candidate for the post of First Minister in the forthcoming Scottish government.

20. The Liberal Democrats held their annual conference in Brighton. The extent to which the party should co-operate with the Labour government was debated. In his leader's speech, Paddy Ashdown gave qualified praise for the Labour government, while urging it to move quicker towards the introduction of proportional representation and a freedom of information bill and to curb its 'control freak' tendencies.

23. The Scottish National Party (SNP) held its annual conference in Inverness. The conference was dominated by preparations for the elections to the Scottish Parliament in 1999. The party's leader, Alex Salmond, urged Scots to drop 'anti-English feeling' and assured observers that Scotland would be a 'good neighbour' to England.

25. The annual conference of Plaid Cymru opened in Cardiff. Elections to the new Welsh Assembly dominated the conference. The party's president, Dafydd Wigley, promised a new style of politics in Wales, and he warned that Plaid would not accept an Assembly controlled by 'Labour cronies'.

27. The Labour Party held its 97th annual conference in Blackpool. New procedural rules were introduced, in which debates and voting on an array of composite and other resolutions was replaced by the tabling of policy documents prepared earlier in the party's national policy forum. The four documents presented on health, welfare reform, crime and European policy were all approved by acclamation.

28. Members of the Marylebone Cricket Club (MCC) voted by the required two-thirds majority in favour of the admission of women to membership.

OCTOBER

1. Metropolitan Police Commissioner Sir Paul Condon appeared before the Macpherson Inquiry into the 1993 murder of a black London teenager, Stephen Lawrence. He apologized for mistakes made during the investigation of the case but denied that police racism or corruption had been the cause of those mistakes. He also strenuously rejected the claim that his force suffered from 'institutional racism'. In contrast, at a session of the inquiry held in Manchester, the Chief Constable of Greater Manchester Police, David Wilmot, did admit that institutional racism existed in his force.

6. The annual conference of the Conservative Party opened in

Bournemouth. It was marked by continued divisions over Europe despite leader William Hague obtaining an endorsement of his policy of opposing the single European currency in a pre-conference referendum of party members. Hague described the referendum result as demonstrating the 'settled will of the party'. Michael Heseltine, former Deputy Prime Minister, described the referendum as 'an irrelevance'.

8. The monetary policy committee of the Bank of England reduced the base UK interest rate by 0.25 per cent, to 7.25 per cent, the first cut since June 1996.

. A Conservative member of the European Parliament, James Moorhouse, joined the Liberal Democrats in protest against the policy of the Conservatives towards the single currency. Later the same day, the party chairman, Michael Ancram, withdrew the whip from two more Conservative MEPs (John Stevens and Brendan Donnelly) who were similarly opposed to the party line.

13. The Committee on Standards in Public Life, chaired by Lord Neill, published proposals for far-reaching reform of the rules governing the funding of political parties and campaigns. The proposals included a ban on all party donations from abroad, disclosure by the parties of all donations over £5,000, a ban on 'blind trusts', more money for the parliamentary opposition parties and the creation of an independent electoral commission to monitor and enforce the new rules. A bill to enact most of the proposals was promised by the government for 1999.

14. Baroness Jay of Paddington, Leader in the House of Lords, announced that a bill would be included in the next parliamentary session which would remove the hereditary component of the House of Lords and also that a Royal Commission would be appointed to consider various options for definitive reform of the upper chamber.

16. David Trimble, leader of the Ulster Unionists and John Hume, leader of the moderate nationalist party, the SDLP, were awarded the 1998 Nobel Peace Prize for their efforts to find a peaceful solution to the conflict in Northern Ireland.

21. The official list of Cabinet Committees and their composition following the July re-shuffle was published. It was noted that Lord (Charles) Falconer of Thoroton, who had become a Minister of State in the Cabinet Office in the re-shuffle, sat on 14 committees, more than all but one other minister. Falconer is a long-time personal friend of the Prime Minister

who was appointed Solicitor-General and made a life peer after the 1997 general election.

26. Nicholas Budgen, former Conservative MP and Eurosceptic, died aged 60.

27. Ron Davies, Secretary of State for Wales, resigned from the Cabinet because of a 'serious lapse of judgement' the previous evening involving him being robbed in south London. Davies repeatedly denied press allegations that either sex or drugs had been involved in the incident. He claimed he had 'a loving relationship' with his second wife. Davies was replaced by Alun Michael, formerly Minister of State at the Home Office.

28. Ted Hughes, Poet Laureate since 1984, died aged 68.

29. The report of the Independent Commission on Electoral Reform, established in December 1997 under the chairmanship of Lord (Roy) Jenkins, was published. It recommended that the existing 'first past the post' electoral system should be replaced with a combination of the alternative vote (AV) in single-member constituencies and 'top-up' seats to ensure greater proportionality between votes and seats. Reports suggested that key members of the Cabinet remained in favour of no change from the present system and the government declined to make any commitment to put the proposals to a referendum before the next general election.
Trade and Industry Secretary Peter Mandelson announced that the proposed purchase of Manchester United by BSkyB would be referred to the Monopolies and Mergers Commission. A report was expected to take about six months to complete.

30. The BBC was fiercely criticized for attempted censorship when it issued a memo to current affairs editors banning any reference in their programmes to the private life of Trade and Industry Secretary Peter Mandelson. This followed three days after Matthew Parris, a columnist on *The Times*, had named Mandelson as one of the homosexual members of the Cabinet on BBC2's *Newsnight* programme.

NOVEMBER

2. In his personal resignation statement to the House of Commons, Ron Davies, the former Secretary of State for Wales, fiercely attacked the

press for spreading rumours about his personal life. He said, 'We are what we are. We are all different, the products of our genes and our experience'.

3. Gordon Brown, the Chancellor of the Exchequer, presented his second pre-Budget report to the House of Commons. He reduced his forecast of economic growth to between 1 and 1.5 per cent but insisted that the government would maintain its plans for increased public spending announced in July.

4. The Government published a Green Paper on a series of proposals for strengthening marriage and the family in the light of the fact that official figures showed divorce ending over 40 per cent of marriages and over one-third of all births in 1997 taking place outside wedlock. Both of these figures were the highest of any country in the European Union.

5. Alun Michael, the new Secretary of State for Wales replacing Ron Davies, announced his candidacy for the Labour leadership in Wales. His challenger was again Rhodri Morgan, who had run against Davies for the post in September.
   The monetary policy committee of the Bank of England reduced the base UK interest rate by 0.5 per cent, to 6.75 per cent. It was the second reduction in successive months.

7. Nick Brown, Secretary of State for Agriculture, Fisheries and Food, announced that he was a homosexual. The acknowledgement was triggered by the intention of the *News of the World* to publish the story of a former partner of Brown. Brown received the full backing of the Prime Minister.

9. The *Sun* carried the front-page headline: 'Tell us the truth Tony: Are we being run by a gay Mafia?' in the wake of the Davies incident and Brown's acknowledgement of his sexuality. In an abrupt change of policy on 12 November, the *Sun* then said it would not 'out' homosexuals in the future except in cases of 'overwhelming public interest'.
   The Human Rights Bill, implementing the Labour government's pledge to incorporate the 1950 European Convention of Human Rights into domestic law, received the royal assent. It is due to come into full effect on 1 January 2000.

11. Prime Minister Tony Blair and Liberal Democrat leader Paddy Ashdown

announced the broadening of Labour–Liberal Democrat co-operation via the special cabinet committee first set up in July 1997. Discussions would now include topics such as welfare, education and UK participation in the single European currency.

The Chief Inspector of Prisons, Sir David Ramsbotham, delivered a damning verdict on conditions within the top security Maze prison in Belfast. Ramsbotham declared the prison to be safe for neither staff nor inmates. The prison was run by an indulgent regime where demoralized staff regarded themselves as little more than 'gophers' for the inmates. The government announced its intention to close the prison by the end of 2000.

13. A government White Paper recommended that the UK Parliament should be given new powers to scrutinize and delay legislative proposals emanating from the European Union as one means of tackling the 'democratic deficit'.

15. The Wales Labour Party announced that its 25,000 members would be allowed to express their individual preferences in the ballot for the leader of the party in Wales, due to take place in February 1999.

18. A court in Paris rejected the UK's request for the extradition of David Shayler, a former officer of MI5, to face charges under the Official Secrets Act in London. Shayler was released immediately after serving three and a half months in prison in France after having been arrested on 1 August.

Paymaster General Geoffrey Robinson apologized to the House of Commons for oversights in his declaration of outside business interests in the register of members' interests. The apology had been requested by the Commons standards and privileges committee.

20. The Crown Prosecution Service (CPS) decided not to prosecute a south London rastafarian who had been charged with the theft of Ron Davies' car in late October. It was felt that the five other people arrested in connection with the incident but not charged were also unlikely to be prosecuted.

23. The European Union agreed to lift the ban on British exports of beef off the bone from young cattle (those aged between six and 30 months old). The ban had first been imposed in March 1996 after a link had been demonstrated between BSE in cattle and CJD in humans. Estimates suggested that the ban had cost British farmers about £5 billion in lost beef exports.

24. The Labour government's legislative programme for the 1998–99 parliamentary session was set out in the Queen's Speech. The main bills concerned the removal of the right of hereditary peers to sit and vote in the House of Lords; four bills on aspects of welfare reform; two bills on the National Health Service and additional bills on the youth justice system, the age of consent for homosexuals and political asylum.

26. In a European Parliament by-election in the Scotland North-East constituency, the Scottish National Party (SNP) retained the seat with 48 per cent of the vote on a much lower turnout (20.5 per cent) than in 1994. Labour was third behind the Conservatives with 18.5 per cent of the vote. SNP leader Alex Salmond said that Labour 'had been given the bum's rush...coming third in a two-horse race'.
   Prime Minister Tony Blair became the first UK Prime Minister to address both houses of the legislature of the Irish Republic. Commenting on the Northern Ireland peace process, Blair said that 'we have come too far to go back now'.

DECEMBER

2. Viscount Cranborne, the Conservative leader in the House of Lords, was dismissed by William Hague, Conservative Party leader, for negotiating a deal with the government, without consulting Hague, to save some hereditary peers. Four frontbench Conservative spokesmen in the Lords resigned in protest at Hague's action. Cranborne was replaced by Lord Strathclyde, hitherto opposition Chief Whip. Under the deal, 91 hereditary peers (out of about 750) would retain their seats in a reformed chamber while definitive reforms were debated. The deal also meant that the European Parliamentary Elections Bill, which had been rejected by the House of Lords five times, would be allowed to pass in time for implement-ation for the elections to the European Parliament scheduled for June 1999.

7. The Trade and Industry Secretary Peter Mandelson set out the government's plans for the Post Office, ruling out privatization but instead allowing the organization more commercial freedom.
   Former Conservative Cabinet Minister Jonathan Aitken was committed for trial at the Old Bailey on charges of perjury, perverting the course of justice and conspiracy to pervert the course of justice.

10. The monetary policy committee of the Bank of England reduced the base UK interest rate by 0.5 per cent, to 6.25 per cent, the third such reduction in three months.

13. Lew Grade, impressario, agent, TV producer and film mogul, died aged 91.

15. The re-introduced Euro-Elections Bill was rejected for the sixth time by the House of Lords (a procedural device) which enabled the government to invoke the Parliament Acts of 1911 and 1949 to override the upper chamber for the third time since 1945.

    The government published a Green Paper setting out its long-awaited plans for reform of the pensions system well into the next century.

16. The Trade and Industry Secretary Peter Mandelson published a government White Paper setting out 100 ways of improving business competitiveness with a view to creating a 'knowledge-driven economy'. UK and US aircraft launched air strikes on Iraq during the evening. The attacks continued until the early hours of 20 December. Operation Desert Fox was intended to 'degrade' Iraq's military capabilities.

17. Widespread concern was expressed at the unprecedented decision of the House of Lords to quash its own decision of 25 November that the former dictator of Chile, Augusto Pinochet, arrested in London on an arrest warrant from the Spanish authorities, did not enjoy immunity from prosecution. The decision was based on the apparent conflict of interest of one of the judges in terms of links with Amnesty International.

20. Dominic Lawson, editor of the *Sunday Telegraph*, categorically denied that he had ever been an agent of MI6 after Labour MP Brian Sedgemore had called for a Commons investigation into the claim made by a former MI6 agent, Richard Tomlinson.

    Deputy Prime Minister John Prescott underlined disagreements within the Cabinet over the government's relationship with the Liberal Democrats by declaring that the government should concentrate upon delivering its own programme backed by a House of Commons majority of 179.

22. Lord (Donald) Soper, Methodist Minister, Christian socialist, pacifist and public orator, died aged 95.

23. Trade and Industry Secretary Peter Mandelson and Paymaster General Geoffrey Robinson both resigned from the Cabinet following the disclosure in the *Guardian* that Mandelson had taken a loan from Robinson of £373,000 to buy a house in London in 1996. Mandelson was replaced by Stephen Byers, who was in turn replaced as Chief Secretary

to the Treasury by Alan Milburn. The post of Paymaster General was given to Dawn Primarolo, hitherto Financial Secretary to the Treasury. Mandelson's responsibilities for the Millennium Dome in London were assumed by Lord Falconer.

Allegations of a conflict of interest, centring on the fact that the Department of Trade and Industry were investigating Robinson's business affairs, were rejected by Mandelson on the grounds that he had deliberately played no part in those investigations. In his reply to Mandelson's resignation letter, Prime Minister Tony Blair noted that 'without your support and advice, we would never have built New Labour' and 'thanks for all you have done' and 'in the belief that, in the future, you will achieve much, much more with us'.

31. In the New Year's Honours List, former Prime Minister John Major was made a Companion of Honour for his contribution to the Northern Ireland peace process. The chairman of the peace talks, former US Senator George Mitchell, was given an honorary knighthood in recognition of his efforts in the same process.

2. Public Opinion Polls 1998

TABLE 2.1 *Voting Intentions in Major Polls 1998 (%)*

Fieldwork	Company	Sample Size	Con	Lab	Lib Dem	Other
Jan						
5–7	Gallup	1014	26	56	12	5
9–11	ICM	1200	30	48	17	5
23–26	MORI	1870	28	54	14	4
Feb						
28/1–4/2	Gallup	1041	29	54	11	5
6–8	ICM	1200	31	47	18	4
20–23	MORI	1792	28	52	15	5
Mar						
27/2–4/3	Gallup	999	29	51	14	6
6–8	ICM	1200	33	46	17	5
20–23	MORI	1879	28	53	14	5
26–1/4	Gallup	985	26	54	16	4
Apr						
3–5	ICM	1212	31	48	16	6
20–22	ICM	1000	29	52	16	3
24–26	MORI	804	30	54	13	3
24–27	MORI	1926	27	55	14	4
23–29	Gallup	1050	25	54	16	4
May						
15–19	ICM	1101	29	50	16	5
21–24	MORI	1832	26	55	14	5
28/5–3/6	Gallup	1011	28	54	12	6
Jun						
5–6	ICM	1201	29	51	16	4
24–26	MORI	1000	28	51	15	6
25–30	MORI	1760	27	56	13	4
25–1/7	Gallup	1008	28	52	14	6
Jul						
3–4	ICM	1200	27	52	17	4
17–21	MORI	1796	28	53	14	6
Aug						
30/7–5/8	Gallup	1003	28	53	13	5
7–9	ICM	1203	31	47	17	4
21–24	MORI	1886	28	52	14	6
26–3/9	Gallup	1005	28	54	12	6
Sept						
4–6	ICM	1178	29	48	17	6
18–21	MORI	1789	24	56	15	5
24–30	Gallup	1028	23	57	15	5
Oct						
1–4	ICM	1120	29	51	15	5
23–26	MORI	1775	26	53	16	5
Nov						
29/10–4/11	Gallup	1036	28	54	14	5
6–7	ICM	1222	27	51	17	5
20–23	MORI	1883	29	53	13	5
26/11–2/12	Gallup	1021	29	55	11	5
Dec						
4–7	ICM	1123	29	49	16	6
11–14	MORI	1864	27	54	12	7

Notes: The figures shown for voting intention are the 'headline' figures published by the polling companies concerned. Both ICM and Gallup now weight their results to produce 'adjusted' figures. MORI, on the other hand, publishes 'unadjusted' figures calculated in the traditional way. Gallup results are normally reported to the nearest 0.5 but all such cases here have been rounded up.

TABLE 2.2 *Voting Intentions in Scotland 1998 (%)*

| | UK Parliament | | | | Scottish Parliament | | | |
	Con	Lab	Lib Dem	SNP		Con	Lab	Lib Dem	SNP
Jan	12	50	11	26		9	44	13	33
Feb	14	46	11	28		12	39	10	38
Mar	12	48	9	28		8	40	10	40
Apr	14	44	10	30		11	36	10	41
May	14	46	10	29		10	35	10	44
Jun	14	43	9	33		9	37	8	45
Jul	13	48	8	28		10	40	9	41
Aug	13	46	8	31		11	41	8	38
Sep	13	45	10	31		12	40	9	39
Oct	14	43	12	29		11	39	12	37
Nov	13	42	13	31		11	38	12	37

Note: System Three do not poll in December but have separate polls in early and late January. The January figures shown are the averages of the two January polls. Rows do not total 100 because 'others' are not shown. From June 1998 respondents were asked separately how they would cast constituency and list votes in the Scottish Parliament elections. The figures shown are for constituency voting intention.

Source: System Three Scotland polls, published monthly in *The Herald* (Glasgow).

TABLE 2.3 *Monthly Averages for Voting Intentions 1998 (%)*

	Con	Lab	Lib Dem		Con	Lab	Lib Dem
Jan	28	53	14	Jul	28	53	16
Feb	29	51	15	Aug	29	52	14
Mar	29	51	15	Sep	25	54	16
Apr	28	53	15	Oct	28	52	16
May	28	53	14	Nov	28	53	14
Jun	28	53	15	Dec	28	51	14

Note: These are the simple means of the figures given in table 4.1.

TABLE 2.4 *Ratings of Party Leaders 1998*

| | Hague | | | Blair | | |
	Pos	Neg	Net	Pos	Neg	Net
Jan	28	55	-27	66	30	+36
Feb	31	55	-24	66	31	+35
Mar	31	50	-19	62	32	+30
Apr	38	49	-11	69	27	+42
Apr (late)	29	56	-27	72	25	+47
May	33	52	-19	70	26	+44
Jun	29	58	-29	68	28	+40
Jul	–	–	–	–	–	–
Aug	29	57	-28	67	30	+37
Sep	29	57	-28	67	28	+39
Sep (late)	28	55	-27	68	27	+41
Oct	32	56	-24	67	29	+38
Nov	33	54	-21	65	30	+35
Dec	33	56	-23	66	29	+37

Notes: The figures are based on responses to the questions 'Are you satisfied or dissatisfied with Mr Blair as Prime Minister?' and 'Do you think that Mr Hague is or is not proving a good leader of the Conservative party?' The difference between 100 and the sum of positive and negative responses is the percentage of respondents who replied 'Don't know'. Gallup appear to have stopped asking a similar question relating to Mr. Ashdown in January 1998.
Source: Gallup Political and Economic Index

TABLE 2.5 *Best Person for Prime Minister 1998 (%)*

	Hague	Blair	Ashdown	Don't know
Jan	11	56	19	14
Feb	11	55	19	15
Mar	13	51	20	16
Apr	12	55	17	16
May	11	60	16	14
Jun	12	59	15	14
Jul	12	57	18	14
Aug	13	55	18	14
Sep	12	55	17	15
Oct	12	57	17	13
Nov	13	57	18	12
Dec	13	56	16	16

Source: Gallup Political and Economic Index. The data are derived from the 'Gallup index', which is an aggregation of all Gallup's polls in the month concerned.

TABLE 2.6 *Approval/Disapproval of Government Record 1998 (%)*

	Approve	Disapprove	Don't know	Approve/ Disapprove
Jan	53	38	10	+15
Feb	52	39	9	+13
Mar	47	41	12	+6
Apr	55	34	11	+21
May	61	29	10	+32
Jun	55	37	8	+18
Jul	55	37	8	+18
Aug	54	38	8	+16
Sep	53	36	11	+17
Oct	56	36	9	+20
Nov	55	36	9	+19
Dec	53	36	11	+17

Notes: These are answers to the question 'Do you approve of the new government's record to date?' The data are derived from the 'Gallup index'.
Source: Gallup Political and Economic Index

TABLE 2.7 *Personal Prospective Economic Evaluations 1997*

	Get a lot better	Get a little better	Stay the same	Get a little worse	Get a lot worse
Jan	4	16	42	25	10
Feb	4	17	41	25	10
Mar	4	15	39	27	10
Apr	4	16	43	24	9
May	4	20	44	21	8
Jun	4	16	44	25	9
Jul	4	18	43	24	9
Aug	4	17	43	24	10
Sep	4	17	45	23	8
Oct	4	17	45	25	8
Nov	3	18	45	23	9
Dec	4	17	44	22	10

Notes: These data are based on the 'Gallup index' and derive from answers to the question 'How do you think the financial situation of your household will change over the next 12 months?' Rows do not total 100 because 'Don't knows' are not shown.
Source: Gallup Political and Economic Index

TABLE 2.8 *Best Party to Handle Economic Difficulties 1998*

	Conservative	Labour	No difference	Don't know
Jan	33	52	8	7
Feb	33	53	6	8
Mar	33	50	8	9
Apr	32	52	7	9
May	31	55	7	8
Jun	32	53	7	8
Jul	34	53	6	8
Aug	34	52	7	7
Sep	32	52	9	7
Oct	31	55	8	7
Nov	32	54	8	7
Dec	31	53	9	7

Note: These are answers to the question 'With Britain in economic difficulties, which party do you think could handle the problem best – the Conservatives or Labour?' The figures are derived from the 'Gallup index'.

Source: Gallup Political and Economic Index

3. Local Elections 1998

The elections held in 166 English local authorities (there were no elections in Scotland or Wales) on 7 May were the first major electoral test of the popularity of the Labour government elected in 1997. The elections covered all 32 London boroughs, the 36 metropolitan boroughs, 88 shire districts and 10 unitary authorities. Over 4,300 council seats were at stake.

The bewildering patchwork of authorities of different types that comprises the system of local government in England makes keeping track of election cycles and interpreting the election results a complicated task. In recent years the problems have been compounded by the piecemeal creation of unitary authorities which themselves have varying cycles. Future complications may include direct elections for mayors of large cities. What follows is a summary of the different types of local authority in Britain and a guide to election cycles.

England

Counties (34)
All members are elected every four years. Elections were held in 1997 (on the same day as the general election) and the next round of elections is due in 2001.

Metropolitan Boroughs (36)
One third of members are elected annually except in those years when there are county elections. Next elections are due in 1999.

Shire Districts with 'annual' elections (88)
Approximately one third of members are elected annually except in those years when there are county elections. Next elections are due in 1999.

Shire Districts with 'all in' elections (150)
All members are elected every four years mid-way between County elections. Next elections are due in 1999.

London Boroughs (32)
All members are elected in another four year cycle. Next elections are due in 2002.

Unitary Authorities (46)
The election cycle varies across authorities.

Scotland

Unitary Councils (32)
All members were elected in 1995 and the next elections will be in 1999.

Wales

Unitary Authorities (22)
All members were elected in 1995 and the next elections will be in 1999.

Election watchers in Britain owe a large debt of gratitude to Colin Rallings and Michael Thrasher whose indefatigable work in collecting and publishing authoritative local election results has smoothed the paths of many others. They have supplied the data presented in the following tables. Full details of the 1998 results, including individual ward results and commentary, can be found in their *Local Elections Handbook 1998* (Local Government Chronicle Elections Centre, University of Plymouth), obtainable from LGC Communications, 33–39 Bowling Green Lane, London EC1R 0DA.

TABLE 3.1 *Summary of 1998 Local Election Results*

	Candidates	Seats won	Gains/ Losses	% Share of vote
London Boroughs (32) Turnout 34.6%				
Con	1805	538	+19	32.0
Lab	1917	1050	+6	40.6
Lib Dem	1578	301	-26	20.8
Other	539	28	+1	6.5
Metropolitan Boroughs (36) Turnout 24.8%				
Con	767	107	+31	26.0
Lab	848	575	-60	45.8
Lib Dem	670	152	+20	22.9
Other	437	15	+8	5.3
District Councils (88) Turnout 30.8%				
Con	1283	423		34.8
Lab	1263	512		33.3
Lib Dem	1105	351		26.4
Other	334	86		5.5
Unitary Authorities (10) Turnout 27.8%				
Con	194	37		26.7
Lab	186	100		40.4
Lib Dem	196	49		26.4
Other	103	18		6.6

Note: Gains and losses for London and metropolitan boroughs are based on a comparison with 1994 results. A straightforward comparison is not possible for shire districts or unitaries as the number of the former has been reduced and the latter have varying electoral cycles.
Source: C. Rallings and M. Thrasher.

TABLE 3.2 *Summary of 1998 Local Election Results (all authorities)*

	Candidates	Seats won	Gains/ Losses	% Share of vote
Turnout 30.0%				
Con	4049	1105	+263	30.4
Lab	4214	2239	-151	40.3
Lib Dem	3549	853	-116	23.5
Other	1413	147	+4	5.8

Note: Net gains and losses are based on estimates provided by Rallings and Thrasher.
Source: C. Rallings and M. Thrasher.

TABLE 3.3 *Monthly Party Vote Shares in Local Government By-elections 1997 (%)*

	Con	Lab	Lib Dem	Others	Number of Wards
Jan	34.2	20.7	31.8	13.3	7
Feb	36.0	18.8	36.2	9.0	13
Mar	25.4	31.9	35.9	6.8	13
Apr	32.1	21.6	37.4	8.9	20
May	38.8	26.9	31.1	3.2	30
Jun	30.2	34.0	23.4	12.4	17
Jul	37.8	28.9	28.7	4.6	36
Aug	4.4	34.5	27.2	33.9	4
Sep	29.4	29.7	35.4	5.5	17
Oct	30.2	31.9	28.0	9.9	22
Nov	28.7	38.2	22.1	11.0	12
Dec	24.2	37.6	25.8	12.4	12

Note: These figures relate to the results of local government by-elections in wards and electoral divisions contested by all three major parties.
Source: C. Rallings and M. Thrasher.

TABLE 3.4 *Quarterly Party Vote Shares in Local Government By-elections 1997 (%)*

	Con	Lab	Lib Dem	Others	Number of wards
Q1	31.5	24.3	35.0	9.2	33
Q2	34.8	27.8	30.2	7.2	67
Q3	32.0	29.7	31.1	7.2	57
Q4	28.4	34.7	26.2	10.7	46

Note: These figures relate to the results of local government by-elections in wards and electoral divisions contested by all three major parties.
Source: C. Rallings and M. Thrasher.

TABLE 3.5 *Seats Won and Lost in Local Government By-elections 1998*

	Con	Lab	Lib Dem	Others
Held	44	81	49	8
Lost	15	56	28	25
Gained	55	9	37	23
Net	+40	-47	+9	-2

Source: C. Rallings and M. Thrasher.

4. UK Referendums 1997–98

1. Referendum on Scottish Parliament 11 September 1997

TABLE 4.1 *Turnout*

Local Authority	%	Local Authority	%
Aberdeen	53.7	Glasgow	51.6
Aberdeenshire	57.0	Highland	60.3
Angus	60.2	Inverclyde	60.4
Argyll & Bute	65.0	North Lanarkshire	60.8
East Ayrshire	64.8	South Lanarkshire	63.1
North Ayrshire	63.4	East Lothian	65.0
South Ayrshire	66.7	Midlothian	65.1
Borders	64.8	West Lothian	62.6
Clackmannan	66.1	Moray	57.8
Dumfries & Galloway	63.4	Perthshire & Kinross	63.1
East Dunbartonshire	72.7	East Renfrewshire	68.2
West Dunbartonshire	63.7	Renfrewshire	62.8
Dundee	55.7	Stirling	65.8
Edinburgh	60.1	Orkney	53.5
Falkirk	63.7	Shetland	51.5
Fife	60.7	Western Isles	55.8
		SCOTLAND	60.4

TABLE 4.2 *Votes cast on first question (Should a Scottish Parliament be established?)*

Local Authority	YES		NO	
	N	%	N	%
Aberdeen	65,035	71.8	25,580	28.2
Aberdeenshire	61,621	63.9	34,878	36.1
Angus	33,571	64.7	18,350	35.3
Argyll & Bute	30,452	67.3	14,796	32.7
East Ayrshire	49,131	81.1	11,426	18.9
North Ayrshire	51,304	76.3	15,931	23.7
South Ayrshire	40,161	66.9	19,909	33.1
Borders	33,855	62.8	20,060	37.2
Clackmannan	18,790	80.0	4,706	20.0
Dumfries & Galloway	44,619	60.7	28,863	39.3
East Dunbartonshire	40,917	69.8	17,725	30.2
West Dunbartonshire	39,051	84.7	7,058	15.3
Dundee	49,252	76.0	15,553	24.0
Edinburgh	155,900	71.9	60,832	28.1
Falkirk	55,642	80.0	13,953	20.0
Fife	125,668	76.1	39,517	23.9
Glasgow	204,269	83.6	40,106	16.4
Highland	72,551	72.6	27,431	27.4
Inverclyde	31,680	78.0	8,945	22.0
North Lanarkshire	123,063	82.6	26,010	17.4
South Lanarkshire	114,908	77.8	32,762	22.2
East Lothian	33,525	74.2	11,665	25.8
Midlothian	31,681	79.9	7,979	20.1
West Lothian	56,923	79.6	14,614	20.4
Moray	24,822	67.2	12,122	32.8
Perthshire & Kinross	40,344	61.7	24,998	38.3
East Renfrewshire	28,253	61.7	17,573	38.3
Renfrewshire	68,711	79.0	18,213	21.0
Stirling	29,190	68.5	13,440	31.5
Orkney	4,749	57.3	3,541	42.7
Shetland	5,430	62.4	3,275	37.6
Western Isles	9,977	79.4	2,589	20.6
SCOTLAND	1,775,045	74.3	614,400	25.7

TABLE 4.3 *Votes cast on second question (Should a Scottish Parliament have tax-varying powers?)*

Local Authority	YES		NO	
	N	%	N	%
Aberdeen	54,320	60.3	35,709	39.7
Aberdeenshire	50,295	52.3	45,929	47.7
Angus	27,641	53.4	24,089	46.6
Argyll & Bute	25,746	57.0	19,429	43.0
East Ayrshire	42,559	70.5	17,824	29.5
North Ayrshire	43,990	65.7	22,991	34.3
South Ayrshire	33,679	56.2	26,217	43.8
Borders	27,284	50.7	26,497	49.3
Clackmannan	16,112	68.7	7,355	31.3
Dumfries & Galloway	35,737	48.8	37,499	51.2
East Dunbartonshire	34,576	59.1	23,914	40.9
West Dunbartonshire	34,408	74.7	11,628	25.3
Dundee	42,304	65.5	22,280	34.5
Edinburgh	133,843	62.0	82,188	38.0
Falkirk	48,064	69.2	21,403	30.8
Fife	108,021	64.7	58,987	35.3
Glasgow	182,589	75.0	60,842	25.0
Highland	61,359	62.1	37,525	37.9
Inverclyde	27,194	67.2	13,277	32.8
North Lanarkshire	107,288	72.2	41,372	27.8
South Lanarkshire	99,587	67.6	47,708	32.4
East Lothian	28,152	62.7	16,765	37.3
Midlothian	26,776	67.7	12,762	32.3
West Lothian	47,990	67.3	23,354	32.7
Moray	19,326	52.7	17,344	47.3
Perthshire & Kinross	33,398	51.3	31,709	48.7
East Renfrewshire	23,580	51.6	22,153	48.4
Renfrewshire	55,075	63.6	31,537	36.4
Stirling	25,044	58.9	17,487	41.1
Orkney	3,917	47.4	4,344	52.6
Shetland	4,478	51.6	4,198	48.4
Western Isles	8,557	68.4	3,947	31.6
SCOTLAND	1,512,889	63.5	870,263	36.5

2. Referendum on Welsh Assembly 18 September 1997

TABLE 4.4 *Turnout*

Local Authority	%	Local Authority	%
Anglesey	57.0	Merthyr Tydfil	49.8
Blaenau Gwent	49.6	Monmouthshire	50.7
Bridgend	50.8	Neath/Port Talbot	52.1
Caerphilly	49.5	Newport	46.1
Cardiff	47.0	Pembrokeshire	52.8
Carmarthenshire	56.6	Powys	56.5
Ceredigion	57.1	Rhondda/Cynon/Taff	49.9
Conwy	51.6	Swansea	47.3
Denbighshire	49.9	Torfaen	45.6
Flintshire	41.1	Vale of Glamorgan	54.5
Gwynedd	60.0	Wrexham	42.5
		WALES	50.1

TABLE 4.5 *Votes cast on referendum question (Should a Welsh Assembly be established?)*

Local Authority	YES N	%	NO N	%
Anglesey	15,649	50.9	15,095	49.1
Blaenau Gwent	15,237	56.1	11,298	43.9
Bridgend	27,632	54.4	23,172	45.6
Caerphilly	34,830	54.7	28,841	45.3
Cardiff	47,527	44.4	59,589	55.6
Carmarthenshire	49,115	65.3	26,119	34.7
Ceredigion	18,304	59.2	12,614	40.8
Conwy	18,369	40.9	26,521	59.1
Denbighshire	14,271	40.8	20,732	59.2
Flintshire	17,746	38.2	28,707	61.8
Gwynedd	35,425	64.1	19,859	35.9
Merthyr Tydfil	12,707	58.2	9,121	41.8
Monmouthshire	10,592	32.1	22,403	67.9
Neath/Port Talbot	36,730	66.6	18,463	33.5
Newport	16,172	37.4	27,017	62.6
Pembrokeshire	19,979	42.8	26,712	57.2
Powys	23,038	42.7	30,966	57.3
Rhondda/Cynon/Taff	51,201	58.5	36,362	41.5
Swansea	42,789	52.0	39,561	48.0
Torfaen	15,756	49.8	15,854	50.2
Vale of Glamorgan	17,776	36.7	30,613	63.3
Wrexham	18,574	45.3	22,449	54.7
WALES	559, 419	50.3	552,698	49.7

3. Referendum on reform of London government 7 May 1998

TABLE 4.6 *Turnout*

London Borough	%	London Borough	%
Barking & Dagenham	25.1	Hillingdon	34.8
Barnet	35.7	Hounslow	32.3
Bexley	35.0	Islington	35.0
Brent	36.6	Kensington & Chelsea	28.2
Bromley	40.2	Kingston upon Thames	28.2
Camden	33.3	Lambeth	32.0
City of London	30.6	Lewisham	30.1
Croydon	37.6	Merton	37.9
Ealing	33.2	Newham	28.7
Enfield	33.2	Redbridge	35.6
Greenwich	32.6	Richmond upon Thames	45.0
Hackney	34.5	Southwark	33.0
Hammersmith & Fulham	34.1	Sutton	35.2
Haringey	30.2	Tower Hamlets	35.6
Harrow	36.6	Waltham Forest	34.1
Havering	34.2	Wandsworth	39.3
		City of Westminster	31.9
		LONDON	34.1

TABLE 4.7 *Votes cast on referendum question (Should there be a directly elected executive mayor?)*

Local Authority	YES		NO	
	N	%	N	%
Barking & Dagenham	20,534	73.5	7,406	26.5
Barnet	55,487	69.6	24,210	30.4
Bexley	36,527	63.3	21,195	36.7
Brent	47,309	78.4	13,050	21.6
Bromley	51,410	57.1	38,662	42.9
Camden	36,007	81.2	8,348	18.8
City of London	977	63.0	574	37.0
Croydon	53,863	64.7	29,368	35.3
Ealing	52,348	76.5	16,092	23.5
Enfield	44,297	67.2	21,639	32.8
Greenwich	36,756	74.8	12,356	25.2
Hackney	31,956	81.6	7,195	18.4
Hammersmith & Fulham	29,171	77.9	8,255	22.1
Haringey	36,296	83.8	7,038	16.2
Harrow	38,412	68.8	17,407	31.2
Havering	36,390	60.5	23,788	39.5
Hillingdon	38,518	63.1	22,523	36.9
Hounslow	36,957	74.6	12,554	25.4
Islington	32,826	81.5	7,428	18.5
Kensington & Chelsea	20,064	70.3	8,469	29.7
Kingston upon Thames	28,621	68.7	13,043	31.3
Lambeth	47,391	81.8	10,544	18.2
Lewisham	40,188	78.4	11,060	21.6
Merton	35,418	72.2	13,635	27.8
Newham	33,084	81.4	7,575	18.6
Redbridge	42,547	70.2	18,098	29.8
Richmond upon Thames	39,115	70.8	16,135	29.2
Southwark	42,196	80.7	10,089	19.3
Sutton	29,653	64.8	16,091	35.2
Tower Hamlets	32,630	77.5	9,467	22.5
Waltham Forest	38,344	73.1	14,090	26.9
Wandsworth	57,010	74.3	19,695	25.7
City of Westminster	28,413	71.5	11,334	28.5
LONDON	1.230,715	72.0	478,413	28.0

4. Northern Ireland referendum on all-party agreement ('Good Friday Agreement') 22 May 1998

TABLE 4.8 *Northern Ireland Referendum Result*

		%
Turnout		81.0
Support Agreement	676,966	71.1
Do not support agreement	274,879	28.9

5. Economic Indicators

TABLE 5.1 *Unemployment, Retail Price Index, Inflation, Tax and Price Index, Interest Rates, Sterling Exchange Rate Index, Balance of Payments (Goods), Terms of Trade Index*

	UN	RPI	INF	TPI	%TPI	IR	SI	BP	TOFT
1993	10.3	140.7	1.6	131.4	1.2	5.50	88.9	-13,319	104.4
1994	9.3	144.1	2.4	135.2	2.9	6.25	89.2	-11,091	102.8
1995	8.0	149.1	3.5	140.4	3.8	6.50	84.8	-11,724	100.0
1996	7.3	152.7	2.4	142.4	1.4	6.00	86.3	-13,086	100.7
1997	5.5	157.5	3.1	145.5	2.1	7.25	100.6	-11,910	101.5
1998									
Jan	4.9	159.5	3.3	147.1	2.4	7.25	104.7	-818	102.3
Feb	4.8	160.3	3.4	147.9	2.6	7.25	104.7	-1,917	102.3
Mar	4.8	160.8	3.5	148.4	2.6	7.25	106.8	-1,518	102.4
Apr	4.8	162.6	4.0	149.7	4.1	7.25	107.1	-1,260	101.9
May	4.8	163.5	4.2	150.6	4.3	7.25	103.4	-1,940	101.7
Jun	4.8	163.4	3.7	150.5	3.8	7.50	105.4	-1,585	102.6
Jul	4.7	163.0	3.5	150.1	3.5	7.50	105.3	-1,366	102.0
Aug	4.6	163.7	3.3	150.8	3.3	7.50	104.6	-1,294	101.7
Sep	4.6	164.4	3.2	151.5	3.1	7.50	103.3	-2,607	102.2
Oct	4.6	164.5	3.1	151.6	3.1	7.25	100.7	-1,752	101.8
Nov	4.6	164.4	3.0	151.5	2.9	6.75	100.6	-2,299	102.4
Dec	4.6	164.4	2.8	151.5	2.8	6.25	100.4	-2,242	102.8

Notes: **UN**=Unemployment. Seasonally adjusted percentage of the workforce defined as unemployed. The current definition is used to estimate the whole series. **RPI**=Retail Price Index. All items. January 1987=100. **INF**=Inflation rate and is the percentage increase in the RPI compared with the same month in the previous year. **TPI**=Tax & Price Index. 1987=100. **%TPI**=Percentage increase in the TPI compared with the same month in the previous year. **IR**=Interest rates based upon selected retail banks' base rates. **SI**=Sterling Exchange Rate Index. Compares the value of sterling with a range of other currencies. 1990=100. **BP**=Balance of Payments (goods) in £millions. **TOFT**=Terms of Trade Index. Price Index of exports as a percentage of the price index of imports.

Sources: Office for National Statistics, *Economic Trends, Monthly Digest of Statistics*.

TABLE 5.2 *Gross Domestic Product, Real Household Disposable Income Index, House Price Index*

	GDP	RHDI	HOUSE
1994	97.3	n.a.	102.5
1995	100.0	100.0	103.2
1996	102.6	102.2	106.9
1997	106.2	106.3	116.9
1998			
Q1	108.0	105.5	122.1
Q2	108.3	106.5	128.6
Q3	108.6	105.4	134.2
Q4	108.7	107.4	133.6

Notes: GDP=Gross Domestic Product at market prices, 1995=100. RDPI=Real Household Disposable Income, 1995=100. HOUSE=Index of House Prices for all dwellings, 1993=100.
Source: Office for National Statistics, Economic Trends.

6. Political Parties

THE CONSERVATIVE PARTY

Main Addresses
Conservative and Unionist Central Office
32 Smith Square
Westminster
London SW1P 3HH
Tel: 0171-222-9000
Fax: 0171-222-1135
http://www.conservative-party.org.uk

Scottish Conservative and Unionist Central Office
Suite 1/1
14 Links Place
Edinburgh EH6 7EZ
Tel: 0131-555-2900
Fax: 0131-555-2869
e-mail: scuco@scottish.tory.org.uk
http://www.scottish.tory.org.uk

Other Addresses
Conservative Research Department
32 Smith Square
Westminster
London SW1P 3HH
Tel: 0171-222-9000
Fax: 0171-233-2065
Director: Roderick Nye
Assistant Directors: Peter Campbell, James Walsh

Conservative Policy Forum
32 Smith Square
Westminster
London SW1P 3HH
Tel: 0171-222-9000
Fax: 0171-233-2065
Director: James Walsh

National Conservative Convention
32 Smith Square
Westminster
London SW1P 3HH
Tel: 0171-222-9000
Fax: 0171-233-1135
Secretary: Chris Poole

One Nation Forum
32 Smith Square
Westminster
London SW1P 3HH
Tel: 0171-222-9000
Fax: 0171-233-1135
Chairman: Sir Graham Bright

Board of the Conservative Party

Michael Ancram	Jean Searle
Archie Norman	Raymond Monbiot
Robin Hodgson	Caroline Abel-Smith
Sir Archie Hamilton	Kim Donald
Lord Strathclyde	Audrey Hull
Michael Ashcroft	Lord Hanningfield
Brian Hanson	Edward McMillan-Scott

Chris Poole (Secretary to the Board)

Officers

Party Chairman	Michael Ancram
Deputy Chairman	Archie Norman
Vice Chairmen	David Prior (Organisation)
	Baroness Buscombe (Development)
	Andrew Lansley (Policy Renewal)
	Richard Ottaway (Local Government)
Chairman of the Party in Scotland	Raymond Robertson

Staff

Directors

Research	Roderick Nye
News and Media	Amanda Platell
Fundraising and Marketing	Jane Keene
Field Operations	Stephen Gilbert
Finance (Acting Director)	Stewart Harris
Membership and Marketing	*Vacant*
Strategy and Campaigns	Andrew Cooper

TABLE 6.1 *Single Currency Ballot, 1998*

The Party Leader and the Shadow Cabinet have agreed that the Conservative Party will oppose British Membership of the Single Currency at the next election as part of the manifesto for the next parliament. Do you endorse the policy of the Party Leader and the Shadow Cabinet?

	N	%
Ballot papers sent out	344,157	
Ballot papers received	202,674	58.9
Invalid ballot papers	624	.3
Valid ballot papers	202,050	99.7
Voting yes	170,558	84.4
Voting no	31,492	15.6

THE LABOUR PARTY

Main Addresses
The Labour Party
Millbank Tower
Millbank
London SW1P 4GT
Tel: 08705-900-200
Fax: 0171-802-1555
e-mail: labour-party@geo2.poptel.org.uk
http://www.labour.org.uk

Scottish Labour Party
Campaign Centre
4th Floor
50 West Nile Street
Glasgow G1 2NA
Tel: 0141-572-6900
Fax: 0141-572-2566
e-mail: general@scottish-labour.org

Welsh Labour Party
Transport House
1 Cathedral Road
Cardiff CF1 9HA
Tel: 01222-877700
Fax: 01222-221153
e-mail: lp-wales@geo2.poptel.org.uk

Information
Tel: 0171-802-1115
Fax: 0171-802-1555

Commercial Marketing Unit	*Elections Unit*
simonp@lp-ho.poptel.org.uk	lp-elections@geo2.poptel.org.uk
International	*Labour Women*
lp-int@geo2.poptel.org.uk	lp-women@geo2.poptel.org.uk
Membership	*Party Development*
lp-membership@geo2.poptel.org.uk	lp-development@geo2.poptel.org.uk

Officers and Staff

Leader	Tony Blair
Deputy Leader	John Prescott
General Secretary	Margaret McDonagh
Assistant General Secretaries	David Pitt-Watson (Finance)
	Phil Murphy (Media Communications)
	Nick Pecorelli (Policy)
	David Gardner (Party Development)
Unit Heads	Carol Linforth (Party Development)
	Alan Barnard (Elections)
	Rachel McLean (Women's Officer)

National Executive Committee 1998–99

Chair	Brenda Etchells
Vice-Chair	Vernon Hince
Leader of the Party	Tony Blair
Deputy Leader of the Party	John Prescott
Leader of the European Parliamentary Party	Alan Donnelly
Treasurer	Margaret Prosser
General Secretary	Margaret McDonagh

Division 1 – Trade Unions

Mary Turner (GMB)	Brenda Etchells (AEU)
Steve Pickering (GMB)	Maggie Jones (UNISON)
Diana Holland (TGWU)	Margaret Wall (MSF)
Derek Hodgson (CWU)	John Allen (AEU)
Michael Griffiths (GPMU)	John Hannett (USDAW)
Anne Picking (UNISON)	Vernon Hince (RMT)

Division 2 – Socialist Societies
Diane Hayter

Division 3 – Constituency Parties

Mark Seddon	Liz Davies
Michael Cashman	Cathy Jamieson
Diana Jeuda	Pete Willsman

Division 4 – Local Government

Jeremy Beecham	Sally Powell

Division 5 – Parliamentary Labour Parties
Clive Soley   Anne Begg
Pauline Green

Youth Representative
Sarah Ward

Three Representatives of the Frontbench
Hilary Armstrong   Mo Mowlam
Ian McCartney

Result of Elections to National Executive Committee 1998–99

Names asterisked were elected. Figures for 1997–98 are shown in brackets if applicable.

Trade Unions
(Twelve places of which at least six must be women)

*	Mary Turner	3,324,000	(3,384,000)
*	Steve Pickering	3,308,000	(3,454,000)
*	Diana Holland	3,303,000	(3,385,000)
*	Derek Hodgson	3,301,000	(3,333,000)
*	Michael Griffiths	3,284,000	
*	Anne Picking	3,279,000	
*	Brenda Etchells	3,267,000	
*	Maggie Jones	3,250,000	(3,365,000)
*	Margaret Wall	3,224,000	(3,310,000)
*	John Allen	3,211,000	(3,263,000)
*	John Hannett	3,208,000	
*	Vernon Hince	2,867,000	(3,405,000)
	Michael Leahy	637,000	(1,061,000)
	Stephen Kemp	120,000	(174,000)

Socialist Societies (One place)
* Diane Hayter (*unopposed*)

Constituency Parties
(Six places of which at least three must be women)
*	Mark Seddon	75,584
*	Michael Cashman	70,256
*	Diana Jeuda	62,509
*	Liz Davies	61,970
*	Cathy Jamieson	61,707
*	Pete Willsman	58,108
	Margaret Payne	55,651
	Christine Shawcroft	53,897
	Terry Thomas	50,412
	Adrian Bailey	46,210
	Rita Stringfellow	39,020
	Sylvia Tudhope	34,768
	Andy Howell	30,305
	Valerie Price	27,079
	Mary Southcott	8,942

Local Government
(Two places to be filled by members of the Association of Labour
Councillors of which one must be a woman)
*	Jeremy Beecham	3,345
*	Sally Powell	3,034
	Georgina Guest	1,372
	Ian Male	900

Parliamentary Labour Parties
(Three places to be filled by members of the PLP or EPLP of which at least
one must be a woman)
*	Clive Soley	259
*	Pauline Green	247
*	Anne Begg	207
	Helen Jackson	186
	Dennis Skinner	182
	Ian Davidson	93
	Alex Smith	43
	Norman Godman	34

Result of Election to Constitutional Committee 1998–99
Names asterisked were elected.

Division 1 – Trade Unions
* Andy Smith (TGWU)   *Elected unopposed*

Division 2 – Socialist Societies
* Bernard Dooley   *Elected unopposed*

Division 3 – Constituency Parties
* Rosina McCrey   62,902
   Bob Hughes   60,398

Division 4 – Women
* Joan Lewis   Elected Unopposed
One vacancy

Parliamentary Committee Elections

Candidates elected
Chris Mullin   182
Jean Corston   177
Ann Clwyd   164
Sylvia Heal   149
Charlotte Atkins   127
Andrew Mackinlay   126

Candidates not elected
Llin Golding   112

A total of 328 MPs were eligible to vote; 223 ballot papers were issued and cast, of which 12 were spoilt.

The Parliamentary Labour Party's Parliamentary Committee

4 officers of the PLP (ex officio)

Leader	Tony Blair
Deputy Leader	John Prescott
Chief Whip	Ann Taylor
Chair	Clive Soley

6 elected Commons backbenchers
Chris Mullin (Deputy Chair)
Charlotte Atkins
Ann Clwyd
Jean Corston
Sylvia Heal
Andrew Mackinlay

4 ministers appointed by the PM

Margaret Beckett	Leader of the House of Commons (ex officio)
Mo Mowlam	Secretary of State for Northern Ireland
Frank Dobson	Secretary of State for Health
Lord Williams of Mostyn	Parliamentary Under-Secretary of State at the Home Office

1 elected Lords backbencher
Lord Williams of Elvel

Formal right of attendance

Chief Whip in the House of Lords	Lord Carter
General Secretary of the Party	Margaret McDonagh

The secretary of the committee is the secretary of the PLP, Alan Howarth (not the MP). The committee meets every week when the House is sitting, at 4.30pm on a Wednesday afternoon.

THE LIBERAL DEMOCRATS

Addresses
The Liberal Democrats
Party Headquarters
4 Cowley Street
London SW1P 3NB
Tel: 0171-222-7999
Fax: 0171-799-2170
e-mail: libdems@cix.co.uk
http://www.libdems.org.uk

Scottish Liberal Democrats
4 Clifton Terrace
Edinburgh EH12 5DR
Tel: 0131-337-2314
Fax: 0131-337-3566
e-mail: scotlibdem@cix.co.uk
http://www.scotlibdems.org.uk

Welsh Liberal Democrats
Bayview House
102 Bute Street
Cardiff CF1 6AD
Tel: 01222-313-400
Fax: 01222-313-401
e-mail: ldwales@cix.co.uk
http://www.cix.co.uk/~ldwales/

Specified Associated Organizations
Association of Liberal Democrat Councillors
President: Jackie Ballard MP
Chair: Sarah Boad
Tel: 01422-843-785
Fax: 01422-843-036
e-mail: aldc@cix.co.uk

Association of Liberal Democrat Trade Unionists
President: Alan Sherwell
Chair: Michael Smart
Tel: 01375-850-881

Youth and Student Liberal Democrats
Chair: Polly Martin
Tel: 0171-222-7999 ext. 587/8

Women Liberal Democrats
President: Baroness Diana Maddock
Chair: Dee Dooley
Tel: 0171-222-7999 ext. 408

Ethnic Minority Liberal Democrats
Chair: Pash Nandhra
Tel: 0181-288-9830

Liberal Democrats for Lesbian and Gay Action
President: Robert Maclennan MP
Chair: Jonathan Simpson
Tel: 0171-222-7999

Liberal Democrats Agent and Organisers Association
President: Candy Piercy
Chair: Bill Morrison
Tel: 0171-222-7999

Liberal Democrat Parliamentary Candidates' Association
Chair: Robert Woodthorpe Browne
Tel: 01279-414-335

Scottish Young Liberal Democrats
Convenor: Tasmin Mayberry
Tel: 0131-337-2314

Party Officers

Party Leader	Paddy Ashdown
President	Baroness Diana Maddock
Vice-Presidents	Paul Farthing (England)
	Ian Yuill (Scotland)
	Lembit Opik MP (Wales)
Chair of Finance	Denis Robertson Sullivan
Treasurer	Tim Razzall

Scottish Party

Leader	Jim Wallace
President	Roy Thomson
Convenor	Ian Yuill
Chief Executive	Willie Rennie

Welsh Party

Leader	Richard Livsey MP
President	Alex Carlile
Administrator	Helen Northmore-Thomas

Federal Party Staff

Chief Executive	Elizabeth Pamplin
Head of Administration and Personnel	Elizabeth Johnson
Campaigns and Elections Director	Chris Rennard
Candidates Officer	Sandra Dunk
Head of Policy and Research	David Laws
Deputy Head of Policy and Research	Christian Moon
International Officer	Kishwer Khan
Financial Controller	Irene Douglas
Director of Membership Services	Appointment Pending
Membership Finance Co-ordinator	Helen Sharman
Conference Organizer	Penny McCormack
Liberal Democrat News Editor	Deirdrie Razzall

OTHER PARTIES

Scottish National Party (SNP)
6 North Charlotte Street
Edinburgh EH2 4JH
Tel: 0131-226-3661
Fax: 0131-226-7373
e-mail: snp.hq@snp.org.uk
http://www.snp.org.uk

President: Winifred Ewing
National Convenor: Alex Salmond
Parliamentary Leader: Margaret Ewing
National Secretary: Colin Campbell
Director of Organisation: Alison Hunter
Communications and Research: Kevin Pringle
Chief Executive: Michael Russell

Plaid Cymru (PC)
18 Park Grove
Cardiff CF1 3BN
Tel: 01222-646-000
Fax: 01222-646-001
e-mail: post@plaidcymru.org
http://www.plaid-cymru.wales.com
President: Dafydd Wigley
Chief Executive: Karl Davies
Chair: Marc Phillips
Chief Whip: Elfyn Llwyd
Communications and Press Officer: Siôn Ffancon

Green Party of England and Wales
1a Waterloo Road
Archway
London N19 5NJ
Tel: 0171-272-4474
Fax: 0171-272-6653
e-mail: office@greenparty.org.uk
http://www.greenparty.org.uk

The Liberal Party
1a Pine Grove
Southport
Lancashire
PR9 9AQ
Tel: 01704-500-115
Fax: 01704-539-315
http://www.libparty.demon.co.uk
President: Michael Meadowcroft
Chair of National Executive: Steve Radford
Communications Director: David Green

Natural Law Party
Mentmore Towers
Mentmore
Buckinghamshire
LU7 OQH
Tel: 01296-662-211
Fax: 01296-662-486
e-mail: info@natural-law-party.org.uk
http://www.natural-law.party.org.uk
Party Leader: Dr Geoffrey Clements

Socialist Labour Party
9 Victoria Road
Barnsley
South Yorkshire
S70 2BB
Tel/Fax: 01226-770-957#
http://www.ifley.demon.co.uk/index.html
President: Frank W. Cave
General Secretary: Arthur Scargill

NORTHERN IRELAND

Alliance Party
88 University Street
Belfast BT7 1HE
Tel: 01232-324-274
Fax: 01232-333-147
e-mail: alliance@allianceparty.org
http://www.unite.net/customers/alliance
Leader: Sean Neeson
Party Chairman: Peter Osborne
General Secretary: Richard Good
President: Philip McGarry

Democratic Unionist Party
91 Dundela Avenue
Belfast BT4 3BU
Tel: 01232-471-155
Fax: 01232-471-797
e-mail: info@dup.org.uk
http://www.dup.org.uk
Leader: Ian Paisley
Deputy Leader: Peter Robinson
Party Chairman: James McClure
Party Secretary: Nigel Dodds
Press Officer: Samuel Wilson
General Secretary: Allan Ewart
Treasurer: Gregory Campbell
Director of Communications: St Clair McAlister

Progressive Unionist Party
182 Shankill Road
Belfast BT13 2BL
Tel: 01232-236-233
Fax: 01232-249-602
http://www.pup.org
Leader: Hugh Smith
Party spokesperson: David Ervine
Chairperson: William Smith

Sinn Féin
Belfast Headquarters
51–55 Falls Road
Belfast BT13
Tel: 01232-624-421
Fax: 01232-622-112
Dublin Office
44 Cearnóg Pharnell (Parnell Square)
Dublin 1
Republic of Ireland
Tel: (00) 3531-872-6100/872-6939
Fax: (00) 3531-873-3074
e-mail: sinnfein@iol.ie
http://www.sinnfein.ie/index.html
President: Gerry Adams
Vice-President: Pat Doherty
General Secretary: Lucilita Bhreatnach
National Chairperson: Mitchel McLaughlin
Six County Chairperson: Gearóid O hÉara
Director of Publicity: Rita O'Hare

Social Democratic and Labour Party (SDLP)
121 Ormeau Road
Belfast BT7 1SH
Tel: 01232-247-700
Fax: 01232-236-699
e-mail: sdlp@indigo.ie
http://www.indigo.ie/sdlp/
Leader: John Hume
Deputy Leader: Seamus Mallon
Party Chairman: Jim Lennon
General Secretary: Gerry Cosgrove
Chief Whip: Eddie McGrady
Director of Communications: *Vacant*
Director of Organisation and Development: Tim Attwood

UK Unionist Party
10 Hamilton Road
Bangor BT20 4LE
Tel: 01247-479-538
Fax: 01247-465-037
e-mail: contactus@ukunionist.freeserve.co.uk
http://www.welcometo/ukup
Leader: Robert McCartney
Party Secretary: Tom Sheridan

Ulster Unionist Party
3 Glengall Street
Belfast BT12 5AE
Tel: 01232-324-601
Fax: 01232-246-738
e-mail: uup@uup.org
http://www.uup.org
Leader: David Trimble
Party Chairman: Dennis Rogan
Secretary: Hazel Legge

7. National Newspapers

TABLE 7.1 *Circulation of National Newspapers*

Average net circulation

Newspaper	Jul 98– Dec 98	Jul 97– Dec 97	Jul 96– Dec 96	Jul 95– Dec 95
Sun	3,675,286	3,779,605	3,980,808	4,027,850
Daily Mirror/Daily Record	3,014,460	3,009,148	3,124,454	3,281,620
Daily Mail	2,350,364	2,237,949	2,090,803	1,876,011
Daily Express	1,118,700	1,202,291	1,195,069	1,261,977
Daily Telegraph	1,054,418	1,098,440	1,084,440	1,052,928
Times	751,862	792,151	790,857	668,756
Daily Star	554,465	619,553	671,494	663,048
Guardian	391,919	403,999	396,800	395,135
Financial Times	366,969	328,793	296,834	295,740
Independent	221,398	260,223	265,037	292,827
London Evening Standard	450,089	449,020	435,028	441,287
News of the World	4,225,599	4,425,708	4,505,632	4,690,563
Sunday Mirror	1,988,579	2,276,089	2,437,662	2,534,566
Mail on Sunday	2,312,329	2,219,430	2,105,566	2,040,758
The People	1,717,277	1,895,121	2,049,509	2,092,056
Sunday Times	1,349,925	1,343,324	1,325,021	1,252,774
Sunday Express	1,027,049	1,140,328	1,177,094	1,362,974
Sunday Telegraph	829,032	887,204	776,231	674,031
Observer	398,983	439,573	453,353	463,301
Independent on Sunday	253,907	287,543	287,282	326,675
Sunday Sport	237,574	275,246	259,366	289,702

Source: Audit Bureau of Circulations

BRITISH ELECTIONS & PARTIES REVIEW

NOTES FOR CONTRIBUTORS

The article should be submitted on hard copy and disk, accompanied by a brief abstract (c. 150 words) and biographical notes, each in a separate file. All pages of the manuscript should be numbered, including those containing figures. The accuracy of the references is the sole responsibility of the author (follow Style Notes below).

FORMAT

Files should be saved in Rich Text Format, named for the author (Jones.rtf). The disk should be labelled with the name of the article, the author's name and the software system used (ideally IBM compatible).

Tables: Set page width to 108mm. Place table in the **text approximate position**, placing a page break at the top and tail: there is no need to include such guidance as '[INSERT TABLE 2 ABOUT HERE]'. **Do not use the 'Table' function** in the word processing package as this causes difficulties at production stage. Instead, use the tab function, as follows: set tabs for columns; align by decimal point; centre column headings. Set the font size of the table to 8pt. The table must fit **within type area 108mm x 175mm**. (Avoid landscape format if at all possible, but for wider tables, use landscape with maximum width 175mm). Tables should be titled and sources given.

Maps and Figures: Following acceptance for publication, articles should be submitted on high density 3½ inch disks (IBM PC or Macintosh compatible) in rich text format (.RTF) together with hard copy. To facilitate the typesetting process, notes should be grouped together at the end of the file. Tables should be saved as text using the appropriate function within your word processor. If this function is not available then tables should be prepared using tabs.

Any diagrams or maps should be copied to a separate disk in uncompressed .TIF or .JPG formats in individual files. These should be prepared in black and white. Tints should be avoided, use open patterns instead. If maps and diagrams cannot be prepared electronically, they should be presented on good equality white paper. If mathematics are included 1/2 is preferred over ½.

STYLE

Headings: (1) Bold, (2) Italics, no underline, (3) Italics, no new paragraph.

Quotation marks: single in text throughout; double within single; single within indented quotations.

Spelling: use the -z- alternative (recognize) except where -yse (analyse); British spellings, e.g. -our rather than -or (favour).

Capitalization: Use capitals sparingly, for titles (the Secretary-General; President Mitterrand) and for unique or central institutions (the European Commission, the International Atomic Energy Authority) but not for general or local organizations and offices (a government minister, the mayor, Brigham parish council). Capitalize party in a title (the British Green Party), otherwise lower case. Lower case for the state and for the left and the right (but the New left, the New Right). Capitalize -isms from names (Marxism), elsewhere lower case (ecologism). In general, lower case for conferences and congresses (the party's tenth congress was held in 1995).

Numbers: words on-ten, afterwards numerals 11, 12, etc; decimals preceded by a nought (0.4).

Dates: 12 July 1994. Abbreviate years: 1983–84; 1908–9; 1920–21; the 1930s (*not* 'the thirties').

REFERENCES

Harvard-style references e.g. (Denver, 1997). References should be cited in the text thus: Denver (1990: 63–4), Denver and Hands (1985, 1990). Use '*et al.*' when citing a word by more than two authors, e.g. (Brown *et al.*, 1991). The letters a, b, c, etc., should be used to distinguish citations of different works by the same author in the same year, e.g. (Brown, 1975a, b).

References cited in the text should be listed alphabetically and presented in full, using the following style. All text references must be included in the list of references. Essential notes should be kept to a minimum and indicated by superscript numbers in the text and collected on a single page at the end of the text, before the references.

Article in journal: Anker, Hans (1990) 'Drawing Aggregate Inferences from Individual Level Data: the Utility of the Notion of a Normal Vote', *European Journal of Political Research* 18: 373–87.

Book: Denver, David and Gordon Hands (1997), *Modern Constituency electioneering*, London and Portland, OR: Frank Cass.

Article in a book: Webb, Paul D. (1994) 'Party Organizational Change in Britain: the Iron Law of Centralization?' in Richard S. Katz and Peter Mair (eds) *How Parties Organize: Change and Adaptation in Party Organizations in Western Democracies*, pp.109–34. London: Sage.